Strategic Event Creation

**Liz Sharples, Phil Crowther, Daryl May
and Chiara Orefice**

 Goodfellow Publishers Ltd

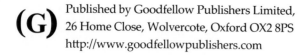 Published by Goodfellow Publishers Limited,
26 Home Close, Wolvercote, Oxford OX2 8PS
http://www.goodfellowpublishers.com

British Library Cataloguing in Publication Data: a catalogue record for this title is available from the British Library.

Library of Congress Catalog Card Number: on file.

ISBN: 978-1-910158-07-4

 Design and typesetting by P.K. McBride, www.macbride.org.uk

Cover design by Cylinder

Printed by Marston Book Services, www.marston.co.uk

Contents

Figures

Tables

Foreword

At one time all planned events emerged organically from the needs and desires of communities. But we now live in a world dominated by instrumentalism, wherein events of all kinds are conceived as instruments of government policy, corporate and industry strategy, entrepreneurs seeking profit, or the service objectives of not-for-profit organisations.

Organizations and destinations bid aggressively to attract events for their tourism and image-making value, while other events are created to fill gaps in ever-larger and more ambitious portfolios of events. The consumers of events have numerous choices, and indeed they expect their communities to offer a wide variety. Events of all kinds have been legitimatized as essential ingredients in modern life.

Consequently, more and more stakeholders are involved in a complex environment shaping both the goals and design of festivals, sports, business and entertainment events, leading to a heightened requirement for professionalism in the events sector. These trends have been accompanied by increasing scrutiny of events by the media, citizens, lobby groups, and accountants representing funders and sponsors.

Events in the private sector must generate positive returns on investment, while those in the public sector, or receiving subsidies and support, must be justified in terms of their demonstrable public good and long-term legacies. Furthermore, there is an expectation that events will be green, strategies will emphasize sustainability, health and safety standards will be rigorously upheld, and corporations will behave in a responsible manner with regard to the community and environment. What a challenge!

This book, *Strategic Event Creation*, is therefore a timely and important contribution to the event-studies literature, and it should be required reading for all those involved in the planning, design, operation and evaluation of events. The contributors use the catchphrase 'outcome obsessed' to describe a new philosophy, one that imposes new standards and procedures, reflecting strategy, professionalism and accountability. Strategy must take into account the voices and needs of numerous stakeholders, and event professionals must be conscious of their complex environment and reflective concerning the outcomes of their actions.

Donald Getz, PhD, Professor Emeritus, The University of Calgary, author of the following books: *Festivals, Special Events and Tourism*; *Event Management and Event Tourism*; *Event Studies*; *Event Tourism*.

Preface

Changes in the wider environment have triggered a new normal for event creation. Heightened attendee expectations, a keener focus upon the return required by funders and wider stakeholders, and, of course, an ever more competitive event marketplace. Couple these with CSR, social media, globalisation and technology and the reasons event creation is now a strategic and multilayered responsibility are clear.

Strategic Event Creation is the contemporary textbook that recognises and articulates this changed reality for students and professionals. It moves away from an older paradigm of simply 'making events work' and managing inputs to show a sector that now needs to be: outcome obsessed, stakeholder centric, strategically focused and driven by strategically aware reflective professionals.

This text is based on a carefully designed framework which

☐ Delivers a clear overview of the key principles

☐ Integrates theory with industry voices, cases and the practitioner perspective

☐ Uses the lens of outcomes to anchor the role of inputs/processes/decisions/budgets

☐ Delivers clear learning summaries and highlights key questions for reflection

The broadly based and experienced author team are widely engaged with the events industry whose voice and insights inform the book throughout. It is designed to move students and professionals beyond event organising to Strategic Event Creation. As the event industry has progressed effective event operations become a prerequisite to exist rather than a recipe to succeed.

It will be an essential text for students studying Events, Festival, Conference and Exhibition Management at all levels, and also of significant use to a wide range of students in Tourism, Hospitality and Marketing. The practical 'real world' perspective means that it can help venue managers, event creators (across many areas), experiential marketing professionals and conference / training managers gain a broader understanding of the business context in which they are competing.

Contributing authors

Phil Crowther, Principal Lecturer, Sheffield Business School, Sheffield Hallam University

Phil enjoyed a career of eleven years working in senior general management roles within the leisure and tourism industries before he left to run his own consultancy business. Since joining the university in 2006 Phil has published within the area of events as strategic live communications and is currently competing his PhD in this area. In addition to his teaching commitments Phil also works heavily with industry, undertaking consultancy roles around the topic of events and strategy.

James Bostock, Senior Lecturer, Sheffield Business School

James joined Sheffield Hallam in 2009 from a background in teaching and management in higher education, of which he has over 10 years' experience. He has predominantly worked within public sector leisure facilities, but also has a wide range of experience of developing partnerships with leisure organisations. James is currently working towards his PhD, investigating how national sport governing bodies have responded to reductions in their funding and the possible impacts on stakeholders within the organisation. This research will investigate such issues as change management, stakeholder management and governance. Teaching and Research Interests: Strategic events policy; Leisure trusts and impacts on leisure provision; Change management within sport, leisure and event organisations; governance within national governing bodies; sustainability within the events sector.

Chiara Orefice, Senior Lecturer, Sheffield Business School

Before joining the university in 2008, Chiara acquired a wide ranging international experience in research and in events management working in the private and public sectors and in international organisations in Italy, Thailand, Switzerland, France, Belgium and the UK for about 15 years. Chiara is Course leader for the MSc International Events and Conference Management and the Sheffield Business School Erasmus coordinator. She is a member of the European Association of International Educators and of Meeting Professional International and is involved in international projects aimed at developing the role of event professionals. Her teaching and research interests are on event design and experience, return on investment and the value of meetings and events, the impact of culture in international events and the internationalisation of the event management curriculum.

Jonathan Moss, Graduate Tutor, Sheffield Business School

Jonathan Moss is a graduate tutor and will complete his PhD in September 2014; its focus is the event experience from a psycho-social perspective and has developed a spectrum model. He is testing this with a new approach, the Descriptive Sampling Method. Jonathan has become an active member of SHU's research community attending a number of conferences and is due to have this first paper published this year in Arts Marketing.

Dr Leah Donlan, Lecturer in Marketing, Manchester Business School,

Since completing her PhD in 2008, entitled *The Contribution of Sports Sponsorship to Consumer-Based Brand Equity*, Leah has researched and published work on sponsorship and brand building, sponsorship objectives and experiential sponsorship activation. Her ongoing research is in the area of experiential sponsorship activation and brand image transfer in sponsorship. Leah has also worked on consultancy projects for a variety of public and private sector organisations in the field of sport.

Gareth Roberts, Senior Lecturer, Sheffield Business School

Gareth Roberts is an academic practitioner - successfully combining industry experience with academic scholarship. He has worked in a variety of roles and sectors across the events and cultural industries for nearly 20 years. Specialist interests include outdoor festivals, community-led change, enterprise start-up and social media technologies. He has taught and supervised research at postgraduate and undergraduate levels, delivered learning activities in business and community settings and been responsible for developing innovative new curriculum for a diverse range of subjects including Cultural Entrepreneurship and Self Employment in the Creative Industries. Teaching responsibilities currently include Events Business and Venues Management, Leisure and Risk and Event Safety Management.

David Strafford, Lecturer, Sheffield Business School

David teaches on the Undergraduate Events Management course, and is currently completing his MSc in International Events and Conference Management and Post Graduate Certificate in Learning and Teaching in Higher Education. His undergraduate degree was in Economics and Politics from the University of Sheffield, graduating in 1998.

David has worked in the Events Industry for over 15 years, mainly in the late night entertainment and nightclub sector For 11 years he was the Senior Events Manager at Sheffield University Students' Union, consistently voted the Number One Students' Union in the UK. He still maintains industry experience, through part-time Event and Tour Management work for BBC Learning, including tours in recent years for C-Beebies characters Mr Bloom and Rastamouse; and is managing this year's BBC Regions' World War One At Home tour, which commemorates 100 years since the outbreak of the war in 1914.

Prof Colin Beard, Professor, Sheffield Business School

Professor Beard is a professor of, and holds a PhD in, experiential learning. He originally trained as a zoologist. He was awarded a UK National Teaching

Fellowship in 2005. He is a Fellow of the Royal Society of Arts, and a Chartered Fellow of the CIPD. He is the owner of a consulting business Experience - the difference. He works with many corporate and public bodies on individual and organisational learning. He has written numerous international books and journal articles on experiential learning. More details can be found on his website: Colinbeard.co.uk

Jane Tattersall, Senior Lecturer, Sheffield Business School

A third generation entrepreneur, Jane became self employed aged19 and in 1998 she became the Managing Director of a fashion footwear retail company and in 2005 co founded a Social Enterprise that helped change the lives of young people through challenging outdoor adventure events, funded by the delivery of corporate and third sector outdoor management development and training activities, conferences and events consultancy to many large clients. Since 2008 Jane has worked as a Senior Lecturer in Events at Sheffield Hallam University and is currently Course Leader for BSc (Hons) Events Management Her teaching and research passion focuses on the development valuable Graduate skills and knowledge for the events sector through experiential and entrepreneurial learning opportunities in the classroom and through work with real clients.

Richard Cooper, Senior Lecturer, Events Team, Sheffield Business School

Richard started by working in sports retailing and outdoor education in the UK and France before moving into project management. This included working on a range of projects from developing a major sports tourism attraction to public art installations. Since moving into higher education in 1999, as well as teaching on UK based courses, he has worked on developing Internet delivered distance learning courses, as well as developing and delivering UG and PG courses in Singapore and Hong Kong. He is an active outdoor sportsman, being involved in the running of a number of sports events, as well as researching and evaluating sports events with the Sport Industry Research Centre at Sheffield Hallam.

Liz Sharples, Principal Lecturer, Sheffield Business School

Liz has worked as an academic at Sheffield Hallam University for 28 years. She first taught Food and Beverage Management for the Hospitality Subject group and now is Subject Team Leader for the Events Management group within the Business School. Previously she worked as a Catering Officer in the public sector and as a Hotel Manager for the Jarvis Hotel group. Liz's personal research and consultancy area lies in the area of Food and Wine Tourism and Food and Wine Festivals and Events. She is particularly interested in the role that local food plays in events, celebration, communities and the wider environment. She has published at an International level with a wide range of collaborators, her most recent book being 'Food and Wine Festivals around the World', co-edited with Michael Hall and published by Elsevier in 2008. She is a regular presenter/key note speaker at national and international conferences, and has acted as an advisor/consultant to a number of national organisations. Currently she sits as

Vice Chair on the Regional Advisory Board of the National Trust for Yorkshire and the North East and is an advisor to the Ludlow Marches Food and Drink Festival in Shropshire. Liz is also a member of the Editorial Board of the British Food Journal.

Dr Richard Tresidder, Senior Lecturer, Sheffield Business School

Dr Richard Tresidder teaches marketing on the MSc programmes within the Centre for Tourism, Hospitality and Events Research the Sheffield Business School. His research interests are in how people interpret marketing campaigns and in particular how signs and images give meaning to the experiences that surround tourism, hospitality, food and events. Richard has managed and undertaken research for many organisations including the Deputy Prime Ministers' Office, the Rural Development Commission and the National Trust.

Dr Craig Hirst, Senior Lecturer, Sheffield Business School

Dr Craig Hirst sits in the Food and Nutrition group of the Sheffield Business School and co-leads the core marketing module of the Tourism, Hospitality, Events and Food Masters programme. His research interests lay in marketing and consumer behaviour and particularly in the socio-cultural dynamics of marketing and consumption and the production of the marketplace more generally. While primarily applying his ideas to food, Craig's interests span Events, Tourism, and Hospitality.

Stewart Hilland, Senior Lecturer, Sheffield Business School

Stewart Hilland has a senior management background in education and has organised a wide range of exhibitions, conferences, ceremonies and international sports and arts events within the education sector. He has worked in the UK, Switzerland and South-East Asia. In 2006, Stewart was awarded an MSc with distinction from the UK Centre for Events Management at Leeds Metropolitan University and received a prize for outstanding academic achievement. He has been part of the Events Management teaching team at Sheffield Hallam University since 2008 and currently he leads on modules relating to business research methods and events policy and planning. Stewart's research interests centre on public sector event delivery and outcomes as well as the teaching, learning and the assessment of student performance in the higher education classroom.

Katrin Stefansdottir Associate Lecturer, Sheffield Business School

Katrin Sif Stefansdottir enjoyed a career within finance and budget planning and evaluation following a degree in Economics from the University of Iceland. After five years of finance work she progressed and gained a MSc. in International Events and Conference Management from Sheffield Hallam University, UK. She is currently working on her PhD at the same university researching event evaluation and business event attendees' experience.

Anjalina Pradhan, Internal Communications and Employer Branding-Corporate Communications at UBM India Pvt Ltd

Anjalina Pradhan is a MSc. in International Events and Conference Management from Sheffield Hallam University, UK, currently working with UBM India Pvt. Ltd. She has worked in parts of India, Nepal and the UK in various roles and industries around travel and tourism, hospitality and marketing. Anjalina takes great interest in reading about learning and delegate engagement in conferences, meeting architecture and content formats, tourism development and culture.

Dr Daryl May, Principal Lecturer, Sheffield Hallam University

Daryl has been conducting research and teaching at Sheffield Hallam University since 2001. His research focus has primarily been on facilities management in the NHS, and specifically workforce development for facilities staff and how to assess the impact of facilities management in terms of health outcomes. Daryl is the Postgraduate Programme Leader for Department of Service Sector in the Sheffield Business School and an executive member of the Association of Events Management Educators (AEME). Prior to working at Sheffield Hallam University, Daryl worked for the Department of Health as a facilities manager.

Lindsey May, Associate Lecturer, Sheffield Hallam University

Lindsey has been teaching with the Events Management team at SHU since 2012, having graduated as a mature student with a first class degree in Public Health Nutrition. She has an industry background in financial management and her current research interests include the impact of major sporting events on the host community's long term physical activity levels and lifestyles. Lindsey is currently completing a masters degree in Sport Business Management, her events management experience stems from involvement in corporate, cycling, sports and nutrition event work.

Howard Lyons, Visiting Fellow, Sheffield Business School

Howard Lyons works with the Events Management Team. Howard recently entered his fifth decade being involved with events management education although the area has been formally recognised by name in the UK for about half that time. His longitudinal view of the events management sector approaches a century and extends to the mid or end of the twenty first century through his decade of involvement with the UK Government Technology Foresight Programme and serving as a member of the Future Analysts Network. Howard is research active in festivals, and in the tertiary businesses associated with Neighbourhood Planning. As an academic he has been a member of faculty at Sheffield Hallam University, a Visiting Fellow at the University of Exeter Business School, and Visiting Professor at North American and European Business Schools. He is also actively involved with Academic Journal refereeing and has a long list of publications. Commercially he has had an on-going involvement in a variety of commercial and consulting firms. However his primary business interests include senior management development in strategy and futures for events, and negotiating skills, as well as small business mentoring.

Acknowledgements

Grimur Atlason, Festival Manager, Iceland Airwaves Music Festival

Sigtryggur Baldursson, Managing Director, Iceland Music Export

Steve Bather, CEO, MeetingSphere, Washington, USA

Carol Bell, Head of Culture and Major Events, NewcastleGateshead Initiative

Claudia Connelly, Operations Director, WRG

Paul Cook, Event Consultant, Managing Director of Planet Planit

Henrietta Duckworth, Executive Producer, Yorkshire Festival

Claire Eason-Bassett, Event Director, Truro City of Lights

Maurice Fleming, Managing Director, Shelton Fleming Associates

Dr Charmaine Griffiths, Director of Strategy and Performance at British Heart Foundation

Tracey Halliwell, Director of Business Tourism and Major Events, London and Partners

Dr Elling Hamso, Meeting Management Consultant, Managing Partner of Event ROI Institute

Eamonn Hunt, CEO Very Creative Ltd

David Jamilly, Co-Founder, Theme Traders Ltd

Emma Kirk, Senior Events Manager, Savvy Marketing

Benita Lipps, Executive Director, DaVinci Institute

Russell Miller, Associate Director Business Relations and Sponsorship, Manchester Business School

Clas Olsen, Booking Manager of the Oya Festival, Norway

Claire O'Neill, Senior Manager, Association of Independent Festivals and Co-Founder of A Greener Festival

Ann Palmer, Director, Event and Roadshow Marketing, Barclays Bank

Alun Pritchard, Partnership Manager, Wales Rally GB

Claire Pulford, Head of Events, Breast Cancer Care, UK

Tony Rogers, Managing Director at Tony Rogers Conference and Events Services, UK

Helen Rowbotham, Director of Consulting at CSM Strategic

Will Russ, Undergraduate Student, Sheffield Business School

Melissa Sharpe, PR Assistant, Clarion Communications

Mark Shearon, Managing Partner, Proscenium, New York

Luke Southern, Marketing and Strategy Director, Glasgow 2014 Commonwealth Games at Virgin Media

Richard Taylor, Executive Director Fundraising and Marketing at Cancer Research, UK

Anna Ásthildur Thorsteinsson, Project Manager, Iceland Music Export

Vladimir Vodalov, Director, EXIT Festival, Serbia

Richard Waddington, Chairman of Events Marketing Association, (EMA)

Nick Woodward-Shaw, Director of Global Events, Forever Living Products International

Part I
New Normal
For Events

1 Strategic Event Creation

Phil Crowther

Learning objectives

- Interpret the changing forces which define the environment for event creation.

- Appreciate why and how the role of event creation is evolving.

- Understand the definition and five pillars of Strategic Event Creation.

Introduction

Changes in the wider environment have triggered a new normal for event creation. Heightened attendee expectations, a keener focus upon the return required by funders and wider stakeholders, and, of course, an ever more competitive event marketplace, are three significant influences which have intensified the challenge of event creation. Whichever sector of the events industry we consider, these forces are influential, to differing degrees, in shaping the environment. Alongside these foremost factors, there are other significant considerations, such as Corporate Social Responsibility (CSR), globalisation, and technology, which transform the contexts within which events are created. All of the above circumstances are interconnected and combine to represent a step change in the environment and challenge of event creation, undoubtedly making it a much more strategic and multi-layered responsibility. Consequently change is required in how we, as event creators and scholars think about, and approach, the discipline of event management.

Although still at an early stage, event education has prospered and matured considerably in the last two decades. This has provoked considerable advancement in academic thinking which is expressed through the growing body of literature. Much of this echoes the event management dominant approach, as characterised by Brown (2014), with events being planned, managed, and process driven as embodied in the influential EMBOK framework (International EMBOK Executive, 2009). Recently, however, there has been a shift in the literature placing renewed emphasis on event design (for example Berridge, 2012; Brown, 2005) as distinct from the more operational tone of event management. This development is significant and in this book we articulate it as the transition from an input orientation to an outcome dominant mindset, which we straightforwardly label 'outcome obsessed'. We argue that inputs are integral, yet they should be subordinate to the outcomes. The mindset and approach of event creators should reflect this. Consequently as the event industry matures, the employability of graduates and the professionalisation of the field are directly linked to, and reliant upon, the outcomes that events generate.

In response, this book proposes *Strategic Event Creation* as both a management approach and an enlightened outlook which is more attuned to this new normal. Strategic Event Creation rises to the challenge of the above circumstances and in so doing offers event students and practitioners a progressive and effectual lens through which to perceive and undertake their quest of event design and delivery. Fundamentally it assumes an outcome obsessed and stakeholder-centric approach, advocating a view that event creators are most appropriately defined as the facilitators of positive outcomes for individuals and groups that are proactively involved with, or implicated as a consequence of the event occurring.

This chapter acts as the bedrock for the remainder of this book, initially in its examination of the changing landscape, secondly in the explanation of Strategic Event Creation and most importantly of the five principles that underpin the approach.

A shifting landscape for event creators

The four interwoven factors discussed below underpin the need for change in how we, as event scholars and practitioners, perceive and execute the creation of events. The developments detailed below are not presented as entirely new phenomena; it is the acceleration in each of these forces, and their combined impact, that specifies a changing circumstance for event creation. They are also not presented as positive or negative, nor are they inherently damaging or destructive, they quite simply reshape the challenge we, as event creators, face.

■ Heightened attendee expectations

Ever since Holbrook and Hirschman (1982) first pinpointed the need for organisations to reconsider their view of consumption and embrace an experiential outlook, successive writers have commented upon the emergence, and growing primacy, of experience. The kind of experiences we, and our forefathers, only experienced in a planned event setting now flood many other aspects of our lives: retail, hospitality, travel, home entertainment and more. Indeed we educators, in colleges and universities, are now encouraged to purposefully generate experiences for our students. In so doing, practitioners, in these settings, are challenged to ponder many of the same considerations as event creators; how do they involve, immerse, generate intensity, individualise, and so forth (see Masterman and Wood's 7 Is, in Wood (2009)). This calculated design of experiences has become very big business.

These pervasive commercial experiences, as interpreted by writers such as Zomerdijk and Voss (2010) and Poulsson and Kale (2004), punctuate our lives. This trend has been accelerated further by the explosion of technology as organisations generate experiences to exceed, and hurriedly re-exceed, our expectations, even when we are not physically in their presence, through television, cinema, gaming, and hand held devices. We therefore perceive how the experience economy, as Pine and Gilmore (1998) labelled it, increasingly engulfs us as we journey through life.

For us, absorbed in the business of event creation, this is all very significant. We must recognise how people's periodic attendance at the planned events we create is interspersed by an abundance of sporadic micro experiences that infiltrate their everyday existence. Generally, our reaction as human beings to this constant exposure to these cleverly designed experiences is that we build immunity and typically demand equal, and greater, stimulation next time, if they are to resonate. As a society, our experience expectations are on an upward trajectory and consequently, as writers such as Schmitt (1999) and Smilansky (2009) allude to, the business of experience creation is inevitably dynamic and fast moving, it has to be. As creators of 'planned events' we do not exist in isolation of this wider experience marketplace. Our role is thus confounded by the glut of experiences our attendees consume elsewhere in their lives.

As event creators we now exist as one grouping within an ever more proliferated and widened community of experience creators – which positively makes our skills much more in demand. Our abilities to interpret attendee antecedents and insightfully shape their experiences become vital. Discussion of attendee experiences is specifically examined in Chapter 4, and clearly illustrated through Claire's voice below.

Industry voice: Claire O'Neill, Senior Manager, Association of Independent Festivals, Co-founder, A Greener Festival , UK

Greater competition amongst festivals brings a sophistication and expectation amongst audience who are, to a degree, spoiled for choice. In addition, there are new audiences attending festivals who would not have done so ten plus years ago. More families and 'glampers' might expect a certain level of comfort and facilities at the events they attend. Events must meet these expectations to compete, and when they succeed to meet expectations more new audiences are attracted.

■ Competitive event marketplace

Favourably, a by-product of society's fondness of experience is that the events industry has, itself, flourished. Live events continue to be foremost providers of experiences; consequently in a world where consumers more than ever before desire experience (see literature on Generation Y, for example Davidson (2008)), and organisations increasingly recognise the rewards of triggering experiences, the marketplace for events will continue to prosper. We therefore see some of the most renowned commentators in the events field charting the increased number, size, scope and significance of events (Bowdin et al, 2011; Getz, 2012; Richards, 2013). As the industry flourishes we predictably see a growing competition between events and event organisations.

Intensified competition triggers the pursuit of differentiation and also logically fuels an escalation in participant expectations. It is within this context that we can recognise the growing value of proficient event creators. Getz (2012) stresses that experience is at the heart of the event, so it logically follows that event creators are the chief facilitator of these experiences (see Chapters 7 and 8 which focus upon experience design). Therefore, as we see busier event marketplaces, populated by more experience-savvy attendees and determined competitors, the abilities of those creating events become increasingly crucial.

The experiences and outcomes that event creators are able to initiate through their proficient and enlightened event design are influential both in ensuring a specific event is perceived as successful, but also in creating the conditions for future event success. The experiences and outcomes stake-holders and participants perceive through their engagement with an event inevitably influence the likelihood of their involvement with future events hosted by that organisation. Most events are not one-offs, and instead link to repeat or related events in future. Therefore the delivery of a given event is also a marketing channel to influence involvement in future events. This inescapable reality of event creation grows in magnitude as the market for events and event venues becomes more and more crowded and dynamic.

1

Case study: Wales Rally GB

Wales Rally GB is the final round of the World Rally Championship that spans the globe, taking place in 13 far flung locations. It is managed, and I am employed, by International Motor Sports, a wholly owned subsidiary of the National Governing Body, the Motor Sports Association, a not-for-profit company whose profits are channelled back into the sport. The Rally has a rich heritage with the Great Britain stage in its 41st year and in 2013 the rally was relocated to North Wales having being based in South Wales for the previous 12 years. The move has turned out to be extremely successful with record spectator attendances both at the event's 'service park' and on many of the rally stages as well. There are many reasons for this success but particularly there has been considerable focus upon enhancing the event beyond the core motor racing audience and ideas such as securing Amy Williams, Winter Olympics Gold Medallist, to be a co-driver for the rally have been very successful in generating an increased buzz and also wider media coverage.

This explosion of interest has been a game-changer for the event, and for the organisers, with shifting and rising expectations of both fans and wider stakeholders. As an example of the breadth of the challenge, beyond the nuts and bolts of the event, we work extremely hard to safeguard the social and environmental impacts of the Rally; the event is supported by the Major Events Unit of the Welsh Government and key to their commitment is that we hit environmental criteria. To achieve this we have an ambition to be the world's first consistently carbon neutral rally. Additionally we work hard with engaging local communities, and also grapple to combat issues such as tree disease and water pollution. To ensure we are best equipped to meet the requirements of all of our stakeholders we constantly analyse best practice from a number of other large scale events, whilst also coming up with in-house ideas of how to achieve our goals. Priority here is information gathering and a thorough market research programme is, for example, taking place during the 2014 event so that we can reflect upon our performance and improve going forward.

A real priority area for us is spectator experience. The public expects to get as close to the action as possible, and we try to facilitate this in a safe way with thorough and rigorous event management procedures. These are now scrutinised more than ever before, both internally and externally, by a variety of relevant organisations. This can quickly lead to increased cost which is a problem in a competitive and price sensitive events marketplace. We are constantly challenged by the tension between delivering exhilarating spectator experiences and operating safe events, which is of course the number one priority. As a result we have to be constantly inventive in our approach and think outside the box to come up with new approaches that solve the issues raised.

Another growing area relates to the commercial agreements that are made with sponsors and other partners, as these organisations become an ever greater consideration in how we put the event together. Previously these would have been straightforward exchanges of equipment or payment for advertising presence, but they are now much more sophisticated and sponsors require more involvement and also evidence of return. Particularly the rise of social media as a tool to activate their sponsorship and to measure results has been a notable recent development.

From our point of view the business of staging events has moved up a gear and as event managers the need to work more strategically, and particularly handle a web of prospective partners, has become a huge part of what we do. Of course the operations and logistics remain but our team has had to expand and mature to ensure we can properly handle the different aspects of making the event happen.

Written by: Alun Pritchard, Partnership Manager, Wales Rally GB

■ Instrumental event investment

There is an established argument across many strands of literature that events are increasingly strategic in their purpose. We discuss the instrumental application of events with funders, sponsors, and partners becoming more calculated and watchful in their event investments. Literature across different event sectors repeatedly identifies the prevalence of the strategic outcomes that investors seek to realise through their event investment (Crowther, 2011; Richards and Palmer, 2010; Vanneste, 2008 to name a few). We are witnessing a notable advancement in how events are purposefully used by organisations, of all shapes and sizes, as a catalyst to achieve wider outcomes.

The required and desired outcomes of event funders and other supporters can, to varying degrees, be achieved within the time and space parameters of the event. Increasingly, however, as a more instrumental approach takes hold, the return on investment perceived by backers, while reliant upon the effectual hosting of an event, are future oriented and therefore aside from the core business of event creation. Consequently, and as discussed partly in Chapter 3, and Chapter 11, events are increasingly invested in as a catalyst rather than an end point. If we accept that events are conduits for wider and future oriented outcomes, we raise important questions about the delineation of the event creator's role and responsibilities. Event creators are primarily delivering events for the here and now but the process of event design and delivery must be infused with a more holistic strategic intent.

Events have always existed in a strategic web whereby the investors who fund and support events do so purposefully. Their collective purpose informs the strategic context of the event and partly defines the event creator's mission. As event investment becomes ever more instrumental, as indicated by Claire in the extract below, event creators typically have more substantial outcomes to realise. We must therefore be increasingly mindful of the importance of the event delivering a return on investment or, given the softer outcomes of many events, a return on objectives. This, again, indicates a more strategic and augmented remit for event creators. This topic is more fully explained in Chapters 3 and 5 in examining the returns expected by clients, sponsors, and event partners. The evaluation of these outcomes is examined in Chapter 13.

Industry voice: Claire Pulford, Head of Events, Breast Cancer Care, UK

The charity sector is increasingly crowded and whilst this has raised the bar for events it means more than ever we need to use them strategically to help us achieve a range of objectives. Ten years ago most charities' engagement with events was rather limited, often it consisted of running events, treks or having places in the London Marathon, but now it's so much more advanced and my team contribute over a third of the charity's total income. Although our main objectives are to realise awareness generation and fundraising goals, events actually offer a much more sophisticated tool than just that, and actually if you just focus upon short term easily quantifiable returns then you miss other opportunities.

The sizeable financial investment our charity makes in event-based activity simply has to be justifiable and is constantly reviewed given the other worthwhile investments the charity could make with those monies. So, for example, we actually assess the value of each event against the organisation goals. Of course we look at audience reach and income but we also look at how the event offers ongoing support to people affected by breast cancer, how it works across the organisation to introduce new donors and improve retention rates of individual and corporate support and its press value, which is essentially advertising spend that's been saved. There are some events that don't have particularly great ROIs and understandably the Exec and Trustees will ask 'Should this event be taking place?' But that is why we constantly monitor and evaluate all our events against a set of objectives that include giving recognition to the added benefits they bring to the organisation. And in the annual planning process if they don't stand up to the thorough assessment, we won't continue doing them.

◾ Responsibility for wider impacts

The above narrative is focussed upon involved stakeholders, those groups and individuals initiating events, positively supporting events and willingly attending events. In understanding the full strategic context of an event it is useful to distinguish between these groups and wider, perhaps less direct and positive, event impacts. This includes stakeholders who are not willing enthusiasts but inadvertently implicated by the existence of the event.

Incumbent upon event creators, more than ever before, is the requirement to adopt an outer layer of consciousness which sharpens awareness of the interplay between the event and the surrounding environment. The inescapable physicality and resource intensiveness of events means that, depending upon the specifics of the event, there are potentially many associated impacts. Therefore an integral consideration for event creators is their impact upon the environment, neighbours, communities, and indeed local and regional economies in which they exist. The strategic context of an event, and therefore the event design, must embrace a sensibility to these wider impacts. This demands a different mindset, and one that affords the event creators opportunities to positively affect a variety of outcome areas as reasoned by Elkington (1994) in his discussion of the triple bottom line.

Besides a moral responsibility, event creators are increasingly hamstrung in this area by legislation, attendee and public expectations, marketing risk and opportunity, and indeed employee, and other stakeholder values. Certainly it will become more and more of a challenge, and a detriment, to behave in an anti-sustainable manner. In years to come it would seem improbable to imagine an event being heralded a success, or an event creator succeeding in their career, were they not to embrace a sustainable mindset. Beyond the outcomes sought by attendees and the objectives commanded by leading stakeholders, event creators must properly consider broader and perhaps less attractive considerations. Discussion of this is contained in Chapter 6.

Strategic Event Creation

The shifting landscape evaluated in the previous section commands that the mindset and approach of those people creating events must evolve accordingly. The future requires event creators who are more outward facing and progressive in their approach, where the budgetary and operational efficacy of the event is subsumed within a more strategic and intuitive appreciation of what success looks like. The new environment demands that event creators move beyond their typecast as operational figures and realise a much more strategic and facilitative role. Event creators are at the heart of the action, recognising the strategic context of the event and through intuitive design they facilitate required and desired outcomes for involved and impacted groups.

You will notice the adoption of words such as shaping, design and facilitation, to depict the event creation process. This is a deliberate attempt to shift the lexicon and you will see a repetition of words of a similar ilk throughout this book: craft, curate, choreograph and so forth. Such words are consistent with progressive thinking around events which embraces a similar perspective (see the recent chapter by Berridge (2012)). We purposefully adopt this language to oppose the unadventurous, underwhelming, and increasingly outdated notions of 'organising' and 'coordinating' that have often dominated the narrative of event literature. These terms now fail to capture the multi-layered requirements of event creation and therefore undersell the role. In the early years of higher education, in this area, event management literature has justifiably adopted a more operational focus, as recently intimated by Rojek (2013). As the event industry has progressed, effectual event operations become a prerequisite to exist rather than a recipe to succeed; therefore the focus of event management literature must respond.

Consequently, this book commentates on the step change that moves beyond event organising and coordinating and towards Strategic Event Creation, which is articulated in the definition and principles expressed below. The sophistication of the event creation role is far reaching and gives an elevated remit and fresh persona to those people charged with the planning, delivery, and evaluation of events. Students and practitioners of events should banish thoughts of themselves as organisers and coordinators, with connotations of 'to-do lists' and where, perhaps, their most important job is to make sure nothing goes wrong. Instead we should open our minds to a far more adventurous and multifaceted responsibility, with a requirement for event creators to be considerably more purposeful, inventive and distinctly facilitative.

Strategic Event Creation can therefore be defined as:

Both a mindset and a management approach to the creation of events which is preoccupied with the characteristics, goals and concerns of involved and impacted stakeholders. Through adopting this perspective, and a proficient and enlightened approach to the design of the event (pre, during, post), the required and desired outcomes can be ably facilitated.

Strategic Event Creation comprises five interwoven principles which are discussed below and shown as interwoven rope threads in Figure 1.1, below. These guiding principles shape the event creation from inception and are integral in facilitating the many and disparate outcomes and impacts represented on the right side of the diagram. Those individuals and event teams who embody this approach are more likely to generate successful outcomes and lessen negative impacts. Event creators will be preoccupied by the specific event consciousness which represents the unique circumstance of any given event; including stakeholders and resources. The global consciousness shown outside of the rope represents the influential macro factors that unavoidably affect an event's creation; whether these are economic, political, social, environmental, and technological or legal. These two layers combine to represent the strategic context of the event which the creator must interpret, engage with and reflect in their behaviour and decisions.

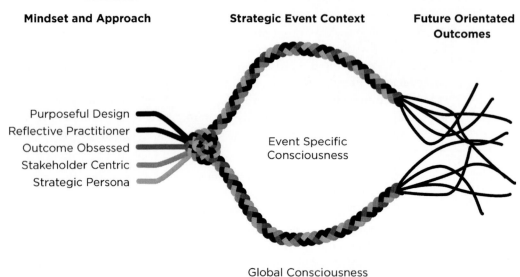

Figure 1.1: The five interwoven principles of Strategic Event Creation

Before considering the five principles individually it is useful to read and reflect upon a case example written by Carol Bell from the public/private partnership charged with marketing Newcastle and Gateshead on a national and international stage. This example embodies the spirit of Strategic Event Creation.

Case study: Spencer Tunick in NewcastleGateshead, UK

We were approached by BALTIC Centre for Contemporary Art to produce and manage an event that would achieve two objectives:

■ Mark and celebrate the opening of the gallery – and, importantly, demonstrate its ambitions beyond the confines of the building itself.

■ Support our (NewcastleGateshead Initiative's) work to change perceptions and create a positive profile for the area.

The event concept centred on Spencer Tunick - an installation artist whose work involves transforming public spaces with nude figures and then capturing these images through photography (see www.spencertunick.com). The aspiration was to attract a large number of volunteers to participate in the installation – in and around Newcastle and Gateshead Quayside – both to be photographed by Tunick and to be filmed for a BBC3 documentary about his work.

The challenges of such a controversial project were clear from the outset – from health and safety, policing and road closure requirements, to the scale of volunteer recruitment and potential negative or critical media coverage. We were, however, convinced that the vision and rationale for the event were so strong that we could and should make it happen. We believed wholeheartedly in the end 'result' - both the creative manifestation and the potential to make a national and international name for NewcastleGateshead as a vibrant, cultural and innovative place that is willing to take risks.

The process of managing this event reaffirmed for me that nothing is impossible – not even...

- Recruiting thousands of ordinary people to take their clothes off, walk around and pose nude in multiple public, city centre locations – all in the name of art.

- Winning the hearts and minds of risk averse public authorities and public service providers, to gain support for such an ambitious event.

- Achieving 100% positive regional, national and international media coverage for an event that could have been perceived as contentious, offensive and/or a significant waste of public money.

How did we do it? Well the key was undoubtedly partnership working...

It was essential that everyone with a role to play or a vested interest in the event, was briefed, engaged and updated throughout – we had to take people along with us or risk dissenting and disapproving voices derailing the project. We quickly established the necessary processes and forums to underpin effective partnership working. These included:

- A Communications Group – involving PR representatives from each of the organisations involved.

- A series of regional media briefings to engage positively with local journalists from the outset – in fact a number even took part in the installation itself!

- A Safety Advisory Group (SAG). At the first of these meetings we shared the vision and the objectives. Whilst these meetings were largely about logistics, it was critical that everyone understood and bought into the reasons for, and benefits of, delivering such an event.

The result:

- We attracted 1,700 people to take part in the installation, many of whom returned to see the resulting exhibition at BALTIC the following February and become positive advocates for the area.

- We secured regional, national and international media coverage worth £1.8m, including a one hour BBC documentary, which not only focused on the event itself but also told the story of the cultural renaissance of NewcastleGateshead.

> ■   We succeeded in raising the profile of BALTIC Centre for Contemporary Art locally, nationally and internationally and importantly put NewcastleGateshead on the map as a culturally vibrant destination at the forefront of contemporary art.
>
> Written by: Carol Bell, Head of Culture and Major Events, NewcastleGateshead Initiative

Strategic Event Creation principles

1   Outcome obsessed

A message that persists throughout this book is that event creators must resist the inclination to routinely fixate on the 'here and now' and instead pause to ensure they possess a considered appreciation of the 'why and how'. A disproportionately operational outlook is not consistent with the ever more strategic context of events, and the delivery of financial and operational effectiveness is a precondition, rather than the definition, of success. Event creators should embrace an outcome oriented perspective where the foremost measures of success are the outcomes received and perceived by involved and impacted stakeholders. The circumstance and expectation of each of these stakeholders consequently acts as the guiding logic which shapes the event design and delivery.

Interpreting the make-up and aspirations of stakeholders, including attendees, is consequently a crucial attribute of capable event creators. Establishing this strategic context is a foremost stage in any event creation process as it serves to provide a harmonising logic that informs, and unifies, the many and diverse decisions that constitute an event's design. Configuring the varied and sometimes competing aspirations, priorities, and concerns that represent this strategic context involves the ability to balance and prioritise, which is an implicit aspect of the event creator's role. For a large scale event this would be a considerable undertaking but even for the smallest events creators should nevertheless pause to map the required outcomes. This point is emphasised by Nick, below, and demonstrates the evolution of events.

When event creation neglects to adopt a more strategic mindset and instead becomes preoccupied by the inputs, outcomes can become overlooked, which seems illogical. This notion is developed through Chapters 3, 4, 5 and 6 which combine to represent the web of outcomes that event creators should be familiar with.

Industry voice: Nick Woodward-Shaw, Director of Global Events, Forever Living Products International, Arizona, USA

In the past, events have been "oh, we've got to hold an event because we have to, haven't we? It's an annual thing" whereas now that's not good enough anymore and you have to focus upon and deliver the return on investment. The microscope is on events and it has been for the past 5 or 10 years. I just think 5 or 10 years ago a lot of companies thought "Yeah, we know we need to do an ROI, but it's difficult to measure and if people go away with a warm, fuzzy feeling that's enough, isn't it?" And what I've noticed, and certainly internally here, is suddenly that's now not enough and actually we need to demonstrate hard facts.

2   Stakeholder centric outlook

The discussion above expresses the need to reflect upon the multiple interests that comprise any given event, and therefore the pivotal notions of mutuality/reciprocity that exist at the heart of event creation. These terms are intentionally used to emphasise the multiple interests, and therefore numerous outcomes, that constitute any given event occurrence. Successful event creation can rarely, if ever, be restricted to satisfaction on the part of a single stakeholder, or even limited to a singular outcome; it is both more diverse, and intricate, than this implies. The challenge is to engage with the multifaceted character of event creation and generate a configuration of outcomes. This acts as the harmonising logic to inform the event design.

Consequently a repeated call, throughout this book, is that successful event creation is typically based upon the adoption of a stakeholder centric approach. Events should be underpinned by a shrewd appreciation of stakeholders' desires and concerns and the business of event creation should, where feasible, be done collaboratively and not in spite of stakeholders, as is emphasised by Claire in the excerpt below. Emphasis is therefore placed upon engaging stakeholders actively in the co-creation of the event, as explored in Chapter 7. Event creation thus becomes, where possible, a collaborative enterprise that is involving and co-innovative, with the prescribed event creators as the lynch-pin.

This approach can be contrasted with three other mindsets which might prevail in event creation, of which the first is 'creator centric' whereby we prioritise operational and financial convenience. The second we consider 'investor centric' whereby the interests of one or two key stakeholders, who are materially supporting the event, are singularly pursued to the exclusion of others. Last we have the 'attendee centric' mindset where there exists an exclusive focus upon attendee gratification. A stakeholder centric outlook is an informed and balanced approach based upon an appreciation of required and desired outcomes for all stakeholder groups. This discussion is expanded first in Chapter 2 and then, as indicated, in Chapter 7.

Industry voice: Claire Pulford, Head of Events, Breast Cancer Care, UK

One example of this is how we often work together on events with new partner organisations – using the event as a tool to engage the organisation with the charity. Often the event provides a softer and more tangible way into an organisation and then the mutual respect and success engendered from an initial collaboration allows us to the build a more lasting relationship.

A great example of this is the work we did in 2005 with Highland Spring at the New York Marathon, which sparked the beginning of a brilliant relationship. The initial event hit lots of key objectives for both parties and off the back of this we developed a corporate relationship that spanned eight years and raised over half a million pounds. All of these partnerships are built upon frankness, where at the outset we both express the returns we hope to achieve and this 'combined ROI' shapes the event's planning and delivery.

3   Purposeful design

Event creators are architects of experience journeys for their attendees and facilitators of outcomes for other involved stakeholders. By interpreting the character and motivations of key stakeholders, you establish a guiding logic to inform your event creation. Understanding the strategic context, as discussed in Principle 1 above, permits an appreciation of the 'configuration of outcomes' which then acts as a distinctive internal logic upon which event design decisions can be made and synchronised. This process supports the need for decisions to integrate with each other to ensure a cohesive event experience for stakeholders.

Of course, the creator's role is restricted to the purposeful crafting of settings in which the groups and individuals can attain their experiences, as experience is unavoidably derived rather than delivered (Ramaswamy, 2009). Through practised understanding of how event settings can be best designed, how attendees experience them, and how event activity can best trigger wider outcomes, event creators can become very effective facilitators and designers. Indeed Berridge (2012) logically discusses how design increases the predictability of experience outcomes. Alternatively, inept event creation results in a mismatch between the rationale and decisions of the event creator and the characteristics of the involved stakeholders. Claire illustrates, in the below extract, how growing competition and heightened experience expectations increasingly challenge event creators to purposefully design events and also to adopt enlightened approaches to ensure a return for the funder and a maximisation of attendee engagement.

Industry voice: Claire Pulford, Head of Events, Breast Cancer Care, UK

Our events have to be distinctive in order to succeed, and they have to reflect us as a charity, so we are obsessive about embedding our core value of caring in the experiences we create. Put simply when you have been to a Breast Cancer Care event you know you have been to a Breast Cancer Care event as we think very carefully about the participant's experience. This is not an easy undertaking and certainly takes us beyond what you might call ordinary event management. It all demands considerably attention, but our events have to feel different. If they don't, we will not reflect our charity values or build the kind of future relationships that will sustain our awareness and fundraising objectives.

A good example of this is our annual 'Ribbon Walk' event where supporters and people who have been affected by breast cancer come together for a walk in the countryside. The values of warmth and care are translated into a vision so that the event feels like you are attending a garden party where everyone is your friend. We then adopt this mindset to meticulously create every stage of the attendee's experience from the moment they arrive to the moment they leave. For example, the welcome they get in the car park through to the route, where we have villages and communities opening up their homes and gardens for refreshment stops, the way that they're cheered over the line by their families and local bands, the cup of tea they get, the medal, the massage, the quality of the food, the warmth of the welcome, all of the extra bits.

4   A strategic persona

A necessary ingredient underpinning Strategic Event Creation is a departure from the stereotypical guise of event creators. The hackneyed reference to planners, coordinators, and organisers was critiqued earlier and must be substituted with more progressive language consistent with the principles of Strategic Event Creation. As interpreters of stakeholder intent, profilers of attendees, and facilitators of multiple outcomes, we are commentating in this book upon a new persona for event creators, which is far removed from the lower-grade identity that often prevails. The importance of event creators behaving at a more strategic level, as guardian of the outcomes, is captured by Nick in his discussion below relating to the selection of event partners and suppliers.

Industry voice: Nick Woodward-Shaw, Director of Global Events, Forever Living Products International, Arizona, USA

When we're dealing with people that haven't worked with us before, we're hugely honest and we tell them up-front very, very clearly what our event objectives are and what our expectations are from a supplier point of view of the services that we expect from you, and we're very demanding because we're very passionate. I think if we're honest with suppliers and stakeholders about our objectives and they come back to us saying "Well, that's not what we're about," then we're cool with that and we'll find somebody else. Also get that honesty out of the way beforehand, because on site it can be pretty stressful because every minute counts. So if a year out from the event you spend a little bit more time trying to find that exact, right partner, then so much the better.

If we move, in our articulation of event creation, beyond a narrower fixation upon financial and operational efficacy and refocus upon the primacy of outcome facilitation, then the event creator moves from being a planner to becoming a deliverer. Consequently they become a strategic partner in the event.

5   Reflective practitioner

Event creators must be reflective practitioners who assess the perceived and achieved outcomes and also capture the many opportunities for learning that each event episode produces. The inclination and ability of event creators to do this directly impacts upon the successes of their future events, their employers, and of course their own career progression. Event creation is a longitudinal and cyclical activity and therefore the act of reflection should be ever-present and not confined to a brief post event activity. Evaluation of outcomes, processes, progress and behaviours, should not be an add-on or postscript but an integral facet of successful Strategic Event Creation.

Reflective practitioners are future orientated in that while they are often seeking to detect event outcomes and to learn from past actions and experience, the purpose of this is to inform future action and behaviours. There are two chapters dedicated to unravelling the issues contained within the above. Chapters 12 and 13 specifically explore the topic of evaluation, however a prevailing theme throughout the book is the requirement for consultation and careful consideration before action.

Concluding remarks

In exploring the interconnected consequences of heightened attendee expectations, an ever more competitive marketplace, instrumental event investment, and widened responsibility for event impacts, we reveal a changed environment that demands a renewed approach to event creation. Therein we foresee event creators as inevitably embracing a more strategic role in the facilitation of outcomes for the involved and implicated stakeholders. Consistent with this requirement, Strategic Event Creation is introduced, underpinned by five defining principles.

The remainder of this book builds upon the core ideas of Strategic Event Creation. The chapters are arranged to convey the five interwoven principles by offering perspectives from contributors, each with different event specialisms and areas of interest. They provide varied, and complementary, perspectives as to how the ideas embodied in this chapter can be applied to the many different aspects of the event creator's remit. The aim is to begin a much needed conversation about how the changing circumstance of event creation, and the underpinning ideas of Strategic Event Creation, fundamentally change the approach of event professionals.

Study questions

1 Identify, and evaluate, specific examples of how the 'shifting landscape for event creators' provides different challenges to the event creator as they seek to achieve successful outcomes.

2 Review the case example of Breast Cancer Care and identify how the messages communicated in Claire's writing correspond with the content of this chapter.

3 Evaluate two of the principles of Strategic Event Creation and examine the challenges event creators would face in embracing these approaches.

References

Berridge, G. (2012). Designing Event Experiences. In S. J. Page and J. Connel (Eds.), *The Routledge Handbook of Events* (pp. 273-288). Oxford: Taylor Francis Group.

Bowdin, G. A. J., Allen, J., Harris, K., O'Toole, W. J. and McDonnell, I. (2011). *Events Management: 3rd Edition*. Oxford: Butterworth-Heinemann.

Brown, S. (2005). Event design—an Australian perspective. Paper presented at the 2nd International Event Management Body of Knowledge Global Alignment Summit, Johannesburg, South Africa.

Brown, S. (2014). Emerging professionalism in the events industry: A practitioner's perspective. *Event Management Journal*, **18**(1), 15-24.

Crowther, P. (2011). Marketing event outcomes: from tactical to strategic. *International Journal of Event and Festival Management*, **2**(1), 68-82.

Davidson, R. (2008). What does Generation Y want from conference and incentive programmes. www.insights.org.uk/articleitem.aspx?title=What%20Does%20Generation%20Y%20want%20from%20Conferences%20and%20Incentive%20Programmes?, accessed 02/01/2013

Elkington, J. (1994). Towards the sustainable corporation: Win-win-win business strategies for sustainable development. *California Management Review*, **36**(2), 90-100.

International EMBOK Executive (2009). Event management body of knowledge: An introduction. www.embok.org/, accessed 10/06/2014

Getz, D. (2012). Event studies: discourses and future directions. *Event Management*, **16**, 171-187.

Holbrook, M. B. and Hirschman, E. C. (1982). The experiential aspects of consumption: Consumer fantasies, feelings, and fun. *Journal of Consumer Research*, **9**(September), 132-140.

Pine, B. J. and Gilmore, J. H. (1998). Welcome to the experience economy. *Harvard Business Review*, **76**(4), 97-105.

Poulsson, H. G. and Kale, S. H. (2004). The experience economy and commercial experiences. *The Marketing Review*, **4**, 267-277.

Ramaswamy, V. (2009). Co-creation of value: Toward an expanded paradigm of value creation. *Marketing Review St Gallen*, **6**, 11-17.

Richards, G. (2013). Events and the means of attention. *Journal of Tourism Research and Hospitality*. doi: http://dx.doi.org/10.4172/2324-8807.1000118

Richards, G. and Palmer, P. (2010). *Eventful Cities: Cultural Management and Urban Revitalisation*. Oxford: Elsevier.

Rojek, C. (2013). *Event Power: How Global Events Manage and Manipulate* London: Sage.

Schmitt, B. H. (1999). *Experiential Marketing: How To Get Customers To Sense, Feel, Think, Act, and Relate To Your Company And Brands*, New York: Free Press.

Smilansky, S. (2009). *Experiential Marketing: A Practical Guide To Interactive Brand Experiences*. London: Kogan Page.

Vanneste, M. (2008). *Meeting Architecture: a Manifesto*, Meeting Support Institute.

Wood, E. H. (2009). Evaluating event marketing: experience or outcome? *Journal of Promotion Management*, **15**(1), 247-268.

Zomerdijk, L. G. and Voss, C., A (2010). Service design for experience-centric services. *Journal of Service Research*, **13**(1), 67-82.

2 Stakeholder Centric Approach

James Bostock

Learning objectives

- To understand the importance of a stakeholder centric approach to event creation.
- To appreciate the various communicative media that promote stakeholder engagement.
- To comprehend the complexities of stakeholder mapping and the importance of locality.

Introduction

The extent to which event creators should dedicate time and careful thought to stakeholder relationships and engagement cannot be overstated. Events are co-produced by a collection of stakeholders, which includes those we immediately think about such as the host organisation who initiated the event, key funders, performers and attendees, but also less obvious stakeholders such as the communities that surround the event. Strategic event creators, as defined in the previous chapter, orchestrate, and more importantly facilitate, the event outcomes by interpreting the contributions, aims and/or concerns, of stakeholder groups and harnesses them to deliver the event and associated activity. Event creators who do this effectively enable truly co-produced events and outcomes, a process that cultivates relationships that endure. This is crucial as one event is a moment in time that very quickly becomes the precursor to future events and other activity. A valuable lasting legacy of an event is the 'orgware', as referred to by Richards and Palmer (2010, p.343), which are the relationships formed and their future potential.

This chapter introduces new ideas to achieve the stakeholder centric approach, introduced in Chapter 1, which lies at the heart of Strategic Event

Creation. It challenges many of the conventional views which can lead to a skewed and hierarchical view of stakeholders, and instead advocates a wider, more consultative, and importantly moral, perspective. It is argued that this approach provides the foundation for more sustainable event creation, economically, socially, and environmentally. It complements the interests of immediate stakeholders such as the key funders, organisers, and audience, with those of the wider community, and ensures that event creation reflects the interests and contribution of wider and often marginalised stakeholders.

The events sector is under increased pressure from a progressively more aware consumer base, the public, authorities and media to consider issues such as Corporate Social Responsibility (CSR), sustainability and the so called triple-bottom line. Consistent with the above paragraph, Pelham (2011) argues convincingly that the sector is adapting its business model in order to counter these changing demands by adopting business practices that seek to achieve a multitude of outcomes – a challenge that was highlighted within Chapter 1. A key part of this 'challenge' is that event creators are being held more accountable by a multitude of stakeholders (Smith, 2009). Indeed, if we wish to deliver events that can achieve strategic objectives then it is important that we seek positive stakeholder involvement, and also ascertain their viewpoints when evaluating whether these outcomes have been achieved (Getz, 2009; Elkington, 2004; Freeman, 1984). Getz (2009, p.65) stresses the importance of the stakeholder by stating that "the event's worth can only be ascertained, and the event deemed responsible and sustainable, if it meets the goals (or at least does not impede them) of all influential stakeholders". Therefore stakeholder approaches that promote wider engagement are integral to the future success of events.

The difficulty for many exisiting events, and in the approaches often advocated, is that too often stakeholder engagement is guided by a shorter term event-centric viewpoint rather than a longer term strategic view that also involves a sense of moral obligation. Traditional thinking places the event at the centre of the relationship between stakeholders, with different individuals seeking to influence the content of the event (Reid, 2011; Hede, 2007; Reid and Arcodia, 2002). This promotes a narrow focus upon immediately obvious stakeholders, and also a hierachical view of these with the implication being that many other parties are marginalised or perhaps ignored. In seeking an antidote to this, it is provocative to reflect on the question posed by Derry (2012, p.263), "Who or what should be at the hub of the stakeholder model?" The argument presented in the latter half of this chapter is that the event should be removed from the centre and replaced with the locality – the actual physical location of event delivery, but shaped within the context of values of those delivering the event and engaging with those who potentially could be affected. Although this is not intended to indicate priority for the economic, social, and environmental wellbeing of the locality, by considering stakeholder mapping in this way it ensures that a wider range of stakeholders are considered, and consulted, which strengthens the possible outcomes the event can generate.

2

Why a stakeholder centric approach is needed

Stakeholder engagement is often viewed as being important to legitimise the event we create. Therefore we need to ask, as event creators, who is it we are legitimising the event for? There is universal acceptance that stakeholders can be seen as those individuals, groups and organisations that are connected to the event and can be affected by or affect the successful outcome of the event - these are defined as legitimate stakeholders (Freeman, 1984). Freeman's view of the stakeholder, applied to an event context, is that they can influence the event creator's ability to achieve specific objectives, and through effective engagement with these stakeholders the event creator can facilitate benefits for all parties. This is significant, from a stakeholder engagement perspective, because single events are increasingly being used to meet a diversity of goals, and therefore touch a growing number of stakeholders, which is evidenced through the discussion in Part Two of this book, and also in Chapter 11. It is easy to see how certain stakeholders within this grouping can become marginalised; often this includes those that comprise the locality. For example, McKercher et al. (2006) found that many so-called tourist attractions actually attracted very few international tourists. Local visitors, in fact, made up the majority of attendees. By prioritising tourists as a primary stakeholder group and making the design decisions about the attraction on that basis, the experience of local visitors is diminished as they do not receive such a positive contextual experience. In many other cases the stakeholder groups that comprise the locality, for example residents, businesses, authorities, and interest groups, who could become advocates and positive contributors to the event, are neglected.

Engaging with a broader range of stakeholders presents the event creator with an opportunity, to not only achieve strategic objectives, but also to minimise adverse impacts. These direct relationships, but also the interplay of these with other stakeholders, have a much greater propensity to leverage positive economic, social, cultural, and environmental impacts for the totality of stakeholders. Consider a community market like that at Sharrowvale in Sheffield (see http://sharrowvalecommunityassociation.co.uk/market) that connects with charities, local groups, and the media, who have a shared interest in creating a socially inclusive event that engages with the different ethnic minorities that live and work in the community. This four way collaboration achieves outcomes beyond the immediate scope of the event but of considerable legacy and place benefit for all. Conversely, if we don't engage with stakeholders in a meaningful way then the gap between their expectations and ambitions and the actual outcomes of an event will only widen (Friedman, et al., 2004). This neglecting of interests limits the achievements of the current event, but also reduces the potential for future collaboration and therefore the sustainability of events going forward (Larson, 2004).

If stakeholders can be engaged in a fashion that seeks to create a consensus between the host organisation and the stakeholders, then events have the potential to operate in a more stakeholder centric manner and avoid what is called a 'democratic deficit' (Noland and Philips, 2010; Green and Houlihan, 2006). This happens when wider stakeholder involvement is limited, or eliminated, and the event becomes exclusively about the key power interests, for example, governmental departments, key funding agencies, commercial sponsorship or private interests. The Hong Kong Government engaged in a communication process that allowed the event creators of the bid to host to 2023 Asian Games to ascertain the needs and wants of the stakeholders concerned, and engage in participatory practices that were not simply tokenistic in nature – see the case study below. Arnstein (1969) would recognize this as an opportunity for the stakeholders to move up the 'participatory ladder' and create a more engaging approach to the decision making process, to ensure better representation of stakeholder values. Through this approach the event creators in Hong Kong could create greater satisfaction when they engage stakeholders in the future as their views and opinions have actually influenced decisions rather than just being listened to and then ignored.

Case study: The Hong Kong 2023 Asian Games Bid

On the 14th January 2011 the finance committee of Hong Kong's legislative council voted overwhelmingly not to finance or support a proposed bid to host the 2023 Asian Games. This decision was made even though Hong Kong had successfully hosted the East Asia Games in 2009, which featured over 260 events and 2,000 athletes in over 20 sports. The proposed bid failed because the council took their commitment to stakeholder consultation very seriously and acted on their views. Whilst the East Asian Games reaped benefits at an economic, social and cultural level the Hong Kong government felt that these benefits could be replicated and enhanced through hosting the much larger Asian Games. This major event would see over 40 countries/regions competing, with an estimated 11,000 athletes competing. Officials felt the event could have significant economic and tourism impact, estimating that over 300,000 spectators would attend the event.

In order for the Hong Kong government to be able to submit a bid, they had to achieve a broad consensus of support for the games from Hong Kong citizens through a consultative exercise. The consultation document proposed that HK$ 10.5 billion would be spent on capital spending and a further HK$3.2 billion to $ 4 billion on operating costs.

The consultation sought responses from Hong Kong citizens through a telephone survey (3,041 Hong Kong residents), public forums (5,271 individuals and 72 organisations), an on-line discussion forum (19,363 messages) and a Facebook page (1,863 persons joined). It should be noted that one person posted 1,631 messages in the discussion forum!

The public consultation revealed that there was a general feeling of animosity towards the event, with around 57% of respondents opposing the bid. The public felt that Hong Kong had more pressing issues to deal with such as soaring property prices and lack of social mobility. There was also a lack of understanding about the games as the government had spent little time communicating the benefits of hosting the games to the population. Most people consulted simply felt the government had better things to spend their money on.

In response the government changed the funding package of the games from HK$14.5 billion to HK$6 billion to try and increase support. This new package, which focused on operational issues rather than capital infrastructure, actually had a negative effect because the general population now felt that the government had little or no control over the costs of the games and disapproval actually went up to 63%. Shortly after this the finance committee voted against funding the games and Hong Kong's bid to host the Asian Games was over.

■ The separation thesis

There exists a tendency in events to focus upon 'who and what really counts' within stakeholder engagement, which Derry (2012) refers to as the separation thesis. Stakeholders are separated in terms of their levels of interaction with the event; primary (those at the heart of the event) and secondary (cooperation is sought) stakeholders (Clarkson, 1995). A subsequent issue may be that the host organisation, facilitated by the event creators, concentrates on how the attributes of the stakeholder can meet the immediate needs of the event, and not how sustainable wider and longer-term beneficial relationships can be formed (Greenwood, 2007). The dominant emphasis of this approach is short term self-interest, with the host and their organisational objectives being placed at the heart of the decision making process (Derry, 2012). However, this approach has its flaws as it unintentionally disregards many other important groups. Sautter and Liesen (1999) reflect on this arguing that by adopting this approach, marginalised groups are created and they will engage less positively with the event and at the extreme may actively seek to hamper the event as was the case for Derby City Council (see the case study later in this chapter).

This approach allows the event creator to make an assessment of the connection of stakeholders through their power (to control the event), legitimacy (the right to be involved) and urgency (importance of related issues) in relation to the event. It will also allow decisions to be made relating to engagement and involvement through a concept called *saliency*, 'the degree to which managers give priority to competing stakeholder claims' (Mitchell et al., 1997, p.854). It is argued by Clarkson (1995) that the event creator should focus on the attributes of the stakeholder and view the interactions more like a business transaction whereby you identify the primary or secondary stakeholder in terms of 'what can we give you and what can you give us?' (See Figure 2.1.) There will be clear winners and losers, which would seem to be flawed as this promotes stakeholder exclusivity and denies certain legitimate stakeholders (the losers) the opportunity to have a voice and positively shape the event.

Figure 2.1: The traditional view of stakeholders. Adapted from Sautter and Leisen (1999, 315)

Stakeholder engagement – A moral and strategic distinction

From an event creation viewpoint, we have argued the importance of the stakeholders collectively influencing the decision making process. The reason for this approach is that: "to be an effective strategist you must deal with those groups that can affect you, while to be responsive (and effective in the long run) you must deal with those groups that you can affect" (Freeman 1984, p.46). This distinction poses a challenge for event creators in how to simultaneously consider and involve such a multiplicity of individuals and groups, and facilitate mutual value creation through the events delivery (Prebensen, 2010; Sautter and Leisen, 1999). Noland and Philips (2010) contend that actually there is no distinction and that 'good strategy' must morally accept this challenge, with the engagement of stakeholders being essential to strategy formulation if the event is to achieve desirable outcomes. In the earlier example of the East Asia Games the engagement of the public, as a group that 'can affect you', demonstrates the necessity of engaging with the full range of stakeholders which is one of the reasons that the business of event creation is strategic and event creators must adopt a strategic persona. It is also noteworthy that by acting in what is a more ethical manner (rather than persistently serving self-interest) the event, the host organisation and partners, will increase legitimacy within the eyes of the stakeholders community as a whole. Indeed Greenwood (2007, p.277) takes this viewpoint further and states 'rather than conceive of stakeholders in either a narrow or broad sense, it may be more useful to consider definitions as depicting the stakeholder as either moral or strategic'. This language opens up a useful perspective for event creators in how they perceive stakeholder engagement.

■ Moral stakeholders

In advocating a view of stakeholders as either moral or strategic, we are not arguing that one group has primacy over the other, or that either group has attributes to be celebrated or neglected. Simply by organising the stakeholders as either moral or strategic, the event creator enables a more transparent approach, which in turn achieves a higher level of engagement clarity (Kaler, 2002). Moral stakeholders are usually those groups that have the potential to be impacted by the event, but have little if any obvious or direct involvements in its delivery, such groups are discussed in Chapter 6 of the book. This distinction helps the event creator identify those stakeholders that are a moral claimant on the event being created, so that all legitimate individuals and groups are engaged. However, we need to be careful and not confuse legitimacy with the interests of powerful groups – it is a broader term to reflect their right to be consulted and involved.

The simple act of engaging with moral stakeholder does not ensure that they are treated in a truthful and honest manner, because traditionally this engagement process has usually focused on the needs and wants of the organisation, with stakeholder views being secondary. In fact Derry (2012) would argue that the event creators could arbitrarily decide who their moral stakeholders actually are (either deliberately or accidentally), seeking only those 'who and what really counts', often ignoring those stakeholders who might be perceived as being unable to bring value to the event. The key here is to remember that these legitimate stakeholders can become obstacles that may even mobilise against the event, either at this time or in the future, and the event creator needs to strive to 'to obtain optimal benefits for all identified stakeholder groups' (Sautter and Leisen, 1999, p.314). Fundamentally, successful event creators represent the interests of all stakeholders and attempt to mitigate any adverse effects of the event.

■ Strategic stakeholders

Strategic stakeholders possess the power and/or urgency attribute rather than legitimacy. There is usually some kind of resource dependency that shapes the relationship between this stakeholder and the event creator, such as financial, marketing or regulatory powers. Event creators can respond to this 'dependency' and simply react to stakeholder issues and pressures, perhaps becoming dependent on one or more powerful actors (Getz and Andersson, 2010). Strategically, the event creator should not be developing the aims and objectives for the event host organisation in isolation. There is a strategic 'sense' to ascertaining the needs and wants of stakeholders, as this can be a method of enhancing the events goals. For example, it would almost be counterintuitive for an event host, who needs to engage with sponsors, local groups, funders and regulatory organisations in order to make financial return, not to align their own aims and objectives with this much wider range of stakeholder (Getz and Andersson, 2010). Thus the event creator's role is to help the event host to improve their reputation and legitimacy and helps the 'organization determine what the nature of their stakeholder management strategies should be' (Greenwood, 2007, p.322).

Derry (2012, p.257) argues that making decisions based on 'competing stakeholder groups as more or less powerful, or more or less legitimate, does not necessarily lead to greater moral sensitivity or firm ethical grounding'. For example, due to a perceived resource dependency a conference facility might routinely decide to hire a large catering chain because of the size of an up and coming event, inadvertently marginalising a local caterer and missing an opportunity to engage a local stakeholder who could have supported the facility to become more sustainable. Had they acted in this manner the organisation could have created more positive outcomes through the event, and for a greater number of stakeholders (Freeman et al, 2007). If the conference facility had engaged with the local caterer, and through them a number of local food producers, it could have communicated a number of sustainable values (food miles, fresh produce, bespoke menus etc.), whilst at the same time acknowledging the concerns of the caterer (cost, keeping money in the local community, partnerships with local firms). In this way the event creator could have interwoven the venue's aims and objectives with that of the local stakeholder to ensure mutual benefit. Once we learn to accept that stakeholder aims and objectives may be different we can seek to create a strategy that, through stakeholder engagement and communication, attempts a convergence of viewpoints. As Noland and Philips (2010, pp.47-48) state:

> A business that is not instrumental in the pursuit of these stakeholder goals is not a successful business... for a firm to determine its strategy without having first engaged its stakeholders would be, literally, to disengage its mission and vision from its identity.

Communicating with stakeholders

Key to this notion of stakeholder-centricity is the aspiration to deepen relationships with stakeholders in order to deliver events that can provide mutually beneficial experiences and outcomes for all concerned. As event creators we need to develop clear strategies for communicating with stakeholders that encourage proactive and straightforward communication, that promotes integrity in the relationship. Communicating in this manner can achieve a transparent discussion between the event creator and stakeholders allowing 'acceptance and subsequent support, for a diverse range of interests' (Hede, 2007, p.20). By interacting in a transparent manner the event creator engages in 'reciprocal communication' where the emphasis is on the opportunities and benefits to the stakeholder, and under these circumstances the other party will be more likely to provide their support and guidance, or be impartial, rather than negative or hostile (Pajunen, 2006). It is important, as shown in Table 2.1, that communication is undertaken in a manner that serves mutual stakeholder interests and not just the goals of the event host and other more powerful stakeholders.

Table 2.1 illustrates how the event creator can create partnerships with different stakeholder groups, and the methods that can be employed to do so. The first column contains the type of stakeholder (which will be explained in more detail in the following section) and the rationale for communication, while the subsequent columns identify different methods for engagement. The event creator will have to spend time and energy building these relationships, but there are clear benefits. First, if the event creator is proactive with stakeholder communication and actively seeks to engage with these groups, there is the potential for the stakeholder to support the development and creation of the event. Second, and probably more beneficial for the event creator, is that the erratic demand for events and high levels of interdependence that exist within event delivery can be more effectively managed (Harrison, and St. John, 1996).

Table 2.1: Communicating with stakeholders. Adapted from Harrison and St.John (1996, p.53).

Stakeholder	Strategic Stakeholders	Moral Stakeholders
The internal		
The event Make a commitment to stakeholders but retain overall direction of the event	Locality is the focus Ensure that stakeholders are not exploited	Locality is the focus Ensure that stakeholders are not marginalized
Involved Open, regular and transparent communications	Long term contracts and future joint ventures	Seek input for key decisions Clear communication links available
The external		
Explicit Keep informed and positive Seek their opinions	Involved in the design team of the event	Public consultations on sensitive issues and advocate local requirement
Implicit Keep informed	Market research that feeds into planning	Community groups informed Public relations advertising
Marginalised Potential/lost Communicate proactively to explain and overcome fears.	Lost stakeholders could be appointed to the board Joint ventures in future events	Public/political relations efforts to offset and protect from negative and promote positive publicity
Hidden	?	?

Table 2.1 gives the event creator a focus for the development of their communication strategy, but should not be seen as a prescriptive method to communicate with stakeholders. The event creator should enter into a substantial amount of face-to-face communication as this has been found to enhance mutual understanding of the event, eliminate mistrust and promote cooperation between stakeholders (Getz and Andersson, 2010; Brown and Eisenhardt, 1997). An event coordinator for a national sport organisation spent a long time engaging with local clubs as their national championships were experiencing decreases in attendance. These communications were presented and structured as a learning process, to understand the views, ideas, and opinions. This proactive stakeholder engagement and consultation identified significant changes in the makeup of the attendee base and the need for much more junior competition rather than adult. By identifying this shift, the event coordinator ensured that the event design altered to reflect the needs of the customer base. By engaging before the future events were designed, the competitions became more co-produced, with involved and interested stakeholders perceiving more of a vested interest in future events.

■ A model of stakeholder communication

We have already argued that two-way, face-to-face communication should be the main tool used by the event creator to engage with stakeholders, however there will be times when this method is simply impractical, unachievable or too expensive. Daft and Lengel (1984) developed a model that evaluated different communication media by the degree of communicative richness they provide. For example, a media that offers 'richness' has a high capacity for carrying information, while 'lean' media has the capacity to carry limited information. This model helps us understand that although non face-to-face engagement does have it merits, these so-called mediated communication methods actually filter non-verbal cues (eye contact, gesture, body movement), verbal cues (tone of voice) and social cues (name, status) out of the communication process, which has increased potential to disengage those who are being communicated with (Keil and Johnson, 2002). Daft and Lengel (1984) explain the concept of richness in terms of asking three questions about the proposed communication media, allowing an assessment of its suitability for stakeholder engagement:

1 Does the media promote and provide feedback quickly, and/or, two-way communication?

2 Does the media allow the opportunity for different communication cues (social, verbal, non-verbal)?

3 Does the media allow customised communication for individual recipients, or for specific situations?

Assessment: Does it promote stakeholder engagement?

It would be a mistake, particularly from a stakeholder engagement viewpoint, to view this as a choice between picking those media which are rich and those that are lean. The model that Daft and Lengal (1986) present (see Figure 2.2) gives the event creator an evaluation tool to decide whether the media they are employing is appropriate for the stated stakeholder group. For example, if the event creator needs to discuss a Temporary Events Notice for an event, that would have a late night finish and would involve the serving of alcohol and involve loud music, then a lean method of communication would fail, disengaging the recipients, as they may only focus on the negative aspects of the event. Through a richer communication method the event creator will be able to alleviate fears, to discuss the positives of the event and through these discussions alter the event to try and create mutual benefit. This would help the event creator to erase any ambiguous feelings that the stakeholders may have towards the event. The process may be complex and involve multiple methods (individual meetings, group consultations, clear lines of communication), however the richer the communication the greater value that is created by the consultation process and the greater the chances of the event meeting the goals of the event creators and wider stakeholder groups (Pajunen, 2006).

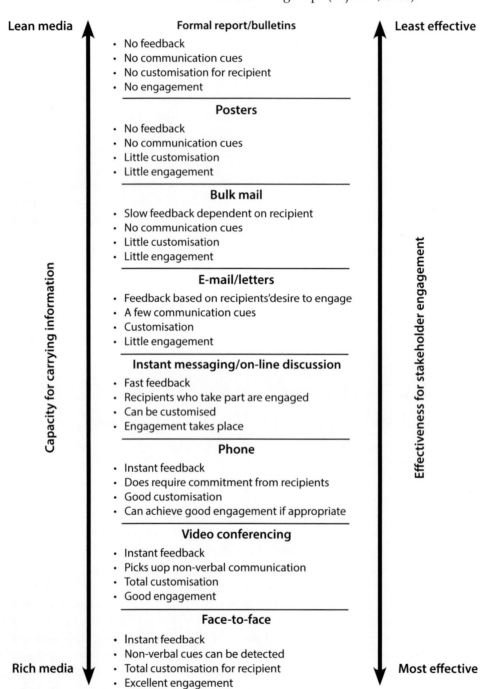

Figure 2.2: Appropriate media for stakeholder engagement. Adapted from Daft and Lengel (1984); Daft and Lengel (1986); Robbins et al (2012, p.301)

Stakeholder mapping and building relationships

As event creators we should endeavour to be accountable for the events we create, and part of this is advancing a more ethical approach to stakeholder engagement. In doing this, it is useful to flip the conventional notion and instead focus on how the events we deliver can have a wider benefit. Derry (2012) holds that if we move the focus of stakeholer engagement and mapping to concentrate more on locality, then we are encouraged to view the event host and key funders as "one of many stakeholders whose needs must be balanced in order to maximize the sustainability of our environment and social well-being" (p.263) - see Figure 2.3.

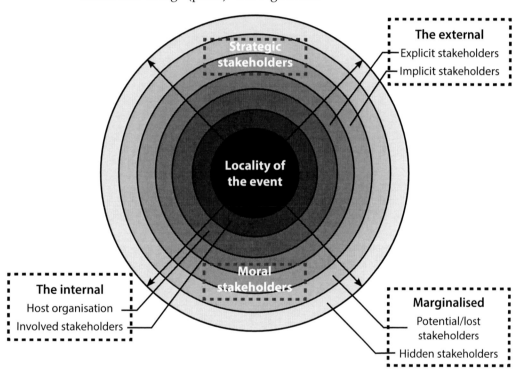

Figure 2. 3: A stakeholder centric approach. Adapted from Getz et al (2007)

To illustrate the implications of this viewpoint we will now follow the decisions of Derby City Council in relation to the building of a new multiple purpose leisure/event venue, and the consequences of not placing the locality of venue at the heart of the stakeholder engagement process - see below for background detail of the case study.

Case study: Derby Arena – An Overview

In April 2011 Derby City Council unveiled proposals to invest £27.5m to build a multi-purpose leisure and event centre. This would not have an indoor cycling track but would have general fitness suites, a sports hall that would accommodate twelve badminton courts and an indoor concert area that could cater for up five thousand people. This project was at the heart of the council's Leisure Strategy, which aimed to:

- Supplement the ageing Assembly Rooms event venue

- Create a new facility that could provide bespoke music, conference, convention and business event facilities

- Invest £50m to improve the city's leisure facilities and to meet residents' dissatisfaction in regards leisure facilities (www.sportengland.org/research)

Building work commenced in November 2012 and appeared to be running smoothly. It was expected to open on time in spring 2014. However, one group, The Sanctuary Bird Reserve, felt their concerns were being ignored. When the project decided to build an additional outdoor cycle track that went through the reserve, despite Richard Winspear stating that the planned track would 'destroy a significant part of the sanctuary', these stakeholders felt Derby City Council were ignoring their viewpoints. They decided to take action.

The following sections of the chapter make reference to this case study.

■ The locality as a focus

By placing locality at the centre of the stakeholder engagement process we are seeking to solve the issue of exclusively serving the self-interest of stakeholders, and the temptation of allocating primacy to individual stakeholders, and instead we are seeking to create value for the greatest number of stakeholders. By using the physical locality of the event as the focus, we seek to understand the wider impacts the event will have. It also provides a more constructive starting point to identify and interpret stakeholders, particularly at a moral level. For example, in the Derby Case study the bird sanctuary group voiced their opposition by calling it 'irresponsible' as the Council had lost sight of the impact on the actual physical location, and in turn alienated stakeholders associated with the locality. While Derby City Council was seeking to create benefit for several moral and strategic stakeholders, its stakeholder approach placed greater importance on its own strategic goals and therefore overlooked, to a large degree, the importance of locality. A locality focus helps anchor the stakeholder mapping process and allows us to envisage how to create value for both the strategic and moral stakeholders. This focus creates greater legitimacy for the event, resulting in the event being 'regarded as desirable, proper or appropriate among its stakeholder' (Larson, 2004, p.11). By ignoring the bird sanctuary group they created unnecessary complications which were negative for both the interest group and the Council.

Figure 2.3 contains several layers. The event creator role is not classified into one of the layers of the diagram but instead is a facilitator that coalesces the varied stakeholder interests, including the interests of the event host, to ensure that outcomes are ably achieved. The event creator may be an individual or group charged with the design of the event. Commissioned, in some way, by the host organisation, their role is to engage with all stakeholders. Their status may be that of employee(s) of the host organisation or agents instructed by them. Having interpreted the stakeholder groups and their interests they will make prioritising decisions about the aims and objectives of the event, and will provide the leadership and event design decisions to achieve the goals. Their role is therefore pivotal.

■ Internal stakeholders

If we move outwards from the centre of Figure 2.3 we encounter a group which Getz et al (2007) would define as internal stakeholders. These are stakeholders that are very closely involved in the creation of an event and are at the heart of the outcomes that are achieved. However, Getz et al (2007) identified a weakness with this approach, suggesting that with the variety of internal stakeholder lines of responsibility can become blurred. Indeed, by looking at the Derby case study, there is an argument to place the bird sanctuary group as internal stakeholders, given their potential to positively or negatively impact the event site and subsequent events. By engaging with them and identifying the contextual issues surrounding the locality they could have become a positive co-creator of the event site and forthcoming events. Instead, by trying to placate them with assurances that the new cycling track was only a proposal, this group moved further away from the centre and became disenfranchised with the whole programme (the model allows for movement between the layers).

Figure 2.3 separates the internal stakeholders into host organisation and those involved to ensure these lines of responsibility remain clear. The host organisation means the principal organisation that hosts and/or initiates the event. There are several reasons for this distinction. First, this enables those with focal responsibility to set a clear and cohesive vision for the event – ensuring that the objectives of all stakeholders, including locality, are carefully considered. Second, it provides a way to avoid the event being hijacked by individual stakeholders for self-seeking proposes which risks distorting the event. Last, it creates a more positive and consultative environment which ensures that decisions are not made arbitrarily and instead the event creator actually seeks interactions with stakeholders to avoid producing what might be referred to as an 'ivory tower event' – a mistake that Derby clearly made with the bird sanctuary group. Here are some general examples relating to the host organisation and internal stakeholders:

- Host organisation
  - ☐ Manufacturing business delivering a product launch
  - ☐ City hosting a major sport event
  - ☐ Company planning a large international conference
  - ☐ Charity hosting a fundraising fun run
- Internal stakeholders
  - ☐ Sponsors and other funders
  - ☐ Partners
  - ☐ Sub-contractors and Employees
  - ☐ Volunteers
  - ☐ Regulatory bodies
  - ☐ Suppliers (invited)
  - ☐ Venue

If Derby City Council had adopted this approach it would have allowed its own aims and objectives to remain at the heart of the process but also be merged with those of other stakeholders, including the locality. This would create the conditions for the event creator to draw in those stakeholders (the bird sanctuary group for instance) that are further away from the centre by inviting them to take a much greater part in the development of the event venue and design of future events.

■ External stakeholders

Organisational literature would argue that because they cannot be managed (controlled) then there is little point in seeking to engage all stakeholders. However, rather than seeking to control their viewpoints, by proactively engaging and creating relationships with these stakeholders, it can generate organisational flexibility (Harrison and St. John, 1996). It enables the event creator to be much more responsive to changes in the external environment, with the stakeholders providing the lens examining and making sense of the business environment within which the event will be delivered (Harrison and St.John, 1996). In the case study, the plans for the cycle track were recommended for approval even though there were 639 letters in support and 826 objecting. The campaigners against the track were left 'absolutely stunned' as the track was built even though public opinion clearly did not support its construction. There was general support for the development of the new event facility, but not the addition of the track. This approach could be seen as being inconsistent with stakeholder engagement, as it viewed that organisations with an outward facing business model generally outperform those that do not (Xu et al, 2003). Through stakeholder engagement, the event creator has a channel through which to locate, engage and communicate with other external stakeholders, improving the organisation's ability to identify threats and opportunities with the event sector (Freeman, 1984).

Again we build on Getz et al's (2007) work in employing the concept of external stakeholders. These are stakeholders who are not directly involved in the operational delivery of the event, but whose contribution can greatly influence the successful outcome of an event. While Getz et al (2007) sub-divide external stakeholders into four distinct categories, this chapter advocates a simpler approach with two types of external stakeholders: explicit and implicit. Explicit stakeholders are those individuals/groups that are targeted through the core aims and objectives of the event, while the implicit stakeholders might still experience the event but are not actively targeted. Implicit stakeholders are therefore likely to have a stronger link to the locality, although it is clearly possible that explicit stakeholders also have this connection. The risk to the event creator is that the decisions they make can easily marginalise implicit stakeholders, particularly when they are not engaged.

If the event creator sought to engage with this group to avoid implicit stakeholders becoming marginalised and becoming an obstacle, then there is a need to build coherent, transparent and equitable relationships with such stakeholders (Quero and Ventura, 2009). This change of 'focus' by the event creator would enable the external stakeholder to make a positive decision to continue the relationship ensuring a long-term relationship because they can see the benefits of cooperation which should ultimately be centred around locality (Alexander et al. 2005). As indicated by Lusch and Webster (2011, p.132) 'a good relationship is one that creates value for both parties and leaves each wanting to continue the relationship in some form'.

■ Marginalised stakeholders

The relationships the event creator is engaged in will be dynamic and will not remain static. For example, as work began on clearing the site for the £900,000 cycle track, Derbyshire Wildlife trust started a legal challenge against the project, stating unless it stopped they would apply for a court injunction. This is just one example of how an internal or external stakeholder can become marginalised through the decisions made by the event creator. Getz et al (2007) does not include this group within his model, but they are an important consideration as this group feels less engaged with the process and often feels powerless to influence the event. The event still has potential to influence them although negatively as they have not been fully engaged. They become disenfranchised and in so doing this becomes a missed opportunity for the event creator in terms of affecting wider positive outcomes. However, this does not mean the group is entirely lost. By working at a strategic level, the event creator can recognise the stakeholders influenced by the event and engage with them, otherwise the event creator would fail to see how these groups and the event fits into the stakeholder's value-creating process (Lusch and Webster, 2011).

Potential stakeholders are those individuals and groups that, if engaged and involved with the event, have the potential to create and generate value. This group might have not been engaged due to lack of planning, lack of understanding of the potential benefit of their engagement or a simple oversight. An example of positively engaging with stakeholders was at the Liverpool European City of Culture 2008, where the organisers identified that school children were a marginalised group within their arts and culture provision. By engaging and involving every child from every school (67,000 in total) the event sought to move individuals from being potential stakeholders to being implicit or even explicit stakeholders. Indeed, young person's participation rates at arts and cultural events, has increased significantly in Liverpool (Garcia et al., 2010).

Derby Council made decisions during the building of the cycle track that were clearly in their best interests, rather than the interests of their stakeholders. The legal challenge by the Wildlife Trust was successful and work was forced to halt by the ruling judge based on planning permission irregularities. The failure of creating a meaningful dialogue with the sanctuary concluded with the relationship completely breaking down and a vital stakeholder group for the project being lost. With the injunction slowing down the building of the track, the council decided to abandon the project due to increased costs. Not only was it evident that the project needed to engage with the group, strategically they will now struggle to achieve their stated aims and objectives. The council stated 'our vision of becoming a regional centre for cycling excellence is now under serious threat'. A further consequence was that the venue was needed to replace another event venue in the area that had been damaged through a fire. This led to several important events being cancelled, including a comedy festival. Another consequence is that other stakeholders have lost trust in the council as they were viewed as showing a 'remarkable degree of misjudgement' over the project, so it is vital that the event creator understands decisions that influence one stakeholder can also influence others. The Arena is due to open in January 2015, a year overdue.

The hidden group is different as it is unseen, unheard and not engaged. This group is clearly the hardest to identify as the event creator is probably unaware of their existence, they are almost impossible to identify and may not even exist – so why include them? We have included this final group as both a challenge and a warning. As events creators, the foremost question we should be asking is not "have we included the main funder in our decision making process?", or "have we attempted to engage with our community groups?", but "have we truly attempted to think about who will affect, or be affected by, the event we plan to deliver?" We support the assertion that Derry (2012, p.263) makes, in that it is not who we engage with that is most important, but when making decisions about the events, the key question is "who are we making disappear?"

Concluding thoughts

As event creators we should be constantly aware of the need to engage and "listen to one's stakeholders" (Derry, 2012, p.263) throughout the event creation process. This is relevant to event creators delivering events in all contexts as they seek to co-produce events with their stakeholders to affect positive and enduring relationships. Central to the argument in this chapter is that in order to create events that properly address stakeholder aspirations and concerns we must place the locality of the event at the centre of our engagement. In this way we engage with the fullest range of stakeholders and do not adopt a blinkered approach. Stakeholder-centricity enhances our ability to create events that are designed to achieve specific objectives for the host organisation and other key funders of the event. Moreover, according to Noland and Philips (2010), it also helps to create an event which places a synergetic link between business objectives, ethical and moral responsibilities and strategic goals.

Study questions

1 Is the stakeholder centric approach achievable within event creation or will there always be certain stakeholders that are seen as having primacy?

2 Look at the communication methods discussed within Figure 2.3. Analyse the communication media that have been omitted and assess their suitability for stakeholder engagement.

3 Conduct some background research into an event (can be a small community event or even a mega-event like the World Cup) and conduct a mapping exercise using the stakeholder centric model. Now take out locality as the focus and replace with a different stakeholder group, maybe one that was stated within the aims and objectives of the event, and re-draw the map. For example, maybe put the Stratford Bangladeshi

community at the heart of London 2012 Olympic stakeholder map? How does this change the stakeholder map and what could be the benefits or limitations of changing the focus?

References

Alexander, C. S., Miesing, P. and Parsons, A. L. (2005). How important are stakeholder relationships? *Academy of Strategic Management Journal,* **4**, 1-7.

Arnstein, S. R. (1969). A ladder of citizen participation. *Journal of the American Institute of Planners,* **35** (4), 216-224.

Brown, S. L. and Eisenhardt., K. M.(1997). The art of continuous change: Linking complexity theory and time-paced evolution in relentlessly shifting organizations. *Administrative Science Quarterly.* 1-34.

Clarkson, M. E. (1995). A stakeholder framework for analyzing and evaluating corporate social performance. *Academy of Management Review,* 20 (1), 92-117.

Daft, R. L. and Lengel, R. H. (1984). Information richness: A new approach to managerial information processing and organizational design. In B. Staw and L. L. Cummings (eds.), *Research in Organizational Behavior,* **6** (191–233). Greenwich, CT: JAI Press.

Daft, R. L. and Lengel, R. H. (1986). Organizational information requirements, media richness, and structural design. *Management Science,* **32**, 554–571

Derry, R. (2012). Reclaiming marginalized stakeholders. *Journal of Business Ethics,* **111** (2), 253-264.

Elkington, J. (2004). Enter the triple bottom line. In A. Henriques and J. Richardson (eds.), *The Triple Bottom Line: Does It All Add Up,* 1-16. Routledge.

Freeman, R. E. (1984). *Strategic Management: A Stakeholder Approach.* Boston: Pitman Publishing

Freeman, R. E., Harrison, J. S. and Wicks, A. C. (2007). *Managing for Stakeholders: Survival, Reputation, and Success.* London: Yale University Press.

Friedman, M., Parent, M. and Mason, D. (2004). Building a framework for issues management in sport through stakeholder theory. *European Sport Management Quarterly,* **4**(3), 170-190.

Garcia, B., Melville, R. and Cox, T. (2010). *Creating an impact: Liverpool's experience as European Capital of Culture.* Liverpool: University of Liverpool/Impacts, 8.

Getz, D. (2009). Policy for sustainable and responsible festivals and events: Institutionalization of a new paradigm. *Journal of Policy Research in Tourism, Leisure and Events,* **1**(1), 61-78.

Getz, D. and Andersson, T. D. (2010). Festival stakeholders: Exploring relationships and dependency through a four-country comparison. *Journal of Hospitality and Tourism Research,* **34** (4), 531-556.

Getz, D., Andersson, T. and Larson, M. (2007). Festival stakeholder roles: Concepts and case studies. *Event Management*, **10** (2/3), 103–122.

Green, M. and Houlihan, B. (2006). Governmentality, modernization, and the 'disciplining' of national sporting organizations: Athletics in Australia and the United Kingdom. *Sociology of Sport Journal*, **23**(1), 47.

Greenwood, M. (2007). Stakeholder engagement: Beyond the myth of corporate responsibility. *Journal of Business Ethics*, **74** (4), 315-327.

Harrison, J. S. and St.John, C. H. S. (1996). Managing and partnering with external stakeholders. *Academy of Management Executive*, **10** (2), 46-60.

Hede, A. M. (2007). Managing special events in the new era of the triple bottom line. *Event Management*, **11**(1-2), 13-22.

Kaler, J. (2002). Morality and Strategy in Stakeholder Identification. *Journal of Business Ethics*, **39** (1), 91–99.

Keil, M. and Johnson, R. D. (2002). Feedback channels: Using social presence theory to compare voice mail to e-mail. *Journal of Information Systems Education*, **13**(4), 295-302.

Larson, M. (2004). Managing Festival Stakeholders. In 13th Nordic symposium in tourism and hospitality research. 4th–7th November.

Lusch, R, L. and Webster E. (2011). A Stakeholder-Unifying, Co-creation Philosophy for Marketing. *Journal of Macromarketing*, **31** (2), 129 – 134.

McKercher, B., Mei, W. S. and Tse, T. S. (2006). Are short duration cultural festivals tourist attractions? *Journal of Sustainable Tourism*, **14** (1), 55-66.

Mitchell, R. K., Agle, B. R. and Wood, D. J. (1997). Toward a theory of stakeholder identification and salience: Defining the principle of who and what really counts. *Academy of Management Review*, **22** (4), 853-886.

Noland, J. and Phillips, R. (2010). Stakeholder engagement, discourse ethics and strategic management. *International Journal of Management Reviews*, **12** (1), 39-49.

Pajunen, K. (2006) Stakeholder influence in organisational survival. *Journal of Management Studies*. **43**, 6, 1261-1288

Pelham, F. (2011). Will sustainability change the business model of the event industry? *Worldwide Hospitality and Tourism Themes*, **3** (3), 187-192.

Prebensen, N. K. (2010). Value Creation Through Stakeholder Participation: A Case study of an Event in the High North. *Event Management*, **14** (1), 37-52.

Quero, M. J. and Ventura, R. (2009). The role of stakeholders in the management of cultural organisations: The case of performing arts organisations in Spain. *Journal of Relationship Marketing*, **8** (1), 17-35.

Reid, S. (2011). Event stakeholder management: developing sustainable rural event practices. *International Journal of Event and Festival Management*, **2**(1), 20-36.

Reid, S. and Arcodia, C. (2002) Understanding the role of the stakeholder in event management, *Journal of Sport and Tourism*, **7**(3), 20-22.

Richards, G. and Palmer, R. (2010). *Eventful Cities: Cultural Management and Urban Revitalisation*. Amsterdam; London: Butterworth-Heinemann.

Robbins, S. P., Judge, T. A. and Campbell, T. T. (2012). *Organizational Behavior 15th Edition*. London: Prentice Hall.

Sautter, E.T. and Leisen, B. (1999). Managing stakeholders a Tourism Planning Model. *Annals of Tourism Research*, **26**, (2), 312-328.

Smith, A. (2009). Theorising the relationship between major sport events and social sustainability. *Journal of Sport and Tourism*, **14**(2-3), 109-120.

Xu, X. M., Kaye, G. R. and Duan, Y. (2003). UK executives' vision on business environment for information scanning – A cross industry study. *Information and Management*, **40**(5), 381-389.

Part II

Outcome Obsessed

3 Setting the Event Host Objectives: a framework for business value creation

Chiara Orefice

Learning objectives

- Analyse the complex environment in which event hosts operate.

- Establish a long term, holistic perspective on objective setting.

- Define strategic and tactical objectives and discuss their contribution to organisational strategy.

Introduction

This chapter looks at the role of one of the key stakeholders in event crea-tion – the event host. Event hosts, also called 'owners' or 'budget holders' are the organisations or individuals that initiate the event. This may be the sole funder or the main financial contributor to the event, or it could be the organisation(s) or group of people that put forward the event concept based on a particular need, cause or mission. Event owners could be managing the event funds rather than directly financing it, raising money for instance through grants, fees and other sources. The variety of event hosts and the different organisational structures that they can take depend on the size, purpose and market in which the event operates. Getz et al. (2007) suggest that as the events field advances, the boundaries of event organisations are becoming fuzzy. Owners can be private companies, not-for-profit organisa-tions or public authorities and, for an increasing number of events, they may be a combination of multiple bodies across these sectors. Sometimes there may be a contractual agreement in place, but often the relationship is more informal. In the case of community events, for instance, Wood (2009) suggests that there can exist different combinations of public sector and community endorsement and support. This can range from little or no engagement in the organisational effort and no funding, to high levels of involvement in the organisation and considerable financial contribution.

As event creation becomes the combined efforts of multiple individuals and organisations, the identification of a single event host becomes more complex and the distinction between owners and stakeholders is blurred (for further discussion on the variety of stakeholders' involvement and interest, refer to Chapter 2). This chapter will analyse the issue of the complexity of host objectives and derive a definition of event host within a Strategic Event Creation perspective. It will challenge the traditional approach that differentiates host objectives by private, public and third sector and it will introduce the concept of mission value[1] to derive a categorisation of objectives that can be shared across the sectors.

Event host objectives – a multi-faceted picture

Traditionally the literature distinguishes between profit making (private sector) event owners, and public and third sector event owners. Events initiated by organisations mainly in the not-for-profit or public sector will often pursue less tangible outcomes such as contributing to the development of community cohesion, knowledge sharing and professional development, the celebration of a certain culture, or encouraging participation in community activities, sport and the arts. Such event objectives connect to longer term aims, such as generating a positive attitude towards local government, attracting more residents and businesses, developing educational and research opportunities, and improving health and quality of life in a city or region (Dwyer et al., 2000; Pugh and Wood, 2004).

The not-for-profit sector, alongside the public sector, is showing an increased market orientation and an improved understanding of the role that events can play as part of cultural or urban regeneration, place promotion, education and research etc, thus growing in its awareness of the long term strategic value of events (Richards and Palmer, 2010; Carlsen and Andersson, 2011). Benita Lipps, Executive Director of the DaVinci Institute, is one of the convenors of the Gender Summit - an annual conference promoting the importance of the gender dimension for research and innovation excellence. In the following quote she explains how the Summit contributes to policy making at European level within a long-term perspective.

---

1   The author would like to thank Dr. Elling Hamso for the significant contribution given to this chapter with his comments and revisions, and in particular for suggesting the concept of mission value.

Industry voice: Benita Lipps, Executive Director, DaVinci Institute, Belgium

For the Gender Summit we have very consciously chosen Brussels as its recurring European location. First, it allows us to create strong connections to the European Union institutions, which helps to create long-term impact on policy making. Second, it makes it easier for us to attract industry partners to the summit, as innovation-focussed companies are eager to showcase their best practice in an EU context. Last, a 'Brussels Summit' sends a symbolic message to our community, making it clear that gender in research and innovation is not just a minority interest, but an essential aspect of European research and innovation policy.

However, although events are acknowledged to be purposefully invested in to achieve such outcomes, the formalisation of quantifiable objectives in these sectors is still progressing slowly. Without attaching clear objectives, and then adequately capturing the outcomes, it is problematic to demonstrate the event contribution to the overall strategy which inevitably generates difficulties in gaining support for future event investment. Benita Lipps describes another conference she is involved with:

Industry voice: Benita Lipps, Executive Director, DaVinci Institute, Belgium

While Graphene Week is probably one of the most respected international scientific meetings in the area of graphene and graphene-based devices, it is hard for us to really measure its impact. What indicators should we use? Number of participants? Number of countries represented? General satisfaction with the programme? While these are relatively easy to measure, they don't really define the 'success' of this conference. Graphene Week is about networking, about creating new connections and collaborations. This is an impact we still find hard to measure.

Events initiated by the private or for-profit sectors, contribute directly or indirectly to an organisation's bottom line, typically through increasing revenues, reducing costs, or improving organisational performance. We can distinguish between external facing (such as roadshows or product launches), internal facing events (such as staff conferences or partner events), or indeed a combination of both and also between financial and non-financial objectives. Non-financial objectives pertain to areas such as staff development, stakeholder relations or team building. These are all areas which ultimately affect the company effectiveness and survival through improved service, enhanced business contacts and so forth (Reic, 2012).

Particularly prominent in the industry is the discussion about the value of events, which has gathered pace in the past few years (see for instance the MPI, 2011 study on the *Business Value of Meetings* and the *Meetings Mean Business Toolkit*, 2013). The economic uncertainty has challenged organisations and event professionals to increasingly engage in systematic ways to justify the event existence by demonstrating more thoroughly the value of the events delivered. Terms such as Return on Investment (ROI) and Return on Objectives (ROO) have therefore become widespread and event creators are increasingly tasked with demonstrating that the investment in the event does provide clear returns. Such a challenge relies upon effective evaluation that crucially goes beyond the typical parameters of attendee satisfaction. As explored in Chapter 12, there are difficulties in engaging in the evaluation process typically due to the perception of high costs, resource requirement, lack of skills and even fear of the results (MPI, 2011). This remains a considerable issue for the industry although there are progressive developments such as the Event ROI methodology which moves forward from simple event evaluation, introducing a framework for setting objectives before the event is designed (Phillips et al, 2007).

Regardless of its profit or not-for-profit orientation, every organisation involved in the initiation of events is required to justify the investment provided. However, a host profit or not-for-profit orientation does not necessarily imply that the event should be generating positive financial returns and vice-versa. For example, some publicly or not-for-profit owned events may have as their main purpose profit making (a typical example are charity fundraising events), whereas private sector funded events may have a focus on community development and contribute to knowledge expansion, or raise awareness about social and cultural agendas. This is illustrated by the words of Claes Olsen, Booking Manager of the Øya Festival in Norway.

Industry voice: Claes Olsen, Booking Manager of the Øya Festival in Norway

When we started Øya festival our goal was not to make money, but to create something for the local music scene that we were all part of, since myself and the others were all running small venues. We wanted to prove that even though we were all competitors, we had good relations and all pursued the same goal. At this time we felt that the other Norwegian festivals did not respect the Norwegian music scene. They either did not know about it, or if the bothered to book Norwegian acts, they did not put them on first, so no one watched them.

The festival started really small with only local acts and 800 tickets sold, but we got what we wanted; a lot of media attention for the local music scene and the artists. We now have 10 year round employees, and 150 staff paid staff who work part time plus 2000 volunteers. This year 85,000 people visited the festival over the four days, and the music scene is healthy. Lots of other festivals have started which also promote Norwegian acts, which for us is great as this has always been our main goal and will always be so.

Overcoming the public/private/third sector distinction – the concept of mission value

The above considerations lead us to argue that, for the purpose of identifying their objectives, it is useful to move away from the traditional categorisation of private, public and third sector to holistically consider each host's specific mission or mandate, its values, strategy and stakeholders as the fundamental driving forces for the events they initiate. Every host organisation, whether not for profit, government, private or educational institution, etc. has a mission. The general mission of a corporation is to increase shareholder value, the mission of a cancer charity is to reduce cancer, the mission of government is to fulfil its promise to the electorate, universities are charged to provide education and research, etc. Everything that an organisation does, including the events it hosts, must ultimately contribute to its mission. Adopting a strategic approach to the creation of events leads to this different perspective, and allows us to identify the commonalities amongst the outcomes that deliver mission value for any type of organisation using events as a strategic tool, rather than focusing on the differences between the sectors they operate in.

The case study below illustrates how the Global Manufacturing Festival in Sheffield contributes to the concept of mission value for the Sheffield City Region and the Sheffield Chamber of Commerce.

Case study: Global Manufacturing Festival, Sheffield, UK

The Global Manufacturing Festival in Sheffield, managed by Sheffield Chamber of Commerce, is becoming an international success. More than 1,500 people attended the 2014 event which included a trade show, a conference with keynote speakers from government and business, and a dinner. A number of international delegates visited the Sheffield City Region for the event which offered an opportunity to build connections, open new business opportunities and showcase successful partnerships. The festival coincided with the International Festival for Business (IFB) in Liverpool, and focused on automotive, rail infrastructure, offshore wind energy, oil and gas and aerospace, all key areas for business development in the region. Richard Wright, executive director of Sheffield Chamber, said: "We established a long-term plan when creating the Global Manufacturing Festival in 2012 - to develop an event which would add value to businesses in the complex engineering supply chains and showcase our advanced manufacturing capabilities to the world. We are on course to deliver these objectives, with the festival growing in stature each year. However, we are keen for momentum and interest to continue, with more delegates, businesses and speakers attending the festival next year, cementing Sheffield City Region as the central foundation of the world's advanced manufacturing and materials industry. (The Business Desk, 2014)

A holistic perspective on host objectives

■ The event portfolio

When characterising the event host's objectives, the first consideration to make is about the differentiation between short term revenue generation and long term mission value generated by the event. This is not specific to a particular type of event or host. Certain events are not about short term financial return, or even financially quantifiable longer term return, whereas others may generate profit and also lead to long-term less tangible positive results. Importantly this perspective signals a movement away from looking at the individual event efficiency, with a narrow focus on inputs including costs, logistics and hospitality, to focus on its effectiveness, i.e. an output orientation. The adoption of an input-orientated, short term perspective, mostly focused on cost savings, generated the wave of cancellations at the height of the economic recession a few years ago. Instead, with this approach, the event is seen as an investment that, integrated with others, in the long term will generate a return for the host. This return may be financial or may need to be expressed in non-financial terms but regardless of the way in which it is expressed, it must be clearly identified for it to be evaluated.

This longer term perspective drives event creators and their clients to analyse in more detail the role of the event as part of a broader organisational strategy and to consider it as part of a portfolio of events and other activities (such as other marketing or organisational development initiatives) aimed at achieving wider strategic objectives involving internal and external stakeholders. Therefore, when analysing the investment needed by an event, rather than looking at each event in isolation, event creators should employ an event matrix (Boone, 2009) which brings together all organisational events/activities, their key stakeholders and the objectives they are delivering. This allows the owner to trace each initiative to the long term organisational goals and see beyond shorter term outcomes. This interpretive process takes into consideration not only how the event contributes strategically into the bigger picture of the organisation but also its relationship to other events and other initiatives over a period of time.

As explained by O'Toole (2011, p.6) events need to be looked at as part of a portfolio "that delivers on the strategic objectives of the key stakeholder be it a country, region, city, association or company" where the benefits (or return on investment) can be perceived over time. The emphasis on a portfolio here, as opposed to a collection of events, is particularly important, as synergies can be identified and leveraged between events and possibly other activities/campaigns aimed at delivering the long term strategy (Ziakas and Costa, 2011). For an in-depth discussion about event portfolios, see Chapter 11.

The quotes below are taken from an interview with event consultant, producer and trainer Paul Cook, discussing the profile of a leader in the events industry. They clearly show how the successful event creator plays an essential role in leading the host (and other stakeholders, as discussed in the next paragraph) to take a step back and look at the interconnection between higher level strategy and the day-to-day activities of the event and in so doing extract the long term and short term objectives. The requisite event outcomes will be determined as a result, which then inform the event design to ensure a coordinated focus upon return on investment.

Industry voice: Paul Cook, event consultant, producer and trainer, UK

A good leader (in the events industry) would not just focus on 'We are having just this event today', but they would also ask 'What else have you got planned? What is your bigger communication plan, potentially?', so that people are being able to see that big picture and know where they need to go with their vision and how they are going to get there. But also [good leaders] are the kind of people that understand that some decisions have to be made and that's the way it has to be because that's part of the leadership process, but they would also be taking on board what other people are saying, so the staff, the volunteers, the customers around them, delegates, those kind of people.

They are going to take all of that knowledge from those people and listen to that and then feel that 'are we really going in the right way with this or do we need to adjust?' So they have to have the ability of being able to look at the long term, the big global picture of what is the vision but also have that situational leadership that has to go on, on a day-to-day basis.

An in-depth discussion about the organisation mission and vision, as precursors of the strategy, is required and may lead to reconsider some fundamental premises of the decision to hold the event. This is a crucial opportunity for event creators to gain visibility and increase their reputation as the facilitators of this discussion and the contributors to the host organisation strategy development.

■ Stakeholder influence

As discussed in Chapters 1 and 2, event creators find themselves at the centre of a network of stakeholders that include event owners, participants, sponsors and the wider community who are all influencing the event and are directly impacted by it. The influence of internal and external stakeholders on the event host's decision making process can be significant since they frequently have conflicting interests, and the event creator plays an integral role in reconciling these. Getz (2002) and Andersson and Getz (2007) discuss stakeholder power in relation to resource dependency and decision making power and explain that these affect the long term sustainability of events. Yet, when setting long term objectives as part of an event portfolio approach, the role of stakeholders is even more crucial. In an event context, the traditional stakeholder power includes a new dimension to influence the event experience by co-creating the value generated by the event (Getz et. al., 2007; Prebensen, 2010). Thus, the influence of stakeholders on the achievement of the event owner's objectives goes beyond the control of scarce resources (i.e. controlling the event inputs) as each stakeholder is now seen a co-creator and co-producer of the event (i.e. they contribute to the outputs). Alongside the attendees, venues, local community groups, associations, charities and all type of suppliers are inextricably linked to each other, being the resource providers, the co-creators, and the recipients of the event-generated value.

Below is an example of how London and Partners is engaging with its stakeholders in order to achieve its objectives, from the words of the Director of Business Tourism and Major Events, Tracy Halliwell, MBE.

Industry voice: Tracy Halliwell, MBE, Director of Business Tourism and Major Events, London and Partners, UK

The thing we are doing this year is to come up with a strategy document – we have always written a business plan – this year what we want to make is a very simple, easy to read document that's for our partners. We are called London and Partners, and that means it's not just about us, it's about all of the stakeholders across the city, the venues, the hotels, the restaurants, and the boroughs in London, the government, the political landscape, anybody that has a vested interest in making London a successful destination. So how can we distil those visions and values across everybody else as well and get everybody else to buy into it? We are using it in everyday life and it's becoming part of who we are and what we do.

Therefore the achievement of the owner's objectives can be guaranteed only in conjunction with the achievement of the other stakeholders' objectives, which need to become complementing and mutually beneficial. This is true for the medium to long term event-generated value, and not only for the experience co-created during the event. It is the reason why the identification of the host objectives is so complex.

■ Balanced Scorecard approach

A consequence of establishing a holistic appreciation of the stakeholders influence on the host objectives, is that the focus on the economic/financial perspective is progressively being replaced with a broader approach aimed at including social/cultural and environmental objectives in an event (portfolio) strategy, in line with the discussion about the Triple Bottom Line (TBL) approach to event planning and design (Hede, 2008). Since the social, cultural and environmental dimensions have to be considered when setting the event objectives, the Balanced Scorecard appears to be a suitable framework to generate a combination of goals allowing an all-inclusive perspective on the value generated by an event (or by a portfolio of events). This combines financial and non-financial measures related to the strategic objectives influenced by key stakeholders (Kaplan and Norton, 1996a; Kaplan and Norton, 1996b).

The Balanced Scorecard approach allows organisations to translate long term strategy into a set of measures that are not only focusing on the evaluation of past performance, but assist in planning for future activities and in communicating the strategy with internal and external stakeholders (Kaplan and Norton, 1996b). This framework is made up of four components:

- ☐ the 'traditional' financial perspective with the related financial/monetary measures;

- ☐ the customer perspective, which includes attendees and also other external stakeholders and focuses on the co-creation of the event experience to generate value for all;

- ☐ the business growth perspective, which looks at internal processes within the host organisation to maximise results; and

- ☐ the learning and growth perspective, which looks at long term growth, innovation and change, improvement and skill development.

These four components should not be seen as independent, and in combination they fulfil the organisation's mission, thus the measures derived must be decided in an integrated manner. The section below will show how these four areas allow the event creator to generate four different sets of objectives.

A strategic framework for event objectives

■ Long term core objectives

Having established that events should be considered as part of a broader organisational strategy and what the influence of stakeholders is, we need to create a framework for the owner's objectives, and this can be adapted from the work of Hussey (1998) and Getz (2005). The foundation of this is the establishment of core objectives, mostly expressed in a qualitative way and set in advance of the event portfolio strategy, and goals and targets (or outputs) which are set as a result of the strategy and are mostly quantitative. The core objectives are directly connected with the organisation's raison d'etre and are typically long term. They state the contribution of the event towards the mission and vision of the organisation and the community growth and development, clarifying the way in which the organisation connects to internal and external stakeholders, and also society in general. They can be characterised as the event mission and vision and provide the required connection between the event and the organisation's mandate and the ideal future state that should be contributed to by the event, as well as the foundation for setting the subsequent event portfolio strategy (Getz, 2005; Hussey, 1998). The external environment, including economic and social market trends will likely affect the setting of core objectives. Internally to the organisation, financial and other risks may affect the decisions but also alternative tools, other than the event itself, that may be available to achieve the long term organisational objectives (Hussey, 1998; Richards and Palmer, 2010). The core objectives should not be unnecessarily restrictive and should still provide space for the event concept(s) to evolve, allowing a degree of flexibility and adaptation, whilst still pursuing the core values of the organisation (Getz, 2005; Hussey, 1998).

British Cycling (2013) Sport Events' core objectives are given below.

Mission: What is common to our events' work is a determination that they deliver a legacy for cycling in terms of inspiring participation in the sport at all levels.

Vision:

- A growing number of major international cycling events in this country;
- A legacy from all major international events which supports the delivery of our objectives;
- An event's structure across the entire spectrum of cycling with clear pathways enabling all cyclists to fulfil their aspirations, ambitions and potential;
- Opportunities for everyone to participate in cycling at their own level, for their entire lifetime;
- A rewarding and enjoyable environment for event organisers and officials

---

The influence of stakeholders is starting to show at this stage, as depending on the type of event owner they may have a significant input on the setting of core objectives. It becomes even more significant when deriving the event-specific medium term objectives as illustrated below.

■ Medium term strategic objectives

Once the core objectives are identified, the event (portfolio) strategy can be derived and with it the event specific goals (or outcome goals). These are results-oriented, providing guidelines for performance that act as milestones in the planning and decision making process. Within this approach Getz (2005) distinguishes between input goals (i.e. the resources and processes needed to deliver the event), output or outcome goals (i.e. what the event will achieve) and avoidance goals (i.e. problems or costs to be minimised). Although controlling inputs and minimising costs is a necessary role of the event creator, as explained earlier, their foremost role is that of the facilitator of strategic outputs, hence the ensuing discussion will focus specifically on outcome goals.

Outcome goals refer to the medium term, strategic objectives that the event should contribute to as part of the organisational portfolio of activities. When working on the event portfolio matrix with the host and identifying outcome goals, the event creator should start with the explicit identification of the stakeholder structure and then with the analysis of their contribution/role to the delivery of the event portfolio (Kenny, 2012). Then, adopting a TBL perspective, social, economic and cultural goals might be identified in terms of visitor expenditure in a destination, increased brand awareness, long-term engagement with a specific cause or brand, new research or development needed, job or training opportunities, improved health or educational facilities and so on.

To assist in the appropriate formulation of these objectives, the Balanced Scorecard approach illustrated above comes into play. Distinguishing between its components can help in formulating several possible sets of behavioural outcomes for an event or a portfolio of events. We combine the Balanced Scorecard approach with Phillips et al. (2007) view that there is no actual value generated by an event unless a change in behaviour is provoked. If stakeholders directly influence and co-create the event value, then a specific behaviour needs to be instigated as a result of the event, or a change in behaviour should become apparent. Although the participants are the primary target of the event activities aimed at stimulating behavioural change, behavioural change can also be generated for some of the other stakeholders. An example could be an increase in media coverage or a different attitude of some suppliers towards sustainability.

Adapting from Kaplan and Norton (1996b) we can identify the following behavioural outcomes:

☐   The desired behavioural changes that the attendee and other external stakeholders should demonstrate as a result of the event (the customer perspective)

☐   The desired behavioural changes that the staff or other internal stakeholders should demonstrate (the business growth perspective)

☐   The organisational or societal innovation or change that should be generated by the event (the learning and growth perspective).

Each set of behavioural outcomes could be achieved through one or more events. Organisations can decide which of the areas their event should focus on, as it would not be recommended to try and achieve them all at once. However, these three areas should not be seen as unrelated. They can be considered as linked by a cause-effect relationship that builds on a set of objectives to deliver the next (Kaplan and Norton, 1996b) and, combined together, all have an impact on long-term core objectives.

Once again this demonstrates that the only way for the event creator to deliver the host objectives is to find a balance amongst all stakeholders' objectives. Regardless of whether they are more hedonic (e.g. in the case of art or sport events) or more instrumental (e.g. in trade shows or professional conferences) their achievement will generate the behavioural change that is required to achieve the host objectives (Prebensen, 2010). The case study of the Medieval Festival in Offagna (Italy) provides a good illustration of how the three sets of behavioural outcomes listed above have been achieved. The festival started on a small scale and with little aspirations, but has developed into a sustainable event that is generating significant behavioural changes in the internal and external stakeholders, with positive long-term societal changes.

Case study: Offagna Medieval Festival, Italy

Offagna is a small town in central Italy, perched on a hill, built around a medieval fortress. Every year since 1988, at the end of July, Offagna hosts a week-long medieval festival that is attracting growing numbers of participants with jousting knights, falconry and acrobatic shows, flag jugglers and street performances. The small town centre becomes the set for the medieval arts and crafts market, street restaurants serving traditional food, street theatre, concerts, and children's shows, and the atmosphere when the night falls is magically recreated through the meticulous work of the local community. Fringe events such as art exhibitions, workshops, talks and conferences with famous scholars and cultural performances also take place during the week. A costume parade requiring months of preparation and research opens the festival and a medieval dinner concludes it, with challenges being set for the four neighbourhoods of the village. The winning neighbourhood will see its flag on top of the fortress for a year.

The festival started from the idea of a group of visionary people and over 20 years has grown well beyond the original expectations to become a professionally created event, based on an accurate historical reconstruction that has brought the whole town together. Every generation is involved in some way in the festival, whether by researching old paintings and manuscripts to recreate the costumes and hair styles, or by actually making and maintaining them over the years, taking part in the street parade or in the drumming group, preparing the script for the 'verbal tournament' or training for the joust (which is based on a real tournament that took place in Offagna in medieval times).

The historical accuracy is guaranteed by the research work carried out by a local cultural association, called Accademia della Crescia, taking the name from a local dish. The association was funded with the main purpose of supporting the festival but has grown in its remit over the years and now looks after the promotion and research of different disciplines that go beyond medieval and renaissance history to look after social development. It organises exhibitions, conferences and other events all along the year. Renowned scholars contribute to the work of the association, which every year appoints a number of 'knights' that are rewarded for their contribution to Italian social and cultural development.

The festival host/owner is Pro Loco, a typical Italian grass-roots organisation which is volunteer-based. Its remit is to organise cultural and leisure activities for the residents and promote the architectural heritage of the area. After years of political division in Offagna, the medieval festival has brought the local community together like never before, contributing to social and economic development and attracting new residents and tourists to the town. With the help of the artistic director of a similar festival who volunteered his cooperation in the very first years, and then calling upon the residents, local businesses, artists, stall holders, public authorities to contribute, the hosts have managed to channel the social tensions into the tournament and to create healthy competition between the neighbourhoods to design and make the most accurate medieval costumes. An important feature in recent years is that the younger generations have been more and more involved in the activities taking place before and during the festival week, and have started groups of drum players, flag jugglers and dancers that are developing their own shows and are called to participate in other events outside Offagna, with positive results on youth cohesion, pride and sense of belonging.

(Feste Medioevali, 2014; Offagna, 2014)

Before concluding this section, we need to discuss the fourth component of the Balanced Scorecard, which does not appear in the above list, although it is not less important. The financial perspective relates to the event outcomes that can be directly expressed in monetary measures, and which are actually a result of the combined effect of the behavioural changes generated by the event (Phillips et al., 2007). If we consider for instance a sales conference with a strong incentive component and some training involved, it should be expected that, once back in the office, the staff show an increased knowledge of a certain product, higher levels of motivation and commitment, which would reflect in the medium term in higher sales and increased profit. In such a case, stating a financially measurable outcome should be quite straightforward. However, as discussed earlier, some event hosts may not want or need to express their objectives in monetary terms and indeed, their events may not be conceived to generate directly a revenue, as explained by Claire Pulford, Head of Events, Breast Cancer Care, London:

Industry voice: Claire Pulford, Head of Events, Breast Cancer Care, UK

Another example is how we intentionally host what we call 'cultivation events' which are not directly about fundraising. They quite simply bring us together with the most important benefactors we have and give us an opportunity to entertain them and in so doing express our gratitude for their continued patronage. We are all too aware of how crowded the charity event marketplace is and we therefore have to work very hard to differentiate the experiences we provide through events.

The aim of the Breast Cancer Care 'cultivation events' is to generate a long-term commitment from the benefactors (i.e. a behavioural change). In the long term these might translate into (possible) financial contributions to the charity, but this is not the main priority of the events. Despite the lack of financial measure, their contribution to the long term mission of the charity is clear. Thus we can conclude that whilst behavioural outcomes must always be identified as part of the definition of medium term outcome goals, there might not be the need to identify a financial outcome and this is the reason why we are keeping this fourth component separate from the others.

The medium term strategic goals combined (whether expressed in financial terms or not) deliver the long term strategy (i.e. the core objectives). However, to directly influence the event design and delivery, they still need to be further broken down into (quantifiable) targets, which Richards and Palmer (2010) call the event outputs. The value added generated by the combined outputs delivers the medium term strategic goal. In other words, behavioural outcomes are the medium term effects of the event, which are achieved through the short term outputs (see Figure 3.1).

■ Short term tactical objectives

Outputs or targets are usually evaluated at the end of the event or a short time after and translate the strategic goal into specific figures which include a time frame. They refer directly to the service or experience generated by the event, and are usually expressed in quantitative terms (absolute figures or percentages) and need to carry specific qualities. They not only have to be SMART (specific, measurable, achievable, realistic and time-bound) but they also have to be understood and shared/accepted by internal and external stakeholders and be compatible with other objectives (Hussey, 1998). They should also allow comparisons of measures over the years. Event outputs could be tickets sold, sales figures directly generated by a product launch, new business leads generated through the event, percentage of returning attendees, increase in donations to a charitable cause, but also number of posts on a social media website. It should be noted that each strategic goal may have a number of related outputs/targets and these in turn may have several performance measures associated with them (Getz, 2005).

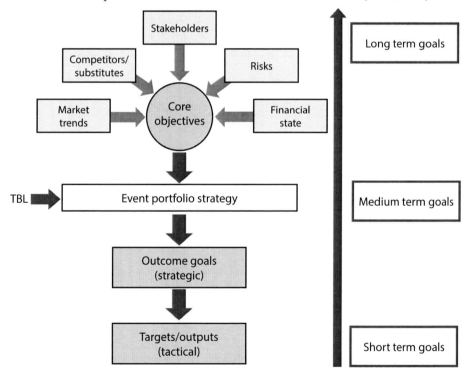

Figure 3.1: A strategic framework for owner's objectives

Below we provide an example of how long, medium and short term objectives can be derived for the Lindau Nobel Laureate Meeting 2013. Other goals and short term outputs could be identified, and these will vary depending on the type of event.

Case study: The Lindau Nobel Laureate Meetings, Germany

The event

The Lindau Nobel Laureate Meetings were founded in 1951 as a European initiative for reconciliation after World War II. Every year Nobel Laureates meet with the world's best young researchers to discuss topics central to future scientific debate on physiology or medicine, physics, chemistry and the economic sciences. In 2013, 34 Nobel Laureates were in attendance and 625 young researchers from 77 countries were selected to participate in the Lindau Meeting. The meetings take place on the banks of Lake Constance between Germany, Austria and Switzerland and involve discussions, presentations, social activities, workshops and debates in an informal atmosphere.

The host

The Meetings are organised, represented and promoted by the Council and the Foundation. The Foundation's mission is 'to promote science, research, and related social activities' as well as 'to ensure the continuance and further development of the Lindau Meetings'. The Council is the operational arm and organises the annual meetings, maintaining the relationships with academic partners around the world, donors and sponsors as well as event participants.

Long term core objectives (mission and vision)

The Lindau ethos is 'Educate, Inspire and Connect'. As stated in their Annual Report, 'the basic principle of the Lindau Meetings was – and still is - to foster the exchange of knowledge, experience, ideas, and inspiration among scientists – across generations, cultures, and nationalities' for the benefit of society and to promote international dialogue and peace.

Medium term strategic objectives (outcome goals)

A   Participants and other external stakeholders

1   To redefine the relationship between professors and students

2   To inspire and motivate young researchers to pursue their passion

3   To foster cross-sector partnerships between the academic community, government and industry

4   To promote links with peers around the globe and foster collaboration

B   Internal stakeholders

1   To create a community of science ambassadors of Nobel Laureates and young researchers

2   To allow donors and supporters to connect to Laureates and young researchers

C   Societal change and development

1   To promote cooperation across scientific disciplines

2   To engage with the general public through global outreach programmes

Short term tactical objectives (outputs)

■ All young scientists have the opportunity to discuss openly with Nobel Laureates in an informal atmosphere (to achieve outcome goals A1, A2, B1)

■ All young scientists have learnt about the life journey of a Nobel Laureate (to achieve outcome goals A2, B1)

■ All Nobel Laureates have the opportunity of rekindle relationships and friendships with peers (to achieve outcome goals A4, B1)

■ The Lindau Alumni network (online community) has grown (of a set percentage) following the meeting (to achieve outcome goals A1, A3, A4, B1)

■ Life stories of young researchers are featured in a prestigious magazine (in 2013, 30 attendees under 30 representing the future of chemistry featured in *Scientific American* prior to the event) (to achieve outcome goals B1, C2)

■ Four video blogs produced by four different participants to share their impression of the meeting and posted on the Lindau Meetings Youtube channel (to achieve outcome goals A4, B1, C2)

■ Print media, TV, radio broadcasts and online media provide coverage in 35 countries (to achieve outcome goals C1, C2)

■ 21 school teachers invited to the Meeting to reward their effort in teaching natural sciences (to achieve outcome goals C1, C2)

(Lindau Nobel Laureate Meetings, 2013)

3

Conclusions

This chapter focused on the key idea that a long term perspective must be adopted when setting event objectives from the host perspective. For the strategic event creator, the consideration of events as investments and not costs leads to the following characterisation of the event host/owner.

The event host is the decision-making unit (an organisation, a committee of people representing different stakeholders' interests, an individual etc.) that has the final word on:

☐ How the budget is spent

☐ How the differences between stakeholders' objectives are resolved (i.e. how they are prioritised)

☐ The event content and format/design.

This implies that financial objectives should not to be separated from strategic ones, as they are all strategic, but it is for the owners to decide which ones to focus on. In this context, the role of event creators becomes critical since they act as the facilitators of the objectives setting exercise which involves the host, the attendees and the other key stakeholders in an iterative way. The aim is to identify each stakeholder's set of objectives at first and then progress the discussion in order to achieve an alignment amongst them, so that the change in behaviour generated by the event delivers as many objectives as possible for all parties involved. This is clearly a challenging balance to achieve and the TBL framework can assist in the exercise. This also implies that the content and format of the event, in fact any decision about the event, should not be made until all objectives are identified and agreed upon. Although this is something generally agreed by everybody on paper, it is much more difficult to fulfil in reality when the pressure to deliver events in a short time frame and with limited resources challenges the job of event professionals.

Study questions

1   Using your experience as an event manager or attendee, discuss specific examples of events where a variety of stakeholders' objectives affect the achievement of host objectives. Provide suggestions as to how the host can be assisted in successfully aligning as many stakeholders' objectives as possible.

2   For a range of events, identify the long, medium and short term objectives divided by internal and external stakeholders, similarly to what has been done in the second Case study.

3   Analyse the contribution of the Triple Bottom Line approach to setting the event objectives from the host perspective and discuss its potential future developments.

References

Andersson, T.D. and Getz, D. (2007). Resource dependency, costs and revenues of a street festival. *Tourism Economics*. **13** (1), 143-162

Boone, M. E. (2009). *The Case for Meetings and Events: Four Elements of Strategic Value*. Boone Associates and MPI Foundation

British Cycling (2013). British Cycling: Our commitment. From www.britishcycling. org.uk, accessed 01/07/2014.

Carlsen, J. and Andersson, T.D. (2011). Strategic SWOT analysis of public, private and not-for-profit festival organisations. *International Journal of Event and Festival Management*. **2** (1), 83-97

Dwyer, L., Mellor, R., Mistilis, N. and Mules, T. (2000). A framework for assessing tangible and intangible impacts of events and conventions. *Event Management,* **6**(3), 175-189

Feste Medioevali (2014). Pro Loco. From www.festemedievali.it, accessed 16/08/2014

Getz, D. (2002). Why festivals fail. *Event Management.* **7**(4), 209-219

Getz, D. (2005). *Event Management and Event Tourism. 2nd ed.* New York: Cognizant Communications

Getz, D., Andersson T. and Larson, M. (2007). Festival stakeholder roles: concepts and case studies. *Event Management,* **10** (2-3), 103-122

Hede, A.M. (2008). Managing events in the new era of Triple Bottom Line. *Event Management,* **11** (1), 13-22

Hussey, D. (1998). *Strategic Management. From theory to implementation. 4th ed.* Oxford: Butterworth Heinemann

Kaplan, R.S. and Norton, D.P. (1996a). Using the Balanced Scorecard as a strategic management system. *Harvard Business Review,* **74** (1), 75-87

Kaplan, R.S. and Norton, D.P. (1996b). Linking the Balanced Scorecard to strategy. *California Management Review,* **39** (1), 53-81

Kenny, G. (2012). From the stakeholder viewpoint: designing measurable objectives. *Journal of Business Strategy,* **33** (6), 40-46

Lindau Nobel Laureate Meetings (2013). Dialogue. 63rd Lindau Nobel Laureate Meeting, Annual Report 2013. Council of the Lindau Nobel Laureate Meetings. www.lindau-nobel.org, accessed 16/08/2014.

Meetings Mean Business (2013). Communications and advocacy toolkit. From www.meetingsmeanbusiness.com/toolkit, accessed 01/07/2014.

MPI (2011). Business Value of Meetings. [online] Meeting Professional International. December 2011. www.mpiweb.org/Education/BVOM, accessed 01/07/2014.

Offagna (2014). Comune di Offagna. From www.offagna.org, accessed 16/08/2014.

O'Toole, W. (2011). *Events Feasibility and Development. From Strategy to Operations.* Amsterdam, London: Butterworth-Heinemann

Phillips, J.J., Myhill, M. and McDonough J.B. (2007). *Proving the value of meetings and events.* ROI Institute and Meeting Professional International

Prebensen, N.K. (2010). Value creation through stakeholder participation: A case study of an event in the High North. *Event Management,* **14** (1), 37-52

Pugh, C. and Wood, E.H. (2004). The strategic use of events within local government: a study of London borough councils. *Event Management,* **9** (1-2), 61-71

Reic, I. (2012). The development of the corporate events sector, in Ferdinand, N. and Kitchin P.J. ed. *Events Management an International Approach.* Los Angeles, London: Sage Publications, pp.267-286

3

Richards, G. and Palmer, R. (2010). *Eventful Cities: Cultural Management and Urban Revitalisation*. Amsterdam, London: Butterworth-Heinemann

The Business Desk (2014). Yorkshire Tourism. businessdesk.s3.amazonaws.com/_files/documents/aug_14/businessdesk__1407105078_HG1636_YK_Tourism6.pdf, accessed 14/08/2014.

Wood, E. (2009). An impact evaluation framework: local government community festivals. *Event Management*, **12** (3-4). 171-185.

Ziakas, V. and Costa, C.A. (2011). Event portfolio and multi-purpose development: Establishing the conceptual grounds. *Sport Management Review*, **14** (4). 409-423

4 The Attendee and the Audience: a strategic approach

Jonathan Moss

Learning objectives

- To gain an understanding of what the attendees hope to gain from an event.

- To demonstrate how a holistic model can be utilised to strategically facilitate attendee outcomes.

- Through case studies illustrate how this model can be adapted for different types of events.

Introduction

This chapter will present a thorough consideration of the attendee and in doing so will discuss why they come to events, what do they get out of it and most importantly, how can we, as event creators, strategically plan our events to deliver what they want?

It will also consider existing theories and research as a platform to develop a conceptual model that can be used to interpret attendee expectations. The discussion will closely link to other chapters that consider the expectations of attendees, particularly Chapter 7. Understanding attendees' expectations provides the basis for much of the discussion in Part III of this book, specifically; facilitate the attendees' experience journey, creatively design the eventscape, and manage other aspects such as marketing and also food and drink. Event design decisions in all of these areas are underpinned by a shrewd understanding of the makeup and expectations of the attendee.

As a foundation for this discussion, this chapter will discuss how events management has previously researched the attendee and what it means to consider their motivations from a strategic perspective. In doing so, the chapter will consider other closely related disciplines to discuss what theories and perspectives can be usefully applied to our field. The last section of this chapter will discuss the future of understanding attendees and how the development of a deeper and broader perspective of motivations will give event creators a more significant insight into the attendee enabling purposeful design. Through the chapter connections to the real world will be made by using two case studies. Due to the events industry being a broad area, the two case studies will be from different sectors: business events and charity events.

The attendee

Many of us have attended a broad range of events, and have enjoyed many and varied experiences. As well as this, we may have been to the same events twice, but at different times with different people and had different or sometimes similar experiences. This variety is fuelled by the fact that we all have different motivations, expectations and preconceptions. Indeed the same person has differences from day to day and event to event. Sometimes our experiences may be similar to other peoples' experiences and what's more, our experiences may be entirely because of, and sometimes entirely unconnected to, the event and even somewhere in-between. To clarify the final point, our engagement with a university open day, for example, might be determined quite heavily by our pre-conception as to whether we like the city and want to study there. A prospective student arriving in high spirits, as they already love the city, would likely consume the open day very differently to the attendee whose parents had persuaded them to come along, even though they had already, in their heart and mind, decided on the one they visited last week.

Some of the above may feel confusing, and perhaps on the face of it, contradictory. It certainly highlights how the ability to understand 'what's in it' for the attendee of events and the prospect of how to facilitate this is a notable challenge, and perhaps it may seem easier if the attendee is not actually considered at all. To make assumptions and decisions based on 'it's worked in the past, so it will work again,' is however a foolhardy and myopic approach and not consistent with the nature of Strategic Event Creation. The interpretation of your attendee and the ability to then transfer that into proficient event design decisions is a core competence of successful event creators.

Industry voice: Nick Woodward-Shaw, Director of Global Events, Forever Living Products International, Arizona, USA

I think in terms of event design and planning if it was a piece of advice I was giving, the biggest one would be know your objectives and know your audience and I think if you know those two, the planets will align.

4

To expand on the view of Nick Woodward-Shaw, without attendees, there are no events and as discussed in Chapter 1, as the industry grows and matures, so does the competition. The key aspect of competition in the events industry is the need to attract attendees – to attract them from other events but also competing with all other distractions. In April 2014, as reported by the BBC , a major music festival event Oxygen was cancelled because the previous year did not consider its audience when developing its music programme. Attendees criticised it, which led to them not being able to attract major artists, the potential attendees moved to other festivals and that was sufficient to ensure the event closed down (BBC, 2014). Each year thousands of events globally suffer the same demise as Oxygen. This demonstrates that the ability to interpret what the attendee wants may well be complex and multi-faceted but it is a core aspect of Strategic Event Creation and one that must be engaged with.

The main reason for this complexity, as Beard in Chapter 7 discusses, is that experience and experiences are not homogenous or static. They are, as Beard and also Schmitt (1999) recognise, ever changing and fluid, inevitably dynamic. It can be argued that experiences are a continual feedback system that instantaneously affect our motivations, expectations and even our sense of self-identity. For example, returning to a music festival for a second time is a different experience. Memories of the previous visit have formed which change and even raise our expectations and motivations. The familiarity of the site will affect how the attendee feels connected to the festival. Perhaps the attendee might feel less of a stranger and enjoy knowing the site. Conversely, they might feel that it hasn't changed and is a bit too similar or uninspiring.

This clearly demonstrates how the repetitious adoption of the same event design, whether that be for a conference, festival, or charity event, leaves events vulnerable and will soon be found to have become outdated as the motivations of the attendees change. Have we all not experienced that sense of change – when something in a market place was incredibly new and exciting and then became common place and then out-dated? The rapid emergence and equally rapid disappearance of flash mobs as a marketing tactic convincingly evidences this point. Understanding the attendee so well that events pre-empt what they would want to be the ultimate goal. This is often expressed by the attendee when using phrases like, "I would never have thought of that but it just worked so well, so original…" or "it felt unique, I can't believe other places haven't done that, I've never seen it before but it was the best, a new high". It is through evaluating the attendees' experience and then continually developing and creating based on what the attendees have experienced that facilitates this pre-knowledge. Understanding the attendee is therefore the foundation upon which purposeful event creation flourishes; it is the platform for creative design which confidently and repeatedly exceeds expectations.

Industry voice: Claire Pulford, Head of Events, Breast Cancer Care, UK

I mean if you've been to a Breast Cancer Care event you know you've been to a Breast Cancer Care event because we think very carefully about the attendee's or the participant's experience and it's very personal, because we as a charity and a brand are all about caring for people.

Claire's appreciation of the attendees' experience is based upon a strategic understanding of the attendees' antecedents as cancer patients, survivors and the carers. The research they do around attendee motivation and event experience provides the insight that enables the charity to ably design future event experience. The discussion now shifts to consider past research and in doing so, strive to understand how the attendee experience can be purposefully designed.

Attendance motivation research

Crompton and McKay (1997) argued that understanding audience motivations was a means to enhance design development, evaluate satisfaction and develop greater insights into the processes of decision making. Since then this area of research has gained considerable attention. This is illustrated clearly by Li and Petrick (2006) who reviewed much of the relevant research and identified all of the motivational factors from across 13 studies. Indeed, their table provides a clear overview of motivation type with many similarities of motivation through each piece of research. Distilling these commonalities down further provides us with clear typology of motivation:

☐   Stimulus seeking/excitement/escape

☐   Social contact/meeting new people/socializing

☐   Family togetherness

☐ Cultural exploration

☐ Novelty/uniqueness/curiosity

These factors however do not account adequately for business events and Getz (2012) argues that these events have their own factors that need to be considered. This is supported by Mair and Thompson (2009) who find the motivational factors of attending business events to be:

☐ Personal and professional development

☐ Networking opportunities

☐ Cost

☐ Location

☐ Time and convenience

☐ Health and well-being

Considering the motivations of sporting events attendants, Wann et al. (2001) and Wann et al. (2008) offer this typology:

☐ Escape

☐ Economic

☐ Eutress (Positive experiences)

☐ Self-esteem

☐ Group affiliation

☐ Entertainment

☐ Family

☐ Aesthetics

Many of these studies of attendees have, however, used quantitative survey research with the focus on either satisfaction, motivation or both (Bowen and Daniels, 2005; Nicholson and Pearce, 2001; Yoon et al., 2010). The logic of which is clear; by understanding what motivates people to attend, the event creators are able to deliver it, and subsequently measure their satisfaction levels. If the process is executed effectively, the satisfaction levels should be high. Indeed, this is logical and promises to provide useful information to event creators. Importantly, as the event industry matures and competition intensifies, a deeper and more holistic understanding is required. A core identification of motivations is a solid base to start from but what more can be done to gain a deeper understanding which can be seen to underpin the success of an event within a competitive experience marketplace? Li and Petrick (2006, p.244) state that:

A gap seems to exist between these research findings and systematic theory building. It is suggested that more efforts in theoretical conceptualization are needed for understanding festival and event attendees' motivations. The related psychology, sociology, marketing and sport marketing literature may provide some useful insights on this issue. Moreover, most festival and event motivation studies have been conducted by a small group of authors. The involvement of more researchers with more diverse backgrounds and disciplinary approaches, and the employment of new research methodologies are strongly encouraged.

The passage above recognises that using surveys to evaluate attendees' experience has limited scope, especially if they don't create robust and lasting theories that can facilitate event creators to design cutting edge events. More in-depth and innovative approaches to understanding the attendee are required, ones that use research from different disciplines so that the understanding of 'what's in it for the attendee' is taken forward.

If event creators, globally, are becoming more strategically proficient in a bid to improve the design of their events, what are the innovative ways to understand motivations and facilitate them? As Beard in Chapter 7 discusses about experience, and Roberts and Strafford in Chapter 6 with expectations, there is a need for a holistic approach, to conceptualise motivations as being interconnected with expectations, both of which are based on their connections to past experiences. Consider the attendees' inner world (their identity and personality) and how this is connected to the external world of the environment (e.g. the festival site or conference centre) and the social world of the event (other attendees, atmosphere, etc.). It is important to remember that these interconnected phenomena are dynamic; they constantly move and flow and are not necessarily bound by time. The following example, with two different experiences, illustrates the previous point.

An event may present some very stunning visual elements that provide moments of physio-psycho responses (goose-flesh, spine-tingles) but across the whole event may leave the attendee with no long lasting positive experiences and the attendee makes statements like, "it was all very flashy but I never felt part of the event and it left me feeling cold." Whereas, a small community festival might not have the same level of technology and therefore not elicit spine tingling moments but across the entirety of the event may provoke statements like, "It wasn't an amazing show but I'm really proud of what they did and to be a part of this community."

We can see then that a positive event experience has to address the attendees' needs on many levels. Dramatic visual effects may positively affect the attendee to some degree and for a limited/specific amount of time. Without addressing other, more social, psychological and emotional needs, it is insufficient and soon forgotten against longer standing motivations. If we look at those previous typologies again we can see that, while there are differences because of the event type, they all consist of psychological, social, emotional, cognitive and environmental factors. Therefore it can be seen that despite the event, what the attendee wants to gain from the experience can be conceptualised from a 'holistic' perspective. This is closely aligned then to the holistic nature of experience as discussed by Beard in Chapter 7.

The depth of analysis involved in the strategic creation of experiences is reflected upon by Nick in the next extract.

Industry voice: Nick Woodward-Shaw, Director of Global Events, Forever Living Products International, Arizona, USA

I constantly think about putting the audience member, or in our case the qualifier, at the head of everything. So every single decision we make about what hotel we're going to have, what trainings we put on, what entertainment, even what music …. we use for our events. I'm constantly thinking about the person sat in the audience and how they're feeling and "What do they want? What's going to excite them?"

The discussion above combines to make a persuasive case of how event creators must adopt approaches to adequately know and understand their audience. As Beard, in Chapter 7 discusses, what are their psychological, emotional, cognitive, social and environmental requirements and what is the relationship between them?

What could this look like as an illustrative model to guide event creators? Figure 4.1 starts as a generic model but which then allows a focus to be made so that it accounts for variations of motivation type and event type.

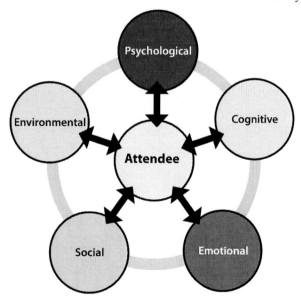

Figure 4.1: The five factors of the attendee

This model is designed to give event creators a tool to start unpacking what they want to deliver for their attendees. It looks in depth at what their attendees want to get from the event. It asks that event creators consider five different factors as a means to developing a holistic view of their attendees. From these five factors, specific considerations can be developed and this can then enhance event design and creation.

The model illustrates that firstly the attendee is affected by the event in five different ways but that also the attendee is an agent of this effect; there is a relationship. As well as this, there is a relationship between all the factors as, for example, the emotional factors can impact the social which then affects environmental factors.

If we take each category and highlight some of the factors involved it can be seen how they affect each other and how an individual can affect other people experiences and how they can influence theirs.

☐   **Psychological** - this involves understanding the attendees' personality, role, status, and image. How do the attendees want to be perceived and how does the event design reflect this?

☐   **Cognitive** - this involves understanding how the psychological considerations affect the attenddees' expectations, motivations and what memories of previous experiences they may have. What are their previous memories and expectations and how can we build on them if we consider the psychological factors?

☐   **Emotional** - this involves understanding how the previous factors can a shape the attendees' emotional needs. For example, stress, anxiety, euphoria, sadness, fear, etc. Can event design enhance the positive/appropriate emotions and minimise undesirable ones?

☐   **Social** - this involves drawing the previous factors together and understanding how the attendees are affected by the other attendees and how they might affect those around them. What is the relationship that the attendees have with each other and how does this feed back into the psychological, cognitive and emotional factors? How can this be developed or enhanced?

☐   **Environmental** - this involves understanding the physical space and requirements of the event. How does the space and place affect the other four factors and are the environmental factors aligned to them?

Before we consider some theories around the five factors let us consider how they might be applied by discussing them within a real world case study.

Case study: abe, France

Advanced Business Events (abe) is a French based company which runs business events. They create small to large trade fairs, business conventions, congresses and summits, delivering 30-40 national and international events a year, ranging from 200 to around 8,000 delegates. Their main audience members are business professionals who are in key roles within their industry; they tend to target original equipment manufacturers (OEM), large contractors and suppliers of companies in the following industries:

- Aviation-space-defence
- Chemistry-pharmaceuticals-cosmetics
- Energy and environment
- Industry and technology
- Packaging and food processing

Their Assistant Manager for Marketing and Communication, Lauren Haney-Wilcox, explained what their key factors are when considering the audience. In the middle column, are the related aspects of the model. The third column shows examples of specific considerations within each of the factors in Figure 4.1.

abe's key factors	Model categories	Specific considerations
Professionalism	Psychological Social Environmental	Identity, personality, motivations Status, role Corporate, high quality
Accessibility	Environmental	Location, building, prestige, facilities
Facilitate needs	Psychological Cognitive Emotional Environmental	Identity, role, personality Expectation, motivation, past experiences Removal of unnecessary stresses, maximise concentration and focus Physical, comfort, transport
Market demand	Environmental	Economic, strategy
Geographical positioning	Environmental Social	Company culture, identity

It can be seen that once the unpacking of the attendee and clients from a holistic perspective begins, it presents what can be referred to as a 'complex mesh', meaning that there are many interwoven elements that define the attendee and their motivations. Nevertheless, while the above example demonstrates the interconnected nature of how this event audience can be perceived, the model provides a basis upon which to interpret what the attendees expect and why.

The following passage, from Lauren Haney-Wilcox, explains why abe see it as important to understand the attendees' needs if you are to provide a premium service and exceed their expectations:

"Experience and satisfaction are of paramount importance to us as a company. We run a Business to Business meetings service within the main event and aim to take care of every last bit of the trade fair experience so that all the client has to do is turn up and meet the right people; this is what we promote as our specialité if you like. We take care of accommodation, lunches, travel, right down to the time and place a client will meet with another in a pre-arranged meeting that they themselves will have requested. If the client doesn't come out the other side of the event with a good level of satisfaction it means all the hard work counts for very little."

When asked about the changing expectations of clients at these business events, a clear environmental change is seen:

"I have only been with my current company just over a year but already I can see that the event expectations are definitely in a period of evolution. Social networking, the instantaneity of information flow and new advances in technology (especially smart-phones, tablets, etc.) have meant that we have to be on the ball and producing newer, more modern ways of communicating with our target audiences. Coupled with this, we have had to develop new methods of distributing our message via social networking as well as more effective and aggressive marketing for example."

It can be seen that these dynamic environmental changes have a direct effect on people's psychological and cognitive levels and show that the speed of information flow is tied to their sense of identity and professionalism. That is to say, the attendees of these events wish to maintain a professional identity, on an individual level and for the businesses they represent.

In the final section of this case study we can see that keeping up with the dynamic nature of the attendee is, in the real world, a taxing job but that it is also a very important one.

"We ask each participant to submit an evaluation questionnaire but…we don't do very well at this because due to budgetary restraints we just don't have the staff. It worries me constantly because we really should be investing more time in new emerging marketing trends instead of being bogged down by old methods… we are constantly trying to find new and more innovative means of spreading our message and extending information about our events. Evolve or die (metaphorically speaking of course)."

From the above answer it can be seen that there is the implicit message to keep up to date with not only the broader developments in events management but also how this affects the experience for the attendee as their individual expectations and world's develop. abe say that this is expensive, so it doesn't get performed as well as it should. It could be argued that this does not add up strategically, and that there are more efficient/innovative/cost-effective approaches available.

The concept of emotions

Returning to the theoretical framework of the model, this chapter will progress to look at how previous theories also show that the psychological, cognitive, emotional, social and environmental factors are all interconnected. This will be done by examining the concept of emotions. Emotions are certainly a key factor in individual attendees' future intentions with Heath and Feldwick (2007) concluding that emotion, and not reason or knowledge, is the key factor in decision making. They state:

> We are continually influenced by subconscious perception and therefore the decisions we make are always influenced by and sometimes entirely driven by emotions and feelings.

(Heath and Feldwick, 2007, p. 50 based on the work of Damasio, 1994 and 2003). '

It is important then to consider the effect that these emotions can have on feelings of satisfaction and memories of the event. This is demonstrated by Mason and Paggiaro's (2012) research at a food festival that showed a strong emotional element to satisfaction. This point is further underlined by Wood and Moss (forthcoming) who researched satisfaction at music events and found that it was an emotional experience.

So, if emotions play a part in attendee experience, how are they connected to memory? According to Stone (2007), emotions and experience are stored in different parts of the memory; emotions are stored in the experiential memory and are thus short lived but memories of emotions are stored in the episodic memory. These episodic memories assist in the formation of beliefs, attitudes and behaviours. These beliefs, attitudes and behaviours can shape an individual's future attendance intentions. It is therefore important to understand them and to do so from a holistic perspective that considers their relationship with other aspects of the attendee. Wilson and Ross (2003) argue that 'we are what we remember,' (p.139), consequently, and given the influence of emotion, the question for event managers is, 'how can we make this event memorable on an emotional level?'

Alea and Bluck (2003) see memory and reflection as being the basis for three other key areas of consideration with regards to the attendee;

☐ The self (identity and self-continuity)

☐ The social (emphasising, sharing and strengthen social bonds)

☐ Directive (problem solving, considering future events).

Looking at the model in Figure 4.1 we can see how memory is linked, directly and indirectly to both personality and experiences. To facilitate your attendees' experiences the event should consider their individual and collective/social personalities.

For example, looking at the earlier event typologies we can see that for festivals:

☐   **Personality** links to   **Seeking stimulus/excitement/escape**

☐   **Social** links to   **Social contact/meeting new people/socializing**

In contrast, for a business event:

☐   **Personality** links to   **Personal and professional development**

☐   **Social** links to   **Networking opportunities**

Benckendorff and Peace (2012, p.2) see personality research as, "a sprawling array of theories, methods and levels of analysis", many of which, because of the experimental research and broad theories, are not currently relevant here but echo the theme of interconnectedness running through this chapter. Mischel's (1968; 1984) perspective argues that personality is best understood in relation to the situation it is placed in and how this affects social motivation and values. This further illustrates the need to understand the attendee from a holistic perspective. Personality is a complex and dynamic phenomenon and needs to be understood in relation to the other factors of the model in Figure 4.1.

It can be seen then that the personality and the environmental factors of the attendee influence their attitudes, beliefs and behaviours by being connected to that of their social and cultural values. These are found externally to the individual but also reinforce or alter their internal states.

For example let us consider a music festival.

Our sense of identity is shaped by the music and the place it occurs (Hudson, 2006). Audiences engage with it through what Kong (1995) sees as texts, contexts and intertexts (t-shirts, posters, dress, etc.) which then feed back into our sense of internal identity and personality.

The last part of this model considers the roles of the social and the environmental. An important question to ask of any event is how we plan to develop a sense of bringing people together? In this context it could encompass many things; it could be a sense of belonging to a team (sports event); a sense of local community (local arts event); to facilitate networking (a business event); a space for shared escape (a music festival).

As a way of illustrating this, the chapter will use a second case study from Shift.ms:

Case study: Shift.ms, UK

Shift.ms is an online charity which supports people newly diagnosed with multiple sclerosis (MS). They run fundraising events, events for people with MS and events for healthcare professionals. They have 5,500 members worldwide.

They involve themselves within many other larger events. For example at the Great North Run they have a supporting event for runners with MS which offers support, food and drinks. They lead and contribute to many of the events on the MS calendar. They also attend run workshops, create art pieces and offer information, leaflets and booklets. They put on continuing professional development courses as well as large fundraisers like the (2014) car rally. The budget for these events range from £500 to £5000 which means much of the staffing is provided on a voluntary basis.

When Community Co-ordinator Cassandra White was asked about their key factors when considering the audience, her response was as follows:

Shift.ms key factors	Model categories	Specific considerations
Accessibility	Environmental	Physical, access, duration
Professionalism of their staff	Psychological	Up to date techniques, well informed, knowledgeable image

It can be seen that similar words are being used to the previous case study but because they have a different audience, they mean different things. Referring back to the social and environmental factors of the model, it can be seen in the next passage that they form an important part of the whole experience for the attendee:

It comes first. We place the MS community at the heart of everything we do, which does sound clichéd, but we really do live this. Our car rally fundraising event has two goals, which are (in order): 1) the MS community having fun together and 2) raising money for our charity. Cohesion within our community is very important to us, so we use events such as our fundraisers to bring MSers together who may have only met previously online. From this, their holistic approach to their attendee can be seen. In this next passage, a number of challenges about the developing expectations of their attendees are discussed.

Accessibility is expected at events now (and rightly so). And as a young, upbeat charity, people expect everything we do to be fun and incorporating the latest trends in social media, etc.

Reflecting on the earlier case study, we can see that a number of the issues are the same, but not for the same reason. Considering them from a holistic perspective, these words and issues can mean the same and different things for both business event attendees and charity event attendees. It should soon become clear that phrases like 'social media' and 'technology' are broad phrases and when unpacked using a strategic approach can mean very different things to different groups of attendees. It is understanding and then

4

delivering these differences which will provide what your attendee wants and will help ensure your events are a success. For example the word 'accessibility' can mean how it is accessed by rail or road but it can also mean ensuring specific access facilities to the event building or site. Another example is that 'social media' could mean ensuring a live Twitter feed and LinkedIn for one event (abe's for example) but if your attendees are a younger audience like Shift.ms's, it could also mean incorporating Snapchat or Instagram.

Lastly a key point in relation to the role of the event is raised. abe's role, shown in the previous case example, is to provide a seamless background service for other professionals to meet and network. On the other hand, the role of Shift.ms'is to make sure they are "accurately reflecting our brand, [ensure] the attendee's enjoyment, use the latest technology and with a low budget."

This provides yet another clear indication of the importance of strategically understanding your attendee from a holistic perspective; so that the event you provide can deliver what the attendee is expecting. For Shift.ms' events it is to be very present, supportive, and engaging while, delivering an enjoyable experience and raising awareness.

It is important to recognise that each of the five initial categories in Figure 4.1 can be broken down further. It is in the developing of these levels and interconnections that complexities of the attendee are realised, showing why it is highly important to strategically consider them in this way and not over-simplify them into the singular considerations of expectations and motivations. This is represented usefully in Figure 4.2 with the connections within this holistic model illustrated at a deeper level than are initially highlighted in Figure 4.1.

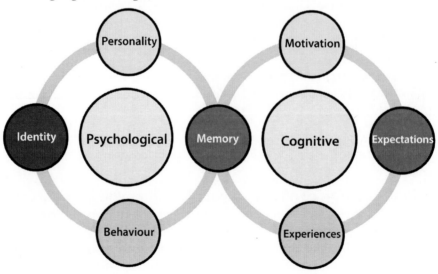

Figure 4.2: The psychological and cognitive factors of the attendee

It is important at this level of the model to start asking specific questions about the attendee, what they would like to get from the event and how this can be facilitated. For example, "What is the identity of our attendees and how we can support and develop that?" or "What aspects of their personality will be most beneficial for us to focus on?"

Conclusion

This chapter has discussed the attendees of events by looking at 'what's in it for them', and by examining previous research that has identified motivations for event attendance. Through discussing the typologies of motivations it has demonstrated differences between event types and highlighted the importance of perceiving attendees' motivations from a holistic viewpoint. The conceptual models illustrated how event creators can identify attendees' motivations and needs. The models starts from a broader, more holistic, perspective but can then be drilled down to be adapted to specific types of events.

The connections, complexities and relationships could be charted and explored in considerable detail through levels and sublevels of analysis. However such analysis is scalable and while larger events may invest considerably in these, smaller events, with much reduced budgets, can also apply them to a lesser degree. The models and their various levels are presented here to provide illustration as to how event creators can adopt such evaluative approaches to better understand their attendee as a precursor to the event design.

Through adopting such an approach, justified decisions can be made, with evidence and confidence, relating to issues such as venues, layout, programme, atmospherics and so forth. This is a far cry from making decisions entirely based upon past experience. It is not an exact science, and human nature and free will do not permit this, but it demonstrates that a strategic approach to event creation should begin, at an early stage, with an evaluation of attendee characteristics and motivations. This analysis is then developed further post event and this post event activity should rightfully become the pre-event evaluation for the next event. The establishment of such an iterative process is highly recommended. Such a process is integral to the abilities of event creators to maintain ingenuity and flexibility in competitive and changing markets, with demanding and proficient consumers of experience. A key point to remember is that if this analysis is executed effectively and proficient event design follows then it theoretically gives the attendee what they want; it is a cyclical process that benefits both the event and the attendees. At the beginning of the chapter a tempting statement was made about knowing what the attendee wants before they do, by using a holistic approach to strategically consider the attendee, facilitating this through the event design, and then effectively evaluating this during and post event. It is understandable how renowned examples of events such as Glastonbury Festival in the UK, Coachella in California, USA and Benicassim in Spain, consistently exceed attendee expectation and sell next year's event within seconds of release.

In conclusion, if the question is asked, "What's in it for the attendee?" The answer is whatever you put into your event; because, if you have strategically considered your audience from a holistic perspective, you'll know what they want to get from it and you'll have purposefully designed the event so that the audience can easily experience and extract the value they seek. Your relationship as an events creator to your audience is like that of the models introduced through this chapter - it is interdependent.

Study questions

1 As an event creator how could you use this holistic model to strategically plan for the short, medium and long term of your business?

2 How could you evaluate that the planned outcomes of your holistic model and what the attendee has gained from your event were aligned?

References

Alea, N. and Bluck, S. (2003). Why are you telling me this? A conceptual model of the social function of autobiographical memory. *Memory*, **11** (2),165-178.

BBC News website (2014). Ireland's 2014 Oxygen music festival cancelled. www.bbc.co.uk/news/world-europe-27094144, accessed 01/05/2014.

Benckendorff, P. and Pearce, P.L (2012). The psychology of events,in S. Page and J. Connell (eds.), *Handbook of Events*, New York: Routledge, pp.1-18

Bowen, H. and Daniels, M. (2005). Does the music matter? Motivations for attending a music festival, *Event Management*, **9**, 155-164.

Crompton, J.L. and McKay, S.L. (1997). Motives of visitors attending festival events, *Annals of Tourism Research*, **24** (2), 425-439.

Damasio, A.R. (1994). *Descartes' Error*, New York: G.P. Putnam's Sons.

Damasio, A.R. (2003). *Looking for Spinoza*, London: Heinemann.

Getz, D. (2012). *Event Studies: Theory, Research and Policy for Planned Events, (2nd edn,* London: Routledge.

Heath, R. and Feldwick, P. (2007). Fifty years of using the wrong model in advertising, *International Journal of Market Research*. **50** (1), 29- 59.

Hudson, R. (2006). Regions and place: Music, identity and place, *Progress in Human Geography*, **30** (5), 626-634.

Kong, L. (1995). Popular music in geography analyses, *Progress in Human Geography*, **19** (2), 183-198.

Li, R. and Petrick, J.F. (2006). A review of festival and event motivation studies, *Event Management*, **9**, 239-245.

Mair, J. and Thompson, K. (2009). The UK association conference attendance decision-making process. *Tourism Management*, **30** (3), 400-409.

Mason, M. C., and Paggiaro, A. (2012). Investigating the role of festivalscape in culinary tourism: The case of food and wine events, *Tourism Management*, **33** (6), 1329-1336.

Mischel, W. (1968). *Personality and Assessment*, New York: Wiley.

Mischel, W. (1984). Convergences and challenges in the search for consistency, *American Psychologist*, **34**, 740-754.

Nicholson, R.E. and Pearce, D.G. (2001). Why do people attend events: A comparative analysis of visitors motivations at Four South Island Events, *Journal of Travel Research*, **39** (4), 449-460.

Schmitt, B.H. (1999). *Experiential Marketing*, New York: Free Press.

Stone, A.A. (2007). Thoughts on the present state of real-time data capture, in Stone, A.A., Shiffman, S., Atienza, A., and Nebeling, L. (eds), *The Science of Real-Time Data Capture*, Oxford: Oxford University Press, pp.361-371.

Wann, D.L., Grieve, G., Zapalac, R.K. and Pearse, D. (2008). Motivational profiles of sports fans of different sports, *Sports Marketing Quarterly*, **17** (1), 6-19.

Wann, D. L., Melnick, M. J., Russell, G. W., and Pease, D. G. (2001). *Sport Fans: The Psychology and Social Impact of Spectators*. New York: Routledge Press.

Wilson, A and Ross, M. (2003). The identify function of autobiographical memory: Time is on our side, *Memory*, **11** (2), 137-149.

Wood, E. and Moss, J. (forthcoming). Capturing Emotion. Experience Sampling at Live Music Events. *Arts Marketing*.

Yoon, Y-S., Lee, J-S. and Lee, C-K. (2010). Measuring festival quality and value affecting visitors' satisfaction and loyalty using a structural approach, *International Journal of Hospitality Management*, **29**, 335-342.

4

5 Understanding Sponsors' and Partners' Motivations

Leah Donlan

Learning objectives

- Identify the range of wider event stakeholders who have an interest and/or involvement in a variety of events.

- Appreciate the objectives of sponsors and other event partners and the impact these can have on event design and delivery.

- Assess strategies that event creators can employ to balance the needs of sponsors and partners to achieve value adding event experiences.

Introduction

Beyond the event creators and the attendees, events of all types and sizes involve a whole host of other stakeholders including sponsors, suppliers and the media. Investment and support from these stakeholders provide a significant and essential source of revenue and other resources for a whole gamut of event types (Andersson and Getz, 2008) including sport, music, art, community and conferences. Without the involvement of these wider stakeholders, events could not take place (Getz et al, 2007) as they are reliant on their support, both monetary and non-monetary in a variety of ways.

As the event creators and attendees have their own motivations for attending, and objectives to be pursued through the event, so do these partners. However, the objectives of sponsors and other partners may differ from those of the attendees and the event creator. As such, in taking a stakeholder-centric view of Strategic Event Creation, it is vitally important that event creators both understand and work with the motivations, objectives and goals of their partners to shape an event's design and delivery. It is the understanding of these objectives and motivations and how they impact upon an event that forms the basis for this chapter.

Who are the event partners?

Regardless of how they are categorised (see Chapter 2 for a comprehensive discussion of different stakeholders), event stakeholders (partners) represent a very wide range of organisations, both for-profit and not-for-profit. The configuration of partners will vary according to the event type. For example, a major sporting event such as the Olympic Games will have a huge number of partners including the media, sponsors, suppliers, governing bodies, governments and local community organisations to name but a few. In contrast, a community real ale festival may have a smaller number of partners, including sponsors, suppliers and the local council. Having a smaller number of partners for an event does not, however, in any way diminish their importance or the attention that event creators should pay to their desired event outcomes.

Client, attendee and community motivations and objectives are dealt with in Chapters 3, 4 and 6 respectively. This chapter will concentrate on the motivations and objectives of sponsors, suppliers, the media, government, general business and tourism organisations, in relation to a range of events. The literature on events primarily talks in the language of stakeholders, however, all of the stakeholders discussed in this chapter contribute to successful event creation and facilitate the desired event outcomes. Therefore, in light of this inter-dependence between the event and these wider stakeholders, this chapter will refer to them as partners. The only exceptions to this will be where other authors being discussed have specifically employed the term 'stakeholder' or where wider event stakeholders, such as attendees, are included in the discussion. These different partners are depicted below in Figure 5.1.

While all of the identified partners can be direct stakeholders of an event, there may also be relationships between different partners, for example sponsors and tourist organisations might work together on a joint advertising campaign to promote the event and their own brands/organisations. These inter-relationships are of particular interest to event creators, as they represent an opportunity not only for partners to derive additional value but also an opportunity to augment the event experience as a result.

Figure 5.1: Wider event partners

In many cases event creators may equate sponsorship with direct revenue generation, implying that sponsors pay in cash for the right to be associated with an event. Indeed sponsors are explicitly identified in Getz et al's (2007) facilitator category as providers of support to make events happen. However, a more comprehensive definition of sponsorship is advocated to encompass all stakeholders who pay in cash or in kind (i.e. through the provision of goods, services or expertise) in return for access to the exploitable commercial potential of an event (Meenaghan,1991). Therefore, the term sponsor, in this chapter, includes both those stakeholders providing financial contributions as well as those adding value in other ways, for example through the provision of a venue, food and drink or marketing and technical support. While the objectives and motivations of sponsors vary according to their individual needs, it is unhelpful to distinguish between sponsors providing monetary and non-monetary support. If a sponsor pays money then this increases the event's revenues. If the sponsor provides resources (perhaps marketing support, venues, staging etc.) this then reduces the event's costs. It can therefore be simply argued that whether the sponsor provides direct monies or 'in kind' goods and services (or indeed a combination of the two), they may both be equally required and desirable to deliver an event effectively.

Regardless of the scale and nature of an event, the pivotal role of sponsors and other partners in delivering event success must not be underestimated and in all cases the event creator must understand and work with their motivations and objectives, i.e. infuse the event design and delivery with a stakeholder-centric strategic intent. It is to the evolution of these sponsor and partner motivations and objectives that the chapter will now turn.

The evolution of partner motivations and objectives

Prior to selecting an event to sponsor or partner with, and certainly prior to selecting an event to become involved with, organisations should consider their overall objectives to ensure that the event aligns with their strategic priorities and allows them to meet their strategic objectives (Papadimitriou et al, 2008). In the same way, events need to be careful to identify and target organisations whose mission complements the event, making for a much more productive relationship. This section will firstly examine the objectives of sponsors and the impact these can have on event design and delivery, before addressing the objectives and related impacts of other partners such as suppliers, the media, government, general business and tourism organisations.

■ Objectives-driven event sponsorship

In line with their strategic priorities, potential sponsors will seek out events which they believe will best allow them to meet their particular objectives. As the need to demonstrate a return on sponsorship investment grows (Donlan and Crowther, 2012) so sponsors are becoming increasingly demanding of the events they sponsor and it is likely that many sponsors will want to influence the event's design and delivery so as to maximise their ability to meet their objectives. As such, it is vital not only for the event creator to have an understanding of the growing array and changing nature of sponsor objectives, but also to appreciate the impact of these on the event itself.

Sponsorship was traditionally used to pursue objectives of media exposure (Head, 1981), brand awareness (Thwaites, 1993) and corporate image benefits (Witcher et al, 1991). However, sponsorship objectives are rapidly evolving and according to both Ukman (2004) and Farrelly et al. (2006) sponsorship is now invested in to achieve a much broader range of business objectives. Clearly, the specific combination of objectives pursued will vary according to the nature and size of the sponsor and the sponsored event. Therefore, there is no one-size-fits-all piece of advice for event creators: they must take the time to understand the unique needs of their event's sponsors if they are to maximise the value creating potential of each sponsorship arrangement.

Industry voice: Russell Miller, Associate Director Business Relations and Sponsorship, Manchester Business School

It's continually surprising to learn of sponsorship practitioners who develop events and present propositions based on their own requirements. Our approach is to understand our prospective partners' objectives and motivations for sponsorship and identify the opportunity that best fits their aims. We don't present a table of rights. We work with our sponsors to develop ideas that help them reach authentic audiences and offer them insights that demonstrate the value of longer-term engagement.

■ Common event sponsorship objectives

Despite the above claims that sponsorship objectives are evolving, this does not in any way negate the continued importance of event sponsorship to meet traditional goals of brand awareness and brand image benefits. While brand awareness has traditionally been pursued through event-based signage, sponsors increasingly want their association to be promoted more widely and as such event creators must consider how sponsors can be creatively involved in promotional materials and the actual content of the event. The concept of image transfer, whereby the image of the event 'rubs off' on the sponsor brand through the association, is at the heart of how sponsorship works and as such it remains a prominent sponsorship objective (IEG/Performance Research, 2012). Where sponsors are pursuing image-related objectives, the importance of a well-executed event is amplified as sponsors seek to maximise positive image transfer from the event to their brand.

In addition to awareness and image benefits, other objectives commonly pursued by event sponsors are targeting specific market segments (Barrand, 2006) and sales (Hartland et al, 2005; Tomasini et al, 2004). However, despite its relative popularity as an objective (IEG/Performance Research, 2012), it has been suggested that sponsorship may not necessarily influence consumers to the extent of impacting on sales (Kitchen, 1999; Sandler and Shani, 1993). Nevertheless, particularly in product categories which lend themselves to on-site event sales such as soft and alcoholic drinks, food and confectionary, sponsors may seek opportunities as part of their sponsorship to sell their products directly to event attendees. In some cases, the needs of sponsors in these product categories may overlap considerably with the needs of suppliers, in that they are focussed on obtaining the optimum opportunity to sell their products on-site. These objectives are likely to impact upon event delivery in terms of the range of food and drink offered and event creators will need to work with sponsors to ensure there is a balance between satisfying the sponsor needs and developing a food and beverage offer which is appropriate and appealing to event attendees.

■ Using events to showcase sponsor and supplier products and services

Another increasingly common objective pursued both by sponsors and suppliers is to showcase their products and services in action (IEG/Performance Research, 2012). This may take the form of providing goods and services that are used in the actual event delivery, such as telecommunications equipment, IT services or catering, or may involve offering on-site product sampling (Nufer and Buhler, 2010). Evidently, such objectives imply a far greater involvement from sponsors and suppliers in the event design and delivery, such that their products and services are demonstrated to their maximum capacity. In these cases, collaboration between the sponsors/ suppliers and the event creator is essential to ensure the interests of all partners are met. By associating themselves with an event, sponsors and suppliers are potentially putting their reputations on the line, were the event to suffer any negative publicity. What the sponsors and suppliers are seeking is a response from consumers that 'if the company is good enough to produce products and services for the event then they are good enough for me'. This is a very powerful association for sponsor/supplier brands as it implies endorsement from an event which consumers value. As such, it is incumbent upon event creators to work with sponsors and suppliers to ensure as far as possible that their products and services are seamlessly and effectively integrated into the wider execution of the event. Not only can the use of sponsor and supplier products and services reduce operational costs of the event, but they can also be used to enhance the attendee experience. For example, having a telecommunications or internet company as a sponsor may allow the event to add value to attendees through offering free wi-fi, and add value to the sponsor by allowing them to showcase their latest broadband and wireless technologies. Here, the event creator brings the different sponsor and partner offerings together to maximise the value to all stakeholders and these sponsors/suppliers facilitate the event experience for attendees.

■ Evolving event sponsorship objectives

Moving beyond objectives linked to showcasing and sales, brands are looking to event sponsorship as a means of achieving their corporate social responsibility (CSR) objectives (Plewa and Quester, 2011; McCullagh, 2009). In this guise, sponsors may seek to work with other partners such as community groups within the event to demonstrate their commitment to, for example, the local community.

If the sponsor's objectives are aligned with those of other involved organisations such as the event owners themselves, public authorities, tourism organisations, as well as attendees, this presents an opportunity for the event creators to shape the event to provide mutually beneficial outcomes. For example, a prominent sponsor may be able to provide marketing support to a local arts festival, such that not only the sponsor benefits, but the achievement of other stakeholder objectives such as promotion of the town as a tourist destination is facilitated. In the context of a growing desire among sponsors to demonstrate their CSR credentials, the event creator has the opportunity to craft an event which generates benefits and value beyond the immediate stakeholders to a much wider set of interested parties. It is when the objectives don't align that the event creator's challenge becomes more difficult, again evidencing the vital importance of stakeholder management.

Industry voice: Claire O'Neill, Senior Manager, Association of Independent Festivals & Co-Founder, A Greener Festival

Sponsorship has become more sophisticated and has evolved alongside event creators and audiences. It is not a branding exercise but a shaper and creator cf content and experiences. What is important is to identify value to improve the event and audience experience, in turn having far greater positive impact for the brand in question associated with the activation. Most sponsors' main objective is to ultimately achieve a connection with the event participants. Sponsors also wish to be a part of the wider opportunity for communication and connecting with audiences outside of the event itself.

Following shifts in marketing focus, as discussed by Gronroos (1994), there is an increasing movement to use sponsorship to achieve relational objectives. This includes enhancing client relations (Hartland et al, 2005), nurturing brand loyalty (Henseler et al, 2011; Levin et al, 2004; McManus, 2002), creating emotional attachments (Ferreira et al, 2008) and crafting opportunities to interact and build relationships with customers (Donlan and Crowther, 2012; Dolphin, 2003). In a traditional event sponsorship context, client relationship-related objectives were typically addressed through the provision of hospitality. However, in the context of greater legal regulations (e.g. the UK Bribery Act 2010) and tightened ethical guidelines, the use of overt hospitality is declining, as evidenced in the IEG/Performance Research 12th Annual Sponsorship Decision-Makers Survey, which found that only 29% of respondents pursued the objective of entertaining clients, down from 33% the previous year (IEG/Performance Research, 2012). Therefore, where event creators may previously have included a hospitality offering within the event design, the changing priorities of sponsors demand a new, creative approach.

With overt hospitality in decline as clients find it harder to accept such invitations, event creators are required to work with sponsors to design event experiences which offer more acceptable and laudable outcomes. For example, a sponsor of a music festival may seek to craft a masterclass from one of the performing artists for their clients, such that there are opportunities for learning and business networking in addition to pure entertainment. Where attendees can reconcile accepting a hospitality invitation with corporate objectives such as learning, continuing professional development, social or environmental contribution, it is more likely that they will be able to attend. This more creative approach to hospitality requires the event creator to adopt a more outcome-based approach and engage in purposeful design with partners so as to facilitate experiences that meet the needs of the sponsor, attendees, and even the local community.

Case study: Cisco and the London 2012 Olympic and Paralympic Games

5

In addition to a wide range of other activations including digital, advertising and PR, an integral part of Cisco's activation of its sponsorship of the London 2012 Olympic and Paralympic Games was Cisco House, a purpose-built interactive experience overlooking the Olympic Park on the roof of Westfield Shopping Centre in East London. Consistent with the brand's business-to-business focus and in line with Cisco's objectives around brand positioning, lead generation, trust and engagement, Cisco House hosted around 11,000 guests before and during the Games, showcasing concepts and ideas relating to business transformation. In the words of one Cisco Manager, Cisco House was crafted as a space for attendees to 'take some time out and [be] inspired to think about business transformation for their organisation.' In line with the notion of Cisco House being an experiential/event space in which attendees could co-create their own experience (Prahalad and Ramaswamy, 2004) with the brand and other attendees, the experiential design and delivery were aligned with the strategy of showcasing Cisco as a platform for change.

In contrast to many experiential sponsorship activations, the focus was not on demonstrating what Cisco does but on what Cisco can make possible. Therefore there was a notable lack of overt Cisco products on display, which was viewed positively by attendees. Through a series of interactive, walk through experiences, offering opportunities for learning, discussion and peer to peer networking, Cisco House facilitated active involvement with attendees. This demonstrated a focus on using the activation to achieve shared outcomes, rather than just as another sponsor mouthpiece. The design of Cisco House addressed many dimensions of the attendee experience, with a walkthrough 3D business transformation experience, spaces for networking with Cisco employees and other attendees and free spaces in which attendees could think about the future of their businesses. In the design and delivery of Cisco House, Cisco importantly realised that their target market of senior executives are very much in demand; therefore for such people to justify taking time out of their busy schedules to attend Cisco House, Cisco needed to craft an event offering that added value, rather than just being another hospitality invitation. While the link to the sponsor brand in traditional corporate hospitality is often weak, Cisco House was designed to allow Cisco to fully immerse its target audience in its desired concepts of business transformation and showcase how Cisco can be a platform for this change.

The keys to the success of Cisco House lie in its strategic execution, with event design and delivery infused not only with the brand's objectives but also with a strong sense of facilitating value for attendees. Therefore, the importance of a focus on mutuality of event outcomes is further reinforced if event creators are to truly work with sponsors (and other partners) to craft events as opportunities for purposeful collaboration and co-creation. While this experiential activation was managed by Cisco itself, it represents a valuable lesson for event creators in terms of what sponsors are looking for and what they might be able to offer them within the main sponsored event itself.

When pursuing relational objectives, sponsors are increasingly seeking opportunities to interact with customers at a sponsored event, such as was the case with Cisco House. As such, they may demand of the event creator specific spaces and time slots within the event which they can 'own'. For example, a sponsor of a conference may require break out rooms in which it can hold meetings with clients or may seek the opportunity for one of its staff to present a keynote speech. In other cases, for example, a sponsor of an art exhibition may seek the opportunity for a private viewing with a select list of invited clients outside of the regular event hours. The specific detail of the sponsor's requests and involvement in these cases will depend upon the nature of both the events and the sponsors, but event creators must be aware of the growing demand among sponsors to exercise their sponsorship rights in these more varied and experiential ways. If effectively managed, this sponsor input can be beneficial to the event creator in that it represents opportunities for enhancing the attendee experience. For example, through giving attendees access to a presentation by a prominent industry figure, or through owning and programming a fringe stage at a music event, the sponsor adds value by bringing content that enhances the overall event experience but at the same time reduces the operational burden on the creator. However, the strategic event creator must balance the needs of all relevant stakeholders and caution must be taken to avoid the event turning into an overt sponsor mouthpiece at the expense of the wider attendee experience. Any sponsor-driven event content should be integrated with the wider event vision to ensure coherence and consistency in event design and delivery.

Industry voice: Melissa Sharpe, PR Assistant, Clarion Communications

Agencies now utilise event sponsorship as a creative platform on which they can actively engage consumers with a brand's personality, whilst achieving the client's objectives. A visitor attraction within the event domain is one strategy commonly proposed by us PRs, as whether this is a pop up restaurant or exciting photo opportunity, it is an activity that will occupy the attendee's senses. Consumers are then naturally immersed in an experience which is both pertinent to the brand and sponsorship, establishing an understanding of the positive impact this product or service will have upon their lifestyle. As a result, this generates an emotional connection which simply cannot be achieved via the traditional sponsorship route.

5

In addition to sponsor requirements for greater involvement in event design and delivery and consistent with the evolving objectives, we see an increasing number of sponsors developing sophisticated experiential sponsorship activation campaigns, such as the example of Cisco given in the case study above. Connecting a brand to an event through sponsorship means that sponsors concede some degree of control over their brand associations as they become dependent on the actions of the event itself (Westberg et al, 2008). When events are successful, then sponsors benefit from the positive associations. However, if there is a problem with a particular event, then sponsors may find themselves suffering from the resultant negative publicity. For example, a bar in Boston vowed not to sell Sam Adams beer as the brewer was a sponsor of the Boston St Patrick's Day parade, which had sparked controversy over the apparent exclusion of LGBT (Lesbian, Gay, Bisexual, Transgender) veterans from the parade. Consequently, Sam Adams decided to withdraw its sponsorship of the event so to distance itself from the negative associations (Garcia, 2014; Robehmed, 2014). As a result of this lack of control, contemporary experiential activation campaigns may involve sponsors developing their own sponsorship-linked events (Donlan and Crowther, 2012). These are distinct from but linked to the sponsored event, allowing them to maintain an increased degree of control over their event-related sponsorship brand communications and place their brands at the heart of the attendee experience (Cliffe and Motion, 2005). One example of such sponsorship-linked events is Cisco House. Another is BT London Live, which was a free sport and music event created by BT and located in Hyde Park during the London 2012 Olympic and Paralympic Games. The event contained a variety of food and beverage outlets, large screens on which attendees could watch Olympic events, live stages with appearances from Olympians, other sponsor installations and live music from high profile artists each evening. Entirely controlled by BT, the event formed a significant part of the brand's activation of their London 2012 sponsorship, augmenting the experience of people in London who wanted to watch the Olympic Games whilst allowing BT to showcase their technologies.

Industry voice: Emma Kirk, Senior Events Manager, Savvy Marketing, UK

Experiential is such a prevalent part of sponsorship at the moment. No longer are brands seeing benefit from just attaching their name to an event. Creative, innovative and engaging brand activity from sponsors at events is now a prerequisite in order to really gain a return on investment. Morrisons Supermarkets utilised the presence of the 2014 Tour de France Grand Depart in Yorkshire to engage with consumers and showcase their quality and convenience in line with the new M Local stores. Morrisons staged activity such as a pop up shop and a fully functioning kitchen serving its own brand produce, creating a unique opportunity for the store to take its cooked produce straight to the customer.

Through staging these sponsorship-linked events, sponsors can more fully shape the outcomes than if they are simply involved in the sponsored event design and delivery. For example, Cisco was able to tailor Cisco House, controlling the presentation of the event space and the brand, ensuring it aligned with their strategic priorities and facilitating a superlative attendee experience. Therefore, Cisco provides a best practice exemplar of what contemporary sponsors are seeking. Importantly, the Cisco case also highlights how event creators can facilitate the type of experiences sponsors are looking for. Event creators should not see these sponsorship-linked events as a threat, but rather they should explore how and why sponsors are crafting their own activation events to better tailor sponsorship offerings for the main event. By understanding the nature and characteristics of sponsorship-linked events created by sponsors themselves, event creators can learn how to facilitate events which will add value to sponsors and even work with the sponsors to shape the sponsored event such that it maximises value not only to the sponsor but also to the event creator and the attendees.

■ Media, government and tourism organisation objectives

Particularly in the case of larger and higher profile events, in addition to sponsors, another prominent partner will be the media, in its many guises, including television and radio broadcasters and print and online media. While the focus of the event creator will be on those physically attending the event, the media cater for the needs of the distant or mediated consumer and as such their objectives might not map exactly onto those of the event creator. For example, the media's objectives are focussed around maximising audience viewing/listening figures, and the viewer experience, as well as their ability to broadcast/report from the event. This might prompt media outlets to request changes to the event's delivery in terms of scheduling and duration, which may conflict with the priorities and preferences, for example, of physical event attendees. Thus the event creator faces the task of juggling these differing but equally important priorities. The case study below, which is based on interviews with Marketing Managers at the sport's UK governing body and several clubs, explores some of the challenges faced by Rugby League's Magic Weekend in balancing the needs of attendees, event creators, sponsors and the media.

Case study: Rugby League Magic Weekend

5

Magic Weekend is a two-day event held in the UK over a weekend in May, where all 14 Super League rugby league teams play a complete round of fixtures. Since 2012 the event has taken place at the Etihad Stadium in Manchester. As part of the wider Super League, Magic Weekend has a range of stakeholders including the clubs, the sport's governing body, the Rugby Football League (RFL), the stadium owners, sponsors, suppliers, media organisations, the local council and the emergency services, as well as the fans themselves. This case is based on interviews with club and RFL representatives, and of particular interest are the sponsors and the media and the impact their objectives have on event design and delivery.

The event sponsors, who in 2013 included Heinz Big Soup, Irn Bru and Foxy Bingo, use the event as an opportunity to reach a wide target audience, as fans of all 14 clubs are in one place over the space of the weekend. As such, the sponsors embrace Magic Weekend as an opportunity to undertake extensive activation, including competitions, giveaways, product sampling and experiential activations such as rugby kicking and tackling challenges with inflatables. The event venue, the Etihad Stadium, is a purpose-built modern stadium, offering the sponsors a large external concourse on which they can set up their activations, which aids them in engaging fans who are mingling outside the stadium throughout the weekend. As facilitators of the event, the RFL work closely with the sponsors to ensure that the activations they put on are appropriate for the event and fit in with the ethos of fans having a fun and enjoyable time. Therefore, Magic Weekend represents a good example of strategic and planned value co-creation, whereby the event creators work with the sponsors to both enhance the attendee experience and achieve the sponsors' objectives. This spirit of collaboration is likely to lead to satisfied sponsors who are more amenable to renewing their sponsorships for subsequent years. As such, the long-term viability of the event is aided by adopting a collaborative and strategic approach to stakeholder management.

Another of the Magic Weekend stakeholders is the television company Sky, which broadcasts all seven matches from the event. The needs of Sky as a broadcaster are of course to drive the maximum viewing audience, which it does by working with the event creators to embed the latest technologies such as ref cam and aerial cam in order to enhance the television viewing experience. In facilitating the media objectives for the event, however, the Magic Weekend event creators must be careful to ensure a balance is achieved with meeting physical attendee objectives. From a fan's perspective, one of the best things about attending Magic Weekend is the ability to come and go as they please thanks to a large amount of unreserved seating in the stadium. However, this results in a very transient crowd that, on television, gives the impression that the event is poorly attended. To the casual viewer, a half empty stadium may give the impression that the sporting fixture is poor, which will tend to discourage them from continuing to watch on television. In contrast, the technology available to aid the television viewing experience is not available to fans in the stadium, who do not get the opportunity for a referee's eye view, or the extreme close up shots available via the aerial cam. As such, it could be argued that for a rugby fan the viewing experience is superior on television to in-person. Clearly, there is some degree of conflict between the objectives of the media and the physical event attendees. The event creators, the RFL are aware of this and face the challenge in future iterations of the event, of balancing the needs such that the broadcaster can maximise its viewing figures but physical attendees do not feel that they have an inferior viewing experience.

Despite the apparent tensions, an important interdependence exists between the event outcomes sought by the media, event creators and other partners. Event creators often seek out media coverage of an event to encourage new visitors to attend the following year (Brown et al, 2002) and to aid with this objective, the media can provide a vivid showcase of both the event and the wider location. Here we also see an overlap between the outcomes sought by the event creator and those sought by host governments and tourism organisations. In many cases, such partners are seeking tourism development outcomes as a result of hosting events (Faulkner et al, 2000). The outcome of increased tourism is likely to also relate to local businesses, who seek to benefit from spending in the local area by event attendees. Aside from the tourism benefits, host governments might also seek more social outcomes from events including regeneration, provision of enhanced recreational opportunities for residents, enhancing national prestige, boosting local pride and creating employment opportunities (New Zealand Major Events, 2013; Getz, 2012; Faulkner et al, 2000). In contrast, the media may be more concerned about providing relevant event-related content to their viewers and readers and less concerned with promoting the event or its locality as a destination.

We can see from the above discussion that not only do motivations vary between the different partners, but they also vary between events, depending on the particular configuration of partners involved. For example, a large scale event such as the Olympic Games will have a complicated interconnected network of local, national and international partners and sponsors. This makes the stakeholder management role considerably more complicated than in the case, for example, of a smaller local festival or one-off seminar. Nonetheless, regardless of the scale and scope of the event, these partner motivations are interrelated with event design and delivery, as conceptualised in Figure 5.2 below. Similarly, the different event partners, all in their own ways, add value to the event through the provision of resources such as revenue, goods and services (which reduce the costs incurred by the event), marketing support, reputational/brand image transfer and, increasingly event content. In many respects, the same rules apply for event creators in managing relationships with other partners as with sponsors. The event creator must understand the motivations and intended return on investment sought by the diverse partners and then work with them, collectively, to achieve these aims as far as possible. The above discussion has highlighted how taking an integrated approach to managing event partners may yield synergies, which can lead to mutually beneficial outcomes for all parties concerned.

Given the unique character of each event, the exact path through the diagram will vary and it is the role of the strategic event creator to create a cohesive event vision around which all of the partners can coalesce to co-create a superlative event experience for all attendees, sponsors and other partners. However, as illustrated through the Magic Weekend case study above, while it may be desirable to conceive of an event where the motivations of all partners coalesce perfectly to a shared vision, there are likely to be multiple iterations and compromises to reach a workable and achievable vision which maximises value to all. In light of this challenge, the next section will look at how event creators can approach the task of balancing diverse partner needs.

Balancing partner needs

Mitchell et al. (1997) argue that stakeholders must possess at least one of the attributes of power, legitimacy and urgency to be considered relevant and of importance to managers. In an event context, the sponsors and other partners discussed in this chapter all possess one or more of these attributes, therefore they are of importance to the event creator, who must understand and manage their different needs and motivations. As discussed above, in some cases, the objectives of the different event sponsors and partners overlap, however, in some cases there is a conflict between the needs of one group and the needs of another. For example, the date and time of sporting events are often dictated to satisfy media requirements. However, this may impact negatively on the event consumption experience of physical attendees.

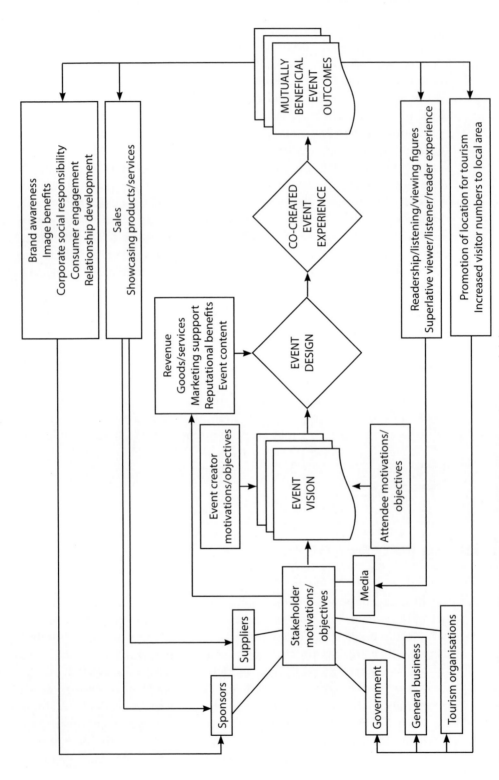

Figure 5.2: Impact of event stakeholder motivations on event design and delivery

Therefore, the strategic event creator is tasked with juggling the demands of different stakeholder groups to choreograph an event experience which delivers mutually beneficial outcomes to as many of these groups as possible (Getz and Fairley, 2004). One such strategy is to bring stakeholders together for mutual benefit (Andersson and Getz, 2008) and involve them in event decision-making (Reid, 2011). By gathering the different sponsors and event partners together in the event design and delivery process and encouraging a collaborative approach to crafting event outcomes, the event creator can create a commonality of purpose and add value to all of the partners, which might encourage their longer-term commitment to the event. However, this relies on a strong event creator and a clear set of event objectives to ensure that wider sponsor and partner objectives don't supersede the objectives of the event itself (Reid, 2011). The management of stakeholders is discussed more fully in Chapter 2 of this book.

Where the objectives of all sponsors and partners connect perfectly with each other and with the objectives of event creators and attendees, events become ripe opportunities for value co-creation (Donlan and Crowther, 2012), as all parties coalesce in the event setting, maximising mutual value. For example, a university careers fair may offer the sponsor, a recruitment company, the opportunity to deliver a talk on interview techniques and promote their services, whilst allowing students to pick up valuable hints and tips to help them in their job search. However, where a larger number of event partners are present, the challenge of balancing their different objectives becomes more demanding. Mitchell et al. (1997) identify that managers are likely to give greater priority to stakeholders possessing all three of the attributes of power, legitimacy and urgency than to those possessing one or two of the attributes. Therefore, this once again reinforces the importance of strategic event creators understanding the relative importance and objectives of the different partners in relation to the event (Reid, 2011) and both prioritising and balancing these needs accordingly.

Maximising value from wider event stakeholders

In some cases, long-standing sponsorship and partner arrangements will be in place. However, where opportunity allows, the event creator should look to be involved in the recruitment and selection of sponsors and other partners for an event. While being aware of the financial and resource requirements of the event, in the selection of sponsors and partners, the event creator should consider the value that particular organisations can bring to the event. For example, in conceiving a business event such as a conference or seminar, the event creator might look to recruit, through local tourism organisations, a series of hotels which can provide a venue and accommodation for the event. Rather than simply thinking what the event can get out of the partnership, the event creator should consider what the sponsors and partners can bring to the event. Looking beyond operational conveniences such as venues and catering, the event creator should seek to understand how sponsors and partners can contribute to the event experience to co-create value with the event hosts and attendees. For example, a mobile phone sponsor could add value to the experience of attending a music event by offering free live track downloads to customers.

In the context of recurrent events (e.g. annual festivals or conferences), event creators should always have an eye on the event's future throughout the event creation process. This is where the notion of Strategic Event Creation comes in: event creators must look to manage their sponsors and partners creatively and strategically so as to engage and re-engage them for future delivery of the same or related events. Through understanding and collaborating with sponsors and other partners, the event creator can use an event as a catalyst for future stakeholder relationships, creating a virtuous circle of satisfaction. If event stakeholders feel valued and are able to derive value from the event, they are much more likely to continue in their role as sponsors, suppliers or media partners or, in the case of governments, continue to offer their support to an event. Sponsors and partners in one event become co-designers of the next. Thus, we see that taking a strategic, stakeholder-centric and outcomes-driven approach to event creation can reap rewards for the event creator and create value for all involved stakeholders.

Concluding remarks

The evolving nature of sponsor and other partner needs heightens the importance of event creators working in a stakeholder-centric manner to interpret their objectives and infuse these into the overall event design and delivery. Balancing the needs of different stakeholders represents a considerable task for event creators and challenges them to adopt much more of a strategic persona. Therefore event creation requires the strategic management of sponsors and partners, such that events can become arenas for value co-creation from which all interested parties can derive relevant and meaningful outcomes.

Study questions

1 For an event with which you are familiar, identify its wider stakeholders and assess their likely objectives for the event. To what extent do these objectives unite or conflict? What are the implications of these different objectives for the event creator?

2 What are the challenges for event creators in managing their sponsors and partners strategically? Are these challenges equally applicable to all types and sizes of events? In your answer you should consider the practical realities facing event creators and the extent to which these might present an obstacle to implementing some of the ideas discussed in this chapter.

5

References

Andersson, T.D. and Getz, D. (2008). Stakeholder management strategies of festivals, *Journal of Convention and Event Tourism* **9** (3), 199-220.

Barrand, D. (2006). Developing and delivering, *SportBusiness International*, June, 34-34.

Brown, G., Chalip, L., Jago, L. and Mules, T. (2002). The Sydney Olympics and brand Australia, in N. Morgan, A. Pritchard and R. Pride (eds.), *Destination Branding: Creating the unique destination proposition*, Oxford: Butterworth-Heinemann, pp. 163–185.

Cliffe, S.J., and Motion, B. (2005). Building contemporary brands: A sponsorship-based strategy, *Journal of Business Research* **58** (8), 1068–1077.

Dolphin, R.R. (2003). Sponsorship: perspectives on its strategic role, *Corporate Communications* **8** (3), 173-186.

Donlan, L. and Crowther, P. (2012). Leveraging sponsorship to achieve relational objectives through the creation of marketing spaces, *Journal of Marketing Communications*. DOI: 10.1080/13527266.2012.684068

Farrelly, F, Quester, P and Burton, R. (2006). Changes in sponsorship value: Competencies and capabilities of successful sponsorship relationships, *Industrial Marketing Management*, **35** (8), 1016-1026.

Faulkner, B., Chalip, L., Brown, G., Jago, L., Marsh, R. and Woodside, A. (2000). Monitoring the tourism impacts of the Sydney 2000 Olympics, *Event Management*, **6** (4), 231–246.

Ferreira, M., Hall, T. K. and Bennett, G. (2008). Exploring brand positioning in a sponsorship context: A correspondence analysis of the dew action sports tour. *Journal of Sport Management*, **22**(6), 734-761.

Garcia, M. (2014). Boston: Major beer sponsor pulls out of St Pat's parade. www.advocate.com/politics/2014/03/14/boston-major-beer-sponsor-pulls-out-st-pats-parade, accessed 10/07/2014.

Getz, D. (2012). *Event Studies: Theory, Research and Policy for Planned Events, 2nd edn*, London: Routledge.

Getz, D., Andersson, T. and Larson, M. (2007). Festival stakeholder roles: concepts and case studies, *Event Management* **10** (2), 103-22.

Getz, D. and Fairley, S. (2004). Media management at sport events for destination promotion: case studies and concepts, *Event Management* **8** (3), 127-139.

Grönroos, C. (1994). Quo vadis, marketing? toward a relationship marketing paradigm, *Journal of Marketing Management* **10** (5), 347-360.

Hartland, T., Skinner, H. and Griffiths, A. (2005). Tries and conversions: are sports sponsors pursuing the right objectives?, *International Journal of Sports Marketing and Sponsorship*, **6** (3), 164-173.

Head, V. (1981). *Sponsorship: The Newest Marketing Skill*. Cambridge: Woodhead-Faulkner.

Henseler, J., Wilson, B. and Westberg, K. (2011). Managers' perceptions of the impact of sport sponsorship on brand equity: Which aspects of the sponsorship matter most?, *Sport Marketing Quarterly* **20** (1), 7-21.

IEG/Performance Research. (2012). 12th annual IEG/Performance research sponsorship decision-makers survey. www.performanceresearch.com/sponsor-survey.htm, accessed 25/03/2014.

Kitchen, P. (1999). *Marketing Communications: Principles and Practice*. London: International Thomson Business Press.

Levin, A. M., Beasley, F. and Gamble, T. (2004). Brand loyalty of NASCAR fans towards sponsors: The impact of fan identification, *International Journal of Sports Marketing and Sponsorship* **6** (1), 11-21.

McCullagh, K (2009). Sponsors placing heavier focus on CSR. www.sportbusiness.com/news/168988/sponsors-placing-heavier-focus-csr, accessed 13/03/2012

McManus, P. (2002). Clubs play the community card, *Sports Marketing*, January, 8-9.

Meenaghan, T. (1991). The role of sponsorship in the marketing communications mix, *International Journal of Advertising* **10** (1), 35-47.

Mitchell, R.K., Agle, B.R. and Wood, D.J. (1997). Toward a theory of stakeholder identification and salience: defining the principles of who and what really counts, *Academy of Management Review* **22** (4), 853-886.

New Zealand Major Events (2013). Strategy. www.med.govt.nz/majorevents/new-zealand-major-events/strategy, accessed 21/03/2014.

Nufer, G. and Bühler, A. (2010) How effective is the sponsorship of global sports events? A comparison of the FIFA World Cups in 2006 and 1998, *International Journal of Sports Marketing and Sponsorship*, **11** (4), 303-319

Papadimitriou, D., Apostolopoulou, A. and Dounis, T. (2008) Event sponsorship as a value creating strategy for brands, *Journal of Product and Brand Management*, **17** (4), 212-222.

Plewa, C. and Quester, P.G. (2011) Sponsorship and CSR: is there a link? A conceptual framework, *International Journal of Sports Marketing and Sponsorship* **12** (4), 301-317.

Prahalad, C.K. and Ramaswamy, V. (2004) Co-creation experiences: The next practice in value creation, *Journal of Interactive Marketing* **18** (3), 5-14

Reid, S. (2011) Event stakeholder management: developing sustainable rural event practices, *International Journal of Event and Festival Management* **2** (1), 20-36.

Robehmed, N. (2014) Sam Adams pulls out of St. Patrick's parade over gay exclusion. www.forbes.com/sites/natalierobehmed/2014/03/14/sam-adams-pulls-out-of-st-patricks-parade-over-gay-exclusion, accessed 10/07/2014.

Sandler, D.M. and Shani, D. (1993) Sponsorship and the Olympic Games: The consumer perspective, *Sport Marketing Quarterly* **2** (3), 38-43.

Thwaites, D. (1993) Sports sponsorship: Philanthropy or a commercial investment? Evidence from UK building societies, *Journal of Promotion Management* **2** (1), 27-43.

Tomasini, N., Frye, C. and Stotlar, D. (2004) National Collegiate Athletic Association corporate sponsor objectives: Are there differences between Divisions I-A, I-AA, and I-AAA?, *Sport Marketing Quarterly* **13** (4), 216-226.

Ukman, L. (2004). *IEG's Guide to Sponsorship*. Chicago: IEG.

Westberg, K., Stavros, C. and Wilson, B. (2008) An examination of the impact of player transgressions on sponsorship B2B relationships, *International Journal of Sports Marketing and Sponsorship* **9** (2), 125-134.

Witcher, B., Craigen, J.G, Culligan, D and Harvey, A. (1991) The links between objectives and function in organizational sponsorship, *International Journal of Advertising*, **10** (2), 13-33.

5

6 Community Outcomes

Gareth Roberts and David Strafford

Learning objectives

- Identify different types of community outcomes of events.

- Define key terms and concepts relating to community outcomes of events.

- Understand the complex nature of community outcomes of events.

- Apply a range of social and cultural theories to effective event creation.

Introduction

Chapter 1 provides a teasing introduction to this chapter by referring to the 'outer layer of consciousness' required by event creators. Ignorance, or perhaps disregard, for the wider outcomes spawned by an event is inconsistent with the notion of Strategic Event Creation, and indeed contemporary business practice. Consequently, along with the previous discussions of event hosts, attendees, sponsors and partners, we now discuss the host community as a similarly significant stakeholder whom event creators must first identify, interpret their concerns, needs and expectations, and then engage with proactively in their designing of the event. This narrative follows on strongly from Chapter 2, which advocated placing locality at the heart of the stakeholder centric approach. This proposed recalibration of stakeholder management is important if event creators are to fully recognise and realise the possibilities of progressive host community engagement. This chapter seeks to map some of the outcomes, considerations, and approaches that event creators must engage with in order to positively contribute to host communities and in so doing forge stronger and longer term relationships.

There exists an intriguing dichotomy when considering the wider, and often indirect, outcomes produced by events. In one sense there exists a moral argument about the need for event creators to act responsibly and work to ensure that the event they are creating is at the very least neutral for the host community in an economic, social/cultural, and environmental sense. Where negative externalities inevitably follow, such as disruption, noise pollution, and so forth, these should be counterbalanced by positive contributions through the event to the host community. Equally there is also a very persuasive strategic argument for the event hosts, and other internal stakeholders, to benefit considerably by engaged and motivated communities. Through progressive event creation, or 'community animation' (see below) outcomes far beyond those provisionally identified can be realised. In this way communities become influential and positive stakeholders, who demonstrate a vested interest in the event, and the event host's success.

A recurring argument in this chapter is that our traditional way of viewing events in established typologies is in some respects unnecessary or perhaps distorting, as we deal with event types in silo. By adopting an outcome obsessed lens we should begin by perceiving the desired outcomes, for the host organisation, attendees, partners, but also, and importantly, the host communities. It is therefore proposed to move beyond these traditional typologies because, even though the event types and scale are varied, there is a substantial cross-over, as argued by Dickinson and Shipway (2007), regarding the outcomes for host communities. Instead it is beneficial to apply a matrix of four interdependent considerations that should preoccupy event creators, whether they are designing a community festival, international conference, or large music event. It is suggested that anticipating and planning host community outcomes using this process enables event creators to responsibly and effectually facilitate their relationship with host communities regardless of the type of event. Therefore, each of these should be prominent in the creation of events and the shaping of the many decisions, activities, and actions that constitute the event design.

1 **Positive and negative outcomes** - the very nature of events as gatherings of people that are often extremely observable and resource intensive means that event creators are inevitably challenged by a combination of potentially positive and negative outcomes.

2 **Intended and inadvertent outcomes** - there exists a tension between outcomes that the event host aims and anticipates to happen, and those that inadvertently occur although they were not planned or previously predicted.

3 **Stimulated or not stimulated outcomes** - linked to both of the above to identify opportunity areas where the event can make a beneficial contribution to the host community and seizing these usually through community engagement.

4   **Mitigated and unmitigated outcomes** – again, by anticipating and
    interpreting 1 and 2 above, and building relationships with the host
    community, the opportunity exists to implement approaches to dimin-
    ish outcome areas that would negatively impact the host community.

In reading the remainder of this chapter we consider how the case
studies, illustrations, and academic discussion are reflective of the above
practicable process. Strategic event creators must internalise the host community as fundamental and adopt approaches through which to deal with
the above considerations and opportunities. A useful illustration of event
creators taking very seriously the concerns and interests of the host community is evidenced below in the thoughts of Claudia Connelly, Operations
Director for WRG Creative Communication, who reflects upon the integral
role of the community as a key stakeholder. WRG were appointed to event
manage the first two stages on the Tour De France in the UK in 2014.

Industry voice: Claudia Connelly, Operations Director for WRG , UK

The event was particularly successful in its engagement with the host community. For
Stages One and Two of the Tour de France, the local authorities were the event organisers and were therefore able to actively engage and interact with the local community
from the outset. This kind of local knowledge and early engagement was key to the
success of the event. The response from the local community before, during and after
the event was overwhelmingly positive. There was undoubtedly an influx of spending brought to the area by the many spectators who travelled far and wide to watch
the event. There was also a feeling of positivity towards the event from the local areas;
they were genuinely excited to host such a prestigious event. We were blessed on the
weekend itself with beautiful weather and the footage of the event was stunning, which
I have no doubt will help attract more visitors to Yorkshire in the future.

There were inevitably some negatives to the event from a community perspective. Large
scale disruption was unavoidable, the event required a huge amount of road closures
across the county. This had a far reaching impact on residents, businesses and blue light
services. Active and early stakeholder engagement was key to minimising disruption as
much as possible. If event planners want to connect their event to the host community
then early engagement is key. It's imperative that event organisers listen and respond
accordingly to the community's needs, their knowledge and support is invaluable to
the success of any event. An event without a positive legacy is counterproductive and
negates the point of hosting a free, un-ticketed event for the local community in the
first place.

Event creator - a community animator

In considering the host community as a foremost stakeholder, and undertaking the above four considerations, the strategic event creator becomes an animator of community outcomes; whether these be economic, environment, or socio-cultural. The argument is that whatever the event, there exists a sliding scale of activity that the event creator can activate in different ways to ensure the event provides appropriate focus upon the host community. This only occurs through the event creator, or creation team, actively stimulating these activities, hence the term 'animation'. Smith (1999) discusses the concept of animation, stating that in English 'animation' is mostly associated with moving images, e.g. film and cartoons. However in French and Italian, animation has a further meaning, whereby animators are informal educators, community workers, and arts workers, seeking to make a positive contribution. Interestingly, and with considerable parallels to event creation, Cabaniss (2007) states in the UK several orchestras employ musicians or composers as animators. The animator's task is to ensure that audiences have the opportunity to connect to the orchestra and its music in new ways, while helping the orchestra to connect with the communities where they play. Applying this more directly to the role of event creator, host communities are given the opportunity to engage more fully with an event and benefit and perhaps learn from it in ways that they may not have done under more traditional approaches where host communities are perhaps considered as relatively inconsequential bystanders.

By embracing such a role, event creators will underpin the longer term sustainability of the event and future events and make a positive contribution to the community. A conference might do this in a fairly modest manner by simply engaging with local suppliers and exposing delegates to the heritage of the area and in so doing provide opportunity for added injections of monies to the local community. A sports event might involve local children in outreach activities and perhaps engage some of the unemployed as volunteers. Whereas the event creator of a large public event, such as a community festival, would orchestrate a whole range of host community outcomes as the community is a key recipient of the event. In such a case their animation might involve local groups bringing content to the event, raising profile and monies for local causes, donating some monies generated to a local initiative, and generally using the event as a direct means of impacting what we later refer to as civic pride.

By seeking to actively involve the community, to whatever extent on the sliding scale, the collaboration this creates leads to a more co-creative emphasis. This sharing is underlined by Smith (1999), who in the context of community participation refers to improved knowledge and a shared sense

6

of creativity. Interestingly, embracing the host community can animate the event for delegate, attendees, and participants also. Consider delegates at a conference where there is a focus upon team work, setting up soup kitchens for local homeless people, or for a festival of entrepreneurship, partnering attendees with local schools or charities to generate entrepreneurial initiatives. A major sports event could run an outreach programme to coach school children and invite representatives to the game to showcase their abilities. The opportunities to engage the host communities in ways that complement the objectives of the event host and other involved stakeholders, such as attendees and sponsors, are considerable.

Henrietta Duckworth discusses below the Yorkshire Festival, a 100 day cultural festival, which accompanied the 2014 Tour de France in Yorkshire.

Industry voice: Henrietta Duckworth, Executive Producer, Yorkshire Festival, UK

Yorkshire Festival's mission was to ensure a broad approach to participation and celebrate community creativity while showcasing Yorkshire's international artistic talent, generating activity to leave a legacy for artists, participants and audiences and animating the county's 6000 square miles in anticipation of the Grand Depart of the Tour de France. This was to be the first ever cultural festival to accompany the Tour de France in all of its 111 years, and the first ever cross-Yorkshire, pan-artform festival bringing together a new partnership between Welcome to Yorkshire, Arts Council of England, the Local Authorities of Yorkshire and principal sponsor, Yorkshire Water. Inspired by the Grand Depart, the majority of the Festival's events were to be totally free to access - just like the largest free annual sporting event itself. 'Be Part Of It' was adopted as the festival slogan at the point of naming the festival in early January and, significantly, adopted comprehensively by new arts sponsors Yorkshire Water. 47 headline projects were selected from a completely open submission process with over 500 fringe arts and cultural projects registered to be part of Yorkshire Festival. 'Be Part Of It' became a reality'.

Placing people at the heart of the Yorkshire festival has been critical to its successful delivery and real engagement. Yorkshire Festival has championed people getting involved creatively and exploring new experiences as audiences. Of the 47 headline projects, more than three-quarters of the events had participation at their core, and as a result over 7,000 people have participated getting involved as cyclists/dancers of Phoenix Dance Theatre and NVA's Ghost Peloton; crocheting woolly bikes; sowing, mowing and nailing land art works across the Worth Valley; dancing in the new dance-theatre version of Kes at Sheffield Crucible; submitting their stories about bikes; sharing their photographs of bikes; creating bike-based creatures for Todmorden's Fantastical Cycle Parade; making a bike from scratch and decorating bikes for Sheffield's Cavalcade; 3000 children singing live together at Scarborough's Open Air Theatre; over 1300 people joining Hope and Social and Grassington Festival's A Band Anyone Can Join for the Tour

> of Infinite Possibility to perform the Festival Song, which also opened the Team Presentation Ceremony to a global broadcast audience.
>
> Over 750,000 people directly attended and engaged with the Yorkshire Festival in celebration of the Grand Depart. This engagement over a sustained period of time, was a significant part of Yorkshire being ready to welcome the world for the Grand Depart and contributed to the successful turnout of 3 million spectators over the race weekend. Furthermore, the Yorkshire Festival has created new experiences of the arts, new creative relationships, new partnerships and new ways of working which will stay with participants, artists and audiences alike long after the peloton has passed, and which will fuel future creative events.

As exemplified in the above illustration, Smith (1999) places emphasis on the active role of animators. He states that animators 'breathe life' into communities and events, which is evident from the considerable orchestration it would have taken to facilitate the Yorkshire Festival. Animators view people as active agents to be engaged with, as opposed to a passive audience who merely observe. Considerable importance must therefore be placed upon the event creator being active, engaging, and generally facilitating outcomes through a free-thinking and facilitative approach. In so doing the event creator is purposefully striving to trigger the positive development of relationships between the event host, internal stakeholders and the host community.

Complexity of outcomes

It is important for event creators, dependent upon the nature and scale of their event(s), to recognise that each host community comprises multiple sub-cultures and sub-communities, which may have different views and concerns. There is a growing body of literature that focusses on outcomes of events for host communities. Historically events have been viewed as something that impacted on the individuals attending, and key funders and research were reflective of this. Faulkner at al. (2003) indicates that these host community outcomes may be apparent before the event takes place, during, or after the event, which is aligned with the suggested approach in the introduction to this chapter, which emphasises careful consideration by event creators of positive and negative, and also intended and inadvertent, outcomes.

Hiller (1998) suggests that the emphasis was unhealthily on positive benefits with negative outcomes remaining largely hidden. As Langen and Garcia (2009) emphasise, these impacts are not always positive, or can perhaps have a positive influence in one domain (e.g. economic) while having a negative impact on another (e.g. environmental). Indeed, for event creators the complex and often counter-intuitive nature of predicting, mitigating and achieving outcomes at the community level should be recognised as one of the more challenging aspects of Strategic Event Creation. Given the more strategic and holistic emphasis, there is a need to engage with wider, often less tangible, and sometimes negative issues associated with host community objectives, particularly in the social and cultural domains as discussed below. This is all a required aspect of the stakeholder centric approach as reasoned in Chapter 2.

It should be acknowledged that there is an argument advanced by writers such as Rojek (2013) who challenge the notion that events are concerned with genuine benefits for a host community. The contention is that events, typically major international events, are actually about power, manipulation, social control, and political gain. The outcomes of these types of event can be more negative than positive for the host community. In this argument the objective of pivotal involved stakeholders dwarf those of wider and marginal stakeholders and any concessions to these groups are tokens to achieve the ends of the pivotal stakeholders. This contrasts with the argument promoted in this chapter, that activity engagement by the event creator, or community animator, must be genuine, and truly collaborate with, and understand the host communities needs and wants, rather than token gestures that exclusively serve the needs of the event host (Smith, 1999).

Assortment of outcomes

Host community event outcomes are apparent in a variety of areas and it is useful to reflect upon these. It is important to recognise that such typologies are misleading and often not helpful as they can mask the inherently interrelated nature of the outcomes. For example a positive environmental initiative which emerges from an event, or event-related project or construction, could feasibly produce outcomes in each of the categories below. Several authors (Dickinson and Shipway, 2007; Langen and Garcia, 2009) have compiled lists of the most frequently noted and more evident host community outcomes of events including:

- ☐ Physical infrastructure

- ☐ Economic (including tourism destination and image)

- ☐ Environmental

- ☐ Social and cultural

The following section focusses upon the final category identified, social and cultural, and presents a range of concepts and ideas that fit well, particularly with the discussion in Chapters 2, 3 and 11. This is an important development of the event creator's role, as a facilitator of wider outcomes, and therefore commands close inspection in this book. Before examining this, it is useful to briefly consider the other categories identified above, which have similarly important implications in relationship to host communities. Each of these outcome areas should demand a whole chapter in order to be adequately discussed – here we are merely seeking to provide a brief overview. The discussion provides signposts to other writers who have considered these areas in more detail.

■ Physical infrastructure

Physical improvement changes, both transitory and permanent, are obvious event outcomes that can understandably cause considerably host community reaction. Often changes are imposed onto communities without adequate, or perceived, consultation. This can lead to developments that the community, or more likely sub groups within the community, believe they do not really need (Rojek, 2013; Taks et al., 2012). Such tangible outcomes can cause tension between the host community and the event creators, and other stakeholders. The impact being lack of community participation and perhaps obstruction as was illustrated through the Derby City Council case study in Chapter 2. As such Hiller (1998) emphasises the need for community involvement.

There is also some evidence (Fredline and Faulkner, 2001) that conflict can occur between host communities and event attendees. This can be especially salient if the host community does not have a positive opinion of the event, and they do not feel that they have been able to be involved with the event planning (Rojek, 2013). Host communities can struggle to contend with the huge, and sudden, demands placed on their infrastructure due to major events (Magalhães et al. undated; Oxford Economics, 2012; Taks et al., 2012). The difficulties of managing increased volumes of traffic and human population can lead to frustration as the host community seek to get on with their day-to-day activities. This can lead to some people from the local community choosing to leave the location during the event (Oxford Economics, 2012), often referred to as the displacement effect (Getz, 2008). Nonetheless, some major events may lead to maintenance of infrastructure to accommodate the increased demands placed on it (Brown and Massey, 2001; Fredline et al., 2006; Janeczko et al., 2002). An example of this being the 6 million pounds spent on local roads ahead of the 2014 Tour De France in Yorkshire (BBC, 2014a).

The case study below, Brazil's FIFA World Cup 2014, illustrates many of the opportunities and tensions alluded to in this discussion of physical infrastructure and also touches on the economic and tourism benefits.

Case study: Brazil's public investment in the 2014 World Cup

After Brazil won the right to host the FIFA World Cup in 2014, Brazilian public opinion was very much split. With a population of 185 million, Brazil is the sixth most populous economy in the world (Brazilian Embassy, 2014), however there is a marked divide between rich and poor; a divide which intensified as the tournament approached. Some could not wait for the World Cup to come 'home' to Brazil, and they championed the short term boost to the economy, the destination marketing benefits and the long-term tourism benefits that a mega event can bring. Business and leisure destination tourism was destined to increase, with the images of Copacabana beach and the Christ the Redeemer statue being broadcast into television sets around the globe.

Others, namely the poorer citizens of Brazil, argued that the investment into the physical infrastructure (i.e. the new stadia, facilities, transport links and communications) necessary to host an event of this size would be better spent on housing and food. The total cost to the Brazilian taxpayer of hosting the tournament amounted to £7 billion, which some argued was too high a cost, in a country where poverty is so widespread. Demonstrations were fierce, especially after two workers died when a crane collapsed during the construction of the stadium in Sao Paolo in November 2013. Another construction worker died on the monorail, which was not even completed for the start of the tournament. Conditions for Brazilian workers were extremely poor, and they worsened as the event drew closer and the pressure to complete construction grew (BBC, 2014b).

Demonstrations turned into riots. Protests outside games were filmed by the world's media as anti-World Cup sentiment grew and demonstrations on the eve of the tournament on 12th June turned ugly as police used tear gas on protesters. One demonstrator said, "I'm totally against the Cup. We're in a country where the money doesn't go to the community, and meanwhile we see all these millions spent on stadiums" (BBC, 2014b).

The bad feeling continued in Brazil. On 20th June 2014, a million protesters took to the streets across the country – in Sao Paolo, twelve were injured and a teenager, eighteen year old Marcos Delefrate, was killed in the most intense night of demonstrations yet. FIFA, football's governing body, were also attacked for their wastefulness and corruption. Nowhere were these feelings better summed up than by the anti-World Cup graffiti that arose around the country's favelas, which supposedly were meant to love the game. "We need food not football" was the message. Paul Ito's image of a crying child unable to eat the football on the dinner table, became an Internet sensation just before the tournament started (Streetartutopia, 2014).

One protest group the Atelier de Dissidências Criativas, which roughly translates to The Workshop of Creative Dissent (Mashable, 2014), used various forms of non-violent protest to raise awareness of this community feeling. They wanted to change the narrative of the World Cup from being a globally commercial sporting mega-event, shifting the focus to the social and community impacts of the event: underpaid workers, increased public transport fares, stadia that wouldn't be used again, millions of Brazilians living in poverty, misspent public money. The Atelier de Dissidências Criativas used art, graffiti, stencils, poetry, dance and sculptures to challenge the accepted international media view of the event, and shine a light on the true social costs to the nation of hosting such an event. The Facebook group Movimento Anti-Copa de Decoração de Ruas (Anti-Cup Movement for the Decoration of the Streets) gained more than 20,000 likes in a little over a month.

Brazil was a country divided, a community divided. As the Brazilian team progressed through the tournament however, the protests dissipated – victory celebrations replacing worker's protests, and demonstrators' voices were silenced. The team itself of course, suffered the ultimate indignation in the semi-finals with a 7-1 loss to Germany; so in the cold light of day after the tournament finished, the nation had to ask itself – was all the expense worth it? And the 'bad news' for Brazil is that Rio de Janeiro has to do it all over again as the host city for the 2016 Olympics. Expect more graffiti.

6

■ Economic (including tourism destination and image)

Economic impacts are widely discussed when considering host community outcomes (see Chhabra, et al, 2003; Crompton et al., 2001; Daniels et al., 2003). Events contribute to the economy of host communities in a number of ways. For instance, Janeczko et al (2002) studied the financial impact of different events: Australian Mountain Bike Association Cup, National Runners Week, Shakespeare Festival, and the Thredbo Jazz Festival. They discovered that these events brought money to the region in the form of more employment for the events, and further business for local restaurants and hotels. Event creators have the opportunity to make decisions which will increase or decrease the likely economic and tourism impact upon the host community. The experience journey of attendees is determined by the decisions they make in terms of locations, timings, programme, and so forth.

Whilst increased employment opportunities, and spending in an area, results in a positive multiplier effect with local businesses benefitting via business by association (OECD LEED Programme, 2012; Oxford Economics, 2012; Taks et al., 2012) this can result in economic outcomes for the host community that do not necessarily translate into longer-term financial benefits or the sustainably positive outcomes sought by event hosts (Brown and Massey, 2001). For instance, the work may be seasonal, inconsistent and temporary (Hiller, 1998; Janeczko et al., 2002). Economic benefits can therefore also be unstable, transient and unsustainable. Nonetheless increases to tourism can also improve civic pride, and can provide essential additional industry to areas whose other industry has declined (Janeczko et al., 2002).

■ Environmental

Elkington (1997) discussed the economic, social and environmental out-comes of businesses activities, which is termed the triple bottom line. The triple bottom line connects well to the breadth of discussion in this chapter and is extremely relevant to event creators in their consideration of host communities. Businesses and, in the case of events, the event creators and internal stakeholders, have a corporate social responsibility (CSR) whereby they have a duty not to put profit before people and the planet. Events have potentially negative impacts on the environment and event creators need to be mindful of potential damage caused by events to ensure their activities remain sustainable. A failure to be environmentally sustainable (and also economically and socially minded) will significantly reduce the likelihood of an event being financially viable into the future, given increased resist-ance and reduced interest from funders and attendees alike. It can therefore be seen that events which pursue an unsustainable approach are ultimately damaging to all stakeholders.

Events are inevitably resource-intensive and therefore can have negative environmental consequences for the host community and planet (Dickinson and Shipway, 2007; Janeczko et al., 2002). Local infrastructure might not be able to cope with increased pressure from tourists e.g., water and waste. Furthermore, it is possible that the host community's landscape and natural environment may be damaged by large scale events (Langen and Garcia, 2009). As a result it is becomingly increasingly important for event creators to anticipate and proactively mitigate the environmental impact of their event, in the interest of sustainability, but also to safeguard stakeholder buy in, achieve cost effectiveness, maximising funding, and reputational issues. Through the combination of these points, and also the pressures from legislation, the media and expectations of attendees, sponsors, partners, suppliers, publics and stakeholder groups of host communities, many com-panies are making 'event greening' a central tenant of their tender process (Pitkin and Shabajee, 2012). 'Event greening' can be defined as the process of integrating socially and environmentally responsible decision making into the planning, organisation and implementation of (and participation in) an event (Pitkin and Shabajee, 2012). Greening an event can reduce the negative environmental impact, and can also leave a positive and lasting legacy for the local community, as it reduces the environmental impact of events, whilst raising awareness of environmental sustainability issues.

■ Social and cultural outcomes

Unlike other outcomes, such as physical infrastructure and economic, social outcomes of events on the host community are less easily quantified; additionally events often generate differential effects on different members of the community. This therefore emerges as an important and somewhat challenging area for event creators to engage with. Examination begins with an important differentiation between social and cultural outcomes. Social outcomes for the host community can be defined as the consequences of the event on the host community that are more direct and noticeable. Cultural changes may be longer term, and refer to changes in the host community's norms and way of life. Research has noted that social and cultural outcomes include shifts in behaviours, perceptions, attitudes, skills, wellbeing and even belief systems (Hodgetts, 20012; Putnam, 2000). These outcomes can be positive for the host community, meaning that the combined outcomes of events over time (or perhaps a one off event if significant enough) result in improved community image, the development of a stronger sense of community, with an enhancement of local traditions, improved initiatives for the local community, and assistance for local groups (Fredline et al., 2003; Hodgetts, 2012).

It would be easy to assume that social and cultural outcomes are entirely the domain of publically funded, or third sector events that are perhaps community oriented festivals and celebrations. Certainly for these events community outcomes are a foremost concern so event creators would be more preoccupied with them. However, all event creators must acknowledge the potential for their events in the shorter and longer term to impact communities in the ways discussed below. A conference venue in a town has the potential to positively contribute socially and culturally through their activities, or not seek to do so.

The Truro case study below provides a vivid illustration of an event that generates social and cultural outcomes for the host community.

Case study: Truro's civic pride: City of Lights

Christmas, in the city of Truro in the heart of Cornwall, UK, is a special time of year. And what makes it special is the spectacular, large-scale City of Lights paper lantern procession which has kick-started the festive celebrations on a Wednesday night in mid-November, for the past 14 years. Back then a mere 100 creative artists paraded the streets of Truro, dazzling bystanders with their paper lantern creations. Now, the parade lasts three hours and is watched by an incredible 25,000 spectators (Truro's population is only approximately 18,000). Civic pride is rife in Truro at this time of year.

The City of Lights is a wonderful example of a true community event, which embodies the heart and soul of the local area, through its celebration of local heritage, culture, history and tradition and building social capital. The event deeply engages the host community's local groups, schools and partners, to such an extent, that the organisers don't particularly feel the need to advertise anymore – in fact the actual date is not widely advertised to tourists, for fear of the city not being able to cope with the influx of visitors.

Claire Eason-Bassett, the City of Lights Event Director since 2007, describes the event as providing Truro citizens with an incredible sense of place. "The people of Truro feel extremely proud of their city during the City of Lights event. There is a real sense of collective togetherness and the event marks the shift of people's mind-set into that Christmas feeling. It provides a clear marker in the calendar year, and has become part and parcel of Truro's festive programme."

Although the event organisers do intend for this feeling of shared connection across the host community, there are many other unexpected benefits. The local media are fully engaged, and marketing images of the city often contain photos of the lantern parade, raising the event's profile. This is not an event that could be picked up and moved to anywhere else in the country, it is a uniquely Truronian experience with cross-generational support widely evident as families and friends bond together watching the children participate in the parade.

School children are at the heart of the event, with Year 6 pupils invited to create lanterns and participate in the parade. It is viewed as a rite of passage, with children in the community growing up watching their older brothers and sisters create lanterns of light, knowing that one day they too will be old enough to carry the lights. Claire thinks it is crucial to involve as much of the host community as possible, on both the creative, artistic side but also the operational side. 2We now have 26 schools taking part with over 700 school children, which is just fantastic. But we also involve other community groups, such as the girl guides; and design students at the University of Falmouth run workshops bringing their creative flair to the event. We also involve students to help with the event management, the stewarding, the music, the graphic design and the photography – the host community are deeply immersed in the artistic and technical aspects of the event.2

The key to the success of the City of Lights, in terms of its deep engagement with the host community, has been that the organisers listen and understand the local traditions, culture and heritage, and don't try to run the event with top-down ideas. The host community's hopes and wishes are embodied by the event. According to Claire, 2we actively want the school children and the other participants to fully engage with the event, and we can only do that by understanding the heart and soul of the host community. We want to create events that people will remember forever. We have to get the balance right between artistic direction and community ownership, but as long as we connect with the heart of the community before we start the event design process, then the City of Lights will remain unique and special. Events are about people at the end of the day, and the City of Lights is all about the people of Truro.

Prepared with help from Claire Eason-Bassett, the City of Lights Event Director

A key concept in the research and understanding of the social outcomes of events such as the Truro City of Lights event is social capital. The pivotal role of the event creator(s) as animators of this is evident, with their event creation decisions and relationships with stakeholders integral to the outcomes that are shaped. Subtly different definitions of social capital exist, though the following definitions encompass the general meaning.

Bourdieu (1983, p. 249) states that social capital is "the aggregate of the actual or potential resources which are linked to possession of a durable network of more or less institutionalized relationships of mutual acquaintance and recognition". Building on this, the World Bank (1999) defines social capital as "the institutions, relationships, and norms that form the quality and quantity of a society's social interactions". This definition takes a Gestalt stance indicating that social capital is more than the sum of bodies within a particular community, which connects with Putnam's (2000) interpretation, suggesting that social capital refers to the connections that exist between individuals in a social network (including host communities). Putnam (2000) refers to the need for trust within the social network, and discusses the concept of civic virtue, stating that this is most powerful when rooted in a network of reciprocal social relations. The role of events as a potential source of virtue, or otherwise, is evident and explored below.

Putnam (2000) believes that social capital could emerge via two distinct roots; bonding capital, created within a like-minded group, and bridging capital, generated through diverse networks. Both strands are important, though bridging capital could be more challenging to achieve, especially with politically, socially, or culturally divided communities. Doherty and Misener (2008) described sport organisations and their events as potential arenas for bonding capital. They suggested that sports organisations may not go beyond this to achieve bridging capital, which may help a host community to get ahead. Hodgetts (2012) discussed how sporting events have been portrayed as an opportunity for the development of social capital, and conducted surveys and interviews into social capital as an outcome of sporting events. She found there was increased bonding capital through a sense of collective identity, a reported sense of community pride and a strong sense of achievement. This appears to relate to the above outcome of increased civic pride following events. Hodgetts (2012) found bridging capital was reported through the establishment of new and enhanced existing relationships with the national and local government, corporate partners, media, police, community service organisations and schools.

There are also potential risks associated with social capital. As Putman (2000) suggests, there are different types of social capital. It is possible that events only develop the bonding capital (Doherty and Misener, 2008). In locations where the community is comprised of different sub-cultures and sub-communities, this could be potentially damaging to the community (Durlauf, 1999). Durlauf suggests that when bridging capital is not promoted by an event or activity, it can lead to divides in a community if bonding capital becomes strong. This is due to bonding capital resulting in a sense of them and us. Though this can have positive outcomes for the in-group, it can have negative connotations for the out-group leading to community division (Brewer, 1999; Durlauf, 1999). Consequently it is important that strategic event creators take into account the need to foster both bonding and bridging forms of social capital.

A number of authors have identified that events can impact on how the host community views itself, but also how it is viewed by others (Derrett, 2003; Wood, 2005). Events of all scales have the potential to induce civic pride in the host community, if people are given the opportunity to engage with the event (Chien et al., 2012; Wood, 2005). The media has a substantial impact in shaping a host community's perception of an event (Chien et al. 2012). It is therefore important for event creators to engage with the host community in partnership and also engage positively with the media as an internal stakeholder. The host community's engagement is largely deter-mined, according to Etiosa (2012), by the extent to which the community is able obtain the social and psychological benefits (such as civic pride) from the event. If this engagement does not occur and the event is viewed negatively by the host community, or by external bodies, then the host com-munity can experience 'civic disgrace', which leads to a negative impact on self-image and self-esteem (Etiosa, 2012).

The overall attitude of a community can greatly affect how an event is received. Bennett (2001) outlined the development of cultural pessimism between the 1970s and the 1990s and stated that to be optimistic was naive and childlike. As such, an invasive sense of pessimism had somehow become the cultural norm, with people and communities exhibiting a more cynical stance. This can impact on how events are received and experienced by the host community en mass. Nonetheless, in more recent work, Bennett (2011) has also explored cultural optimism, identifying an 'optimism of everyday life'. This optimism performs important psychological, social and cultural functions and can have a significant benefit to an individual's psychological and physical health, as well as having wider societal benefits, including enhanced relationships with family and friends. Bennett suggests that optimism can enhance social cohesion which links to the event specific discussion above and the role of the event creator as a community animator.

Azmat et al (2014), discuss how through the arts and cultural events a sense of togetherness can be created and recreated for local communities, promoting discussion of their needs as a community. They argue that such events give communities the chance to experience and acknowledge the importance of community when it is often not tangible. When implemented effectively and sensitively, strategic events do not negatively impact on the public sphere, but can enhance it. This appears to be via processes akin to the bonding capital as outlined above. In this sense an outcome of some events may be seen as promoting cultural resistance, as opposed to diminishing the public sphere. This indicates that there can be a divide in the impact of events on a host community. Where events are used as a tool to control the community, decisions are made via top-down means, and the needs of the event host take priority over the host communities. This may result in the event negatively impacting on the public sphere as individuals within the host community feel undervalued and unheard. However, where strategic events genuinely consult and engage the host community, then there is some scope to enhance the public sphere by bridging the community.

Conclusion

The prevailing argument presented in this chapter is that the event creator is at the heart of the interface between the event and the host community and that their approach is highly influential in facilitating short, but particularly medium and longer term outcomes. There exists, what might be considered, a fragile and often precarious eco-system of event outcomes at the community level. The event creator acting as a 'community animator' should consider the four inter-related outcomes outlined in the introduction in order to effectively navigate and doing so create a mutuality of benefit.

Points one and two of the list emphasise the identification, interpretation, and consideration of positive and negative community outcomes and also intended and inadvertent outcomes. These are an essential precursor to the event design process. This should ordinarily be undertaken through conversation with the host community and not in a detached manner. Once this context is clearly mapped the event creators, through relationships with the community, should seek to undertake measures to both stimulate positive consequences and also mitigate areas of risk and possible negativity.

Through such a transparent and progressive process the host community, as an integral stakeholder, can experience the best possible outcomes from the event. This is not only the morally correct course of action but also the most prudent course of action for the development of future relationships and events. In so doing the notion of the event creator as a 'community animator' provides a useful direction to inform future development of thinking in this area.

Study questions

1   What are the factors that strategic event creators need to consider when organising and delivering an event in order to achieve specified community outcomes?

2   How does the scale and type of event influence the outcomes of the event?

References

Azmat, F., Fujimoto, Y., Rentschler, R. (2014). Exploring cultural inclusion: Perspectives from a community arts organisation, *Australian Journal of Management*, **27**, doi: 10.1177/0312896214525180

Bennett, O. (2001). *Cultural Pessimism: Narratives of Decline in the Postmodern World.* Edinburgh: Edinburgh University Press

BBC (2014a). Yorkshire Tour de France roads get £6m in repairs. wwwbbc.co.uk/news/uk-england-york-north-yorkshire-28053498, accessed 15/08/2014.

BBC, (2014b). Brazil World Cup: Clashes at Sao Paulo and Rio protests.www.bbc.co.uk/news/world-latin-america-27811657, accessed 08/08/2014

Bennett, O. (2011). Culture of Optimism. *Cultural Sociology*, published online 4 April 2011 DOI: 10.1177/1749975511401270

Bourdieu, P. (1983). Forms of capital, in J. C. Richards (ed.). *Handbook of Theory and Research for the Sociology of Education*, New York: Greenwood Press

Brazilian Embassy (2014). Population. www.brazil.org.uk/brazilinbrief/population.html, accessed 16/08/2014

Brewer, M.B. (1999). The psychology of prejudice: Ingroup love and outgroup hate?, *Journal of Social Issues*, **55**, 429–444.DOI: 10.1111/0022-4537.00126.

Brown, A. and Massey, J. (2001). *Literature Review: The Impact of Major Sporting Events. The sports development impact of the Manchester 2002 Commonwealth Games: Initial baseline research*, Manchester Institute for Popular Culture, Manchester Metropolitan University

Cabaniss, T. (2007). An animateur's journey: A report from the field, Polyphonic.org, from www.polyphonic.org/article.php?id=127

Chien, P.M., Ritchie, B.W., Shipway, R., Henderson, H. (2012) I am having a dilemma: Factors affecting resident support of event development in the community, *Journal of Travel Research*, **51**, 451-463. Doi: 10.1177/0047287511426336.

Chhabra, D., Sills, E., Cubbage, F.W. (2003). The significance of festivals to rural economies: Estimating the economic impacts of Scottish Highland Games in North Carolina, *Journal of Travel Research*, **41**, 421-427

Crompton, J.L., Lee, S., Shuster, T.J. (2001). A guide for undertaking economic impact studies: The Springfest example, *Journal of Travel Research*, **40**(1), 79-87

Daniels, M.J., Backman, K.F., Backman, S.J. (2003). Supplementing event economic impact results with perspectives from host community business and opinion leaders, *Event Management*, **8**(3), 117-125

Derrett, R. (2003). Festivals and regional destinations: How festivals demonstrate a sense of community and place, *Rural Society*, **13**(1), 35-53

Dickinson, J. and Shipway, R. (2007). *Resource Guide: The Impact of Events*, Oxford: The Higher Education Academy Hospitality, Leisure, Sport and Tourism Network. www. hlst.heacademy.ac.uk

Doherty, A., and Misener, K. (2008). Community sport networks, in Nicholson, M. and Hoy, R, (Eds.), *Sport and Social Capital* (pp. 113–141), London: Elsevier Butterworth Heinemann

Durlauf, S.N. (1999). The case 'against' social capital, *Focus*, **20**; 1-50

Elkington, J. (1997). *Cannibals with Forks: The Triple Bottom Line of 21st Century Business*, Oxford: Capstone Publishing

Etiosa, O. (2012). The impacts of event tourism on host communities, Case: the City of Pietarsaari, Thesis Central Ostrobothnia University Of Applied Sciences Degree Programme in Tourism. http://publications.theseus.fi/bitstream/handle/10024/43714/omoregie_etiosa.pdf?sequence=1, accessed 08/06/2014.

Faulkner, B., Chalip, L., Brown, G., Jago, L. March, R., and Woodside, A. (2003). Monitoring the tourism impacts of the Sydney 2000 Olympics, *Event Management*, **6**(4), 231-246

Fredline, E., Deery, M., Jago, L. (2006). Host community perceptions of the impact of events a comparison of different event themes in urban and regional communities, CRC for Sustainable Tourism. www.crctourism.com.au/wms/upload/resources/bookshop/fredline_comparevicevents.pdf

Fredline, E., Faulkner, B. (2001). Residents' reaction to the staging of major motorsports events within their communities: A cluster analysis. *Event Management*, **7**, 103–114

Fredline, E., Jago, L., Deery, M. (2003). The development of a generic scale to measure the social impact of events, *Event Management*, **8**, 1, 23-37

Getz, D. (2008). Event tourism: Definition, evolution, and research, *Tourism Management* **29**, 403-428.

Hiller, H.H. (1998). Assessing the impact of mega-events: a linkage model, *Current Issues in Tourism*, **1**(1), 47-57

Hodgetts, D. (2012). Social capital as a legacy from a major sporting event, presentation from the Sport Management Association of Australia and New Zealand (SMAANZ) 2012 Conference. danyahodgetts.com/2012/12/06/447/, accessed, 06/05/2014.

6

Janeczko, B., Mules, T., Ritchie, B. (2002). Estimating the economic impacts of festivals and events, a research guide, CRC for Sustainable Tourism. www.crctourism.com.au/wms/upload/resources/bookshop/Mules_EcoImpactsFestivals_v6.pdf

Langen, F.and Garcia, B. (2009). *Measuring Impacts of Cultural Events: A Literature Review*, Impacts 08: European Capital of Culture Research Programme

Magalhães, F., Serdoura F., Xavier, H.N. (undated). Positive and negative impacts of major events in two cities - the case of Rio Carnival and Lisbon Football Championship. www.isocarp.net/Data/case_studies/159.pdf, accessed 07/06/2014

Mashable (2014). Protest ignite in Brazil as World Cup nears. mashable.com/2014/06/25/world-cup-protests-struggle-brazil, accessed 08/08/2014

Organisation for Economic Co-operation and Development (OECD) Local Economic and Employment Development (LEED) (2012). *Local Development Benefits from Staging Global Events: Achieving the Local Development Legacy from 2012, A Peer Review Of The Olympic And Paralympic Legacy For East London Proposed By The Department Of Communities And Local Government*, United Kingdom

Oxford Economics (2012). *The economic impact of London 2012: Olympic and Paralympic games*, Commissioned by Lloyds Banking Group

Pitkin, K. and Shabajee, P. (2012). *Best Practices for Event Amplification: a Greening Events II Report*. Other. UKOLN, Bath, UK. http://isc.ukoln.ac.uk/2011/10/01/event-amplification-report

Putnam, R. (2000). *Bowling Alone: The Collapse and Revival of American Community*, New York: Simon and Schuster

Rojek, C. (2013). *Event Power: How Global Events Manage and Manipulate*, London: Sage

Smith, M. K. (1999). Animateurs, animation and fostering learning and change, The Encylopaedia of Informal Education. www.infed.org/mobi/animateurs-animation-learning-and-change, accessed, 04/05/2014

Streetartutopia (2014). www.streetartutopia.com/?p=14459, accessed 14/08/2014

Taks, M., Chalip, L., Green, B. C. and Misener, L. (2012). Exploring the impact of sport events on sustainable sport participation outcomes in local communities, In Sport between Business and Civil Society: European Association of Sport Management conference (144), Aalborg: EASM/UCN.

Wood, E.H. (2005). Measuring the economic and social impacts of local authority events, *International Journal of Public Sector Management*, **18**, 37-53. Doi: 10.1108/09513550510576143

World Bank (1999). 'What is Social Capital?', PovertyNet. www.worldbank.org/poverty/scapital/whatsc.htm, accessed 04/05/2014

Part III
Purposeful Design

7 Designing and Mapping Event Experiences

Colin Beard

Learning objectives

- To know and understand the six main elements which underpin the human experience.
- To understand, and apply an experience design modelling process.
- To understand, and apply an experience design mapping process.

Introduction

The first chapter of this book commented on the heightened attendee expectations in an increasingly competitive event marketplace. For these reasons event creators are rightfully preoccupied with the design of engaging and memorable experiences for attendees. This chapter will scrutinize the fluid and complex nature of the human experience and present an overarching model that brings together many of the core dimensions of the human experience to advance our understanding of how to design and deliver event experiences. This model is supported by a range of tools that enable us to better understand the experience design processes. The conceptual notions presented here are illustrated through the exploration of a UK charity event, and two international case studies.

The event experience: a complex concept

Whilst the events industry is very much concerned with the challenges of designing and delivering experiences, we must firstly systematically define what constitutes the human experience (Poulsson and Kale, 2004). Early in the 1980s Holbrook and Hirschmann (1982) made a significant contribution to the understanding of the experiential perspectives of consumer experiences, with Holbrook (1999, pp.8-9) later noting the central position of experience in the creation of consumer value:

> Finally, by experience, I mean that consumer value resides not in the product purchased, not in the brand chosen, not in the object possessed, but rather in the consumption experience(s) derived therefrom

It is noteworthy that a number of authors were simultaneously arriving at rather similar conclusions. In the final year of the 20th century Schmitt produced a key text on Experiential Marketing, referring to a 'new century of marketing' (1999, p.11), and Pine and Gilmore (1991) produced their key work on the Experiential Economy. This focus on experience persists, evidenced convincingly by the fact that customer-facing staff, in what is reputedly the most successful adventure company in the world, operating in more than one hundred countries, and serving more than 100,000 customers every year, are given the title of CEO. For G-Adventures the title does not mean Chief Executive Officer, but Chief Experience Officer (Poon Tip, 2013).

Event creators are in effect designers of experiences, which somewhat elevates the role given that the concept of experience is complex and multidimensional. Our understanding of the human experience has its roots in many fields and disciplines, covering both the social sciences and the natural sciences. The more insight event creators can gain, then the more the design of event experiences can develop into a predictive skill, based upon informed and purposeful action (Berridge, 2012).

So what is an event experience, and how is it special in the way it might differ from an 'everyday' experience?

People construct their own unique experiences, based on their perception, and the experience will be heavily influenced by factors such as personal needs, past experiences, and selective sensory focusing (McIntyre and Roggenbuck, 1998). A number of authors talk of an experience, rather than everyday experiencing, and suggest that for events there should be a 'wow' factor, and be memorable, special, and conceivably unique (Pine and Gilmore, 1999; Berridge, 2012; Mehmetoglu and Engen, 2011). Schmitt (1999, p.22) suggests that people want experiences to 'dazzle their senses, touch their hearts, and stimulate their minds'. Schmitt also notes that experiences are not static, but fluid, creating an ever changing perceptual novelty. Experience is a slippery concept, and no matter how hard we try to grasp it there will always be parts that will escape the homogenizing grasp. The meaning derived from any event is uniquely perceived and processed by individuals; given the disparate nature of event audiences the facilitation of attendee experience is always going to be an inexact science. This unpredictability, integral to the appeal of events, is captured by Sheets-Johnstone

(2009, p. 380) who describes how experiences can create 'instances in which we are at a loss for words, so stunned by something we cannot speak'. This elusive dimension within event design is also recognised by Burr (2003) who suggests that we should regard such forms of experience as existing outside the realm of language, i.e. as 'extra discursive' or resistant to description. This does not necessarily mean that such experiences cannot be designed; the short case study below illustrates an unusual experience which cannot easily be described. This fits with the notion that event creation is indeed an art, as well as a science, with creators adopting the guise of choreographers, facilitators and curators rather than organisers.

Case study: Kadoorie Farm and Botanical Garden, Hong Kong

At Kadoorie Farm and Botanical Garden in Hong Kong (website: www.kfbg.org.hk) a series of events are offered for the public each year that work with the notion of the 4Hs: Head, Hands, Heart and Home. These events include experiences that involve the 'more than human world' (MTHW), with exciting possibilities for transformative encounters with other people and the animal, plant and spiritual world. Two dimensions of the human experience, notably the sense of being and belonging can involve more complex design (see Baumeister, and Leary, 1995). Their events include, for example; a half-day and a full day of silence and personal transformation, a low carbon living event, Good Life Sunday Events, working with self-sufficiency methods that use the 24 solar rhythms of the Chinese calendar, Sensory Days with Plants, and many other more than human world 'encounters'.

The half day and day events of silence and transformation have attracted over one hundred people during the first two years of delivery. The event involves facilitators taking participants through a peaceful and uplifting experience in the serene surroundings of beautiful tropical forest and gardens in a remote part of the island of Hong Kong. The core physical activity is a slow walk up to the summit of Kwun Yum Shan Mountain, at an altitude of 552 metres. On this slow walk participants experience mindful walking, sitting silently in nature, story-telling, stretching activities, sharing and showing gratitude to nature. The experience involves time out, with others, to contemplate life, quieten the mind, and generally slow down. Many participants remarked that sitting listening to the sounds of flowing water was very special.

In the instructions sent to participants people are 'requested to respect other participants by maintaining silence throughout the journey'. Many of the participants reported that they experienced a significant quieting of the mind, a special closeness to nature, and inner peace and well-being. A significant number of participants expressed a wish to return to experience more of these events. In the future the experience may involve being alone, lying and gently rocking in hammocks for a short while in the tropical forests, simply contemplating life and just being.

7

The tension between the experience and writing or talking about it is evocatively portrayed by Robert Kull in his book *Solitude: Seeking Wisdom in Extremes*, Kull writes about a life changing experience when he spent a year in remote Patagonia immersing himself in a state of solitude. He skilfully describes how language obstructs the process of understanding, designing and describing events from an experiential perspective.

> There is no dance between word and world. What I see and feel begs a sensuous tango, but my words march static and stiff in lines across the page.

(Kull, 2008, p.184).

The one dimensional form of written and spoken word can thus create significant limitation for event design. We simply cannot entirely comprehend experience, and similarly the art of experience creation is imperfect. To add to the challenge of designing event experiences, the sensory experience that event designers create, such as music, décor, or performance, will be experienced differentially by individuals and groups within the audience. This experience will be determined by their own antecedents. Consider an eager teenager at a music event with their favourite band. Significantly for design, the intention, anticipation, and expectation of the audience prevail, providing the pre-conditions for the experience to be memorable, linked to their heightened sensory state. The same sensory stimuli is available to their protective parent who has accompanied them to the concert but their intention, anticipation, and expectation are dissimilar, and their senses are less likely to be similarly stimulated by the experience. The experience is 'read' differently. In extending this principle it is not surprising therefore that Petterson and Getz (2009, p.310) contend that "(event) experiences cannot be fully designed, they are both personal (i.e. psychological) constructs that vary with the individual, as well as being social and cultural constructs related to influences on the individual and the (often) social nature of events".

Despite the above discussion, event designers remain highly influential in shaping whether attendee experiences are basic, memorable, or transforming (Hover and Mierlo, 2006). As Berridge (2012) indicates, if we don't design, we leave the experience to chance, if we do design, we increase the predictability of the event outcome. It can be further suggested that if we inadequately design, we adversely affect the experience outcome.

The fundamental dimensions of the event experience

Many authors have attempted to understand the complex nature of human experience within their specific fields of study, such as experiential learning, experiential marketing, outdoor leisure and adventure programming and economics, to name a few. Whilst all have sought to investigate the key components that make up the human experience, they have done so to differing degrees and the result is that there is much contention over what 'experience dimensions' are most important. Discrepancies exist concerning the extent to which an experience is socially (with other people), psychologically (inner psyche/self), emotionally (feelings), cognitively (mind/thinking), environmentally or otherwise constructed.

Mannell and Kleiber (1997) suggest that all experiences have three essential dimensions: the cognitive (thinking), the conative (acting/doing) and the affective (feelings). These three elements are commonplace considerations in the literature on event design, but some authors suggest other important experience dimensions. Berridge notes the work of Rossman (2003) (in Recreation Programming: Designing Leisure Experiences) who suggests the six important aspects of interacting people, physical setting, objects, rules, relationships, and animation. Figure 7.1 captures the considerable diversity of views on the core dimensions of the human experience.

7

Author/s	Important dimensions of the event experience	No. of core dimensions
Mannell and Kleiber (1997)	The cognitive (thinking), the conative (acting/doing) and the affective (feelings).	3
Rossman (2003)	Interacting people, physical setting, objects, rules, relationships, and animation.	6
Schmitt (1999)	Acting, feeling, relating, sensing, feeling. 'Dazzle their senses, touch their hearts, and stimulate their minds'. The experience involves the entire living 'being'.	5
McIntyre and Roggenbuck (1998)	Environment/nature; self and internal thoughts; others; emotions; and task/activity.	5
O'Sullivan and Spangler (1998)	Physically, mentally, emotionally, socially, or spiritually.	5
Bitner (1992)	Cognitive, emotional, physiological.	3
Mannel (1984)	A state of mind.	1

Figure 7.1: The contested and complex nature of human experience

Berridge, 2012 (p. 279) references a more comprehensive overarching notion of event experience presented by O'Sullivan and Spangler (1999, p.23) on Experience Marketing, who suggest that any experience involves:

> participation and involvement; the state of being physically, mentally, socially, spiritually and emotionally involved; the changing knowledge, skill, memory or emotion; a conscious perception of having intentionally encountered, gone to live through an activity or event; and effort that addresses a psychological need.

An event experience clearly has many dimensions underpinning the design, some being major dimensions and others being micro components. The following case study from Malaysia highlights exciting design possibilities when many of the core macro and micro ingredients outlined above are creatively utilised. These are highlighted in italics in the text.

Case study The Great Langkwai Race, Malaysia: Applying design fundamentals

The Great Langkawi Race was a specialist event organised for ninety very senior and talented clients who were responsible for the financial management of a whole nation. The race took place on Langkawi Island, Malaysia in 2012. The event was designed and designed by Wilderness Malaysia.(www.wildernessmalaysia.com).

Over forty experienced outdoor events staff were involved in delivering this very complex outdoor experience. The clients demanded perfection: much was at stake, and a very professional delivery was expected by the clients HR department. Nothing was to go wrong and health and safety was not to be compromised. The water activities for example involved specific briefings and participation from the local fire brigade: 'Fire and Rescue' specialists were on standby on jet skis, two instructors were to be located nearby in kayaks, and several staff were present on the nearby beach.

The event creators designed and sequenced many themes, generating social, cognitive, psychological and physical experiences (O'Sullivan and Spangler, 1999; Rossman, 2003; Schmitt, 1999). They applied many supplementary design principles to assist in the creation of this corporate motivational learning event. The Great Langkawi Race challenged the creators to identify clear goals and objectives, generate a sense of pre-event anticipation and focus, plan multiple journeys within the event, and facilitate experiences where participants had to demonstrate many forms of aptitude. The competitive race experience had elements of collaboration, and organisation skills, involving a mass of data to sort before making strategic team decisions. There were rules, regulations, penalties and restrictions to take into account, with time constraints, obstacles, and complex procedures to follow. Real and perceived challenge or risk was included, as was success and failure and the stretching of personal boundaries. These were the micro-design features.

The 90 clients were divided into three teams of 30. Prior to the event each team of 30 was asked to divide their teams into three sub-groups of 10 people to belong to and take part in the major experiential activities under the headings of (1) Fast and Furious, with physical demands requiring fitness (2) Slow and Steady, for less physically able, but with greater intellectual 'stretch' and (3) and the Hybrid (mixture of both capacities). The organisers recommended the required profile requirements for each of these categories: the Fast and Furious sub group were asked to identify staff who were prepared, for example, to paint Langkawi red, to think on their feet, to get muddy and wet, and to flex their muscles. It was also suggested that the member profile should be active, energetic, risk taker, puzzle solver, have attention to detail, daring, versatile, and food connoisseurs. In contrast the slow and steady sub-group had a suggested member profile of patience, logical analytical abilities, mechanical knowledge, and handyman skills! This design process allowed the team and individual choice, so that everyone could, to some extent, journey through the event so that they could gain the best experience. The design of major dimensions involved options revolving around the balance between physical and intellectual, the social and emotional/psychological, and active and passive experiences (see Schmitt, 1999). This approach created a sense of involvement, team belonging, anticipation and excitement prior to the event.

A diverse range of experiences took place across the whole island, with complex transport logistics evolving for the total of one hundred and thirty events staff and clients. The activities contained both competitive and collaborative experiences, all under a set of detailed time and logistical constraints. The conative (active and doing) experiences, for example, included asking the public if they could serve them at a petrol station, making kapok (natural seed) pillows with staff from a local cottage industry, feeding and riding buffalo, solving cryptic clues, completing physical challenges, and building bikes from parts (that were earned by completing other activities) to give to a charity supporting children in need, to name but a few of the variety of experiences (see Beard, 2010). Points were handed out for completing these activities. Success and failure were of course at stake for these highly competitive and successful people.

7

An overarching explanatory model

In order to give more clarity and structure to these micro and macro event design principles, an overarching model to assist effective event design will now be introduced. The model was initially developed in 2002 and subsequently updated and refined in 2006 and 2013 (Beard, in Beard and Wilson, 2013). It is of particular use by designers to ensure the understanding and application of seven distinctive dimensions of the human event experience.

By answering the following questions, event design decisions can be purposefully applied, to trigger the desired human experiences. The crucial event design questions that need to be asked as they underpin the human experience model are as follows:

1   Where, and with whom does the experience take place? (people, such as other attendees, speakers, performers, service staff etc., places, and props such as staging, seating, decoration etc.)

2   What kind of activities will people be engaged in? (the doing or conative element of the experience)

3   What sensory experiences will be stimulated by the experience? (perceptual novelty)

4   Will there be emotional engagement? (the affective, 'heart' of the experience)

5   How can knowledge thinking be engaged? (the cognitive - knowledge - experience)

6   In what way did personal change occur? (being/identity)

All these core dimensions of the human experience are of course only artificially separated in a model. In an event experience they are inextricably interwoven.

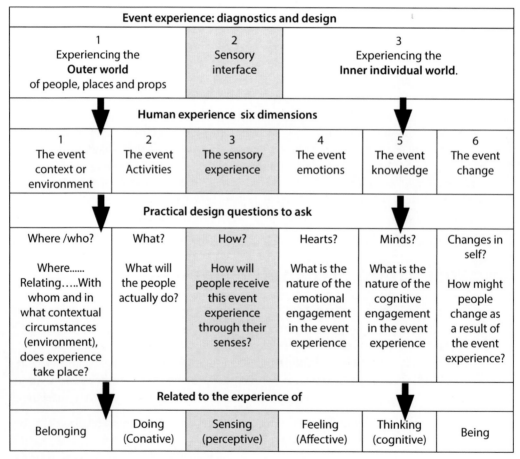

Figure 7.2: The human experience model

An event designer is presented with two major interrelated dimensions of the human experience, notably the inner experience (self) and outer world experiences (others/human and non-human). Given our quest, which is to shape and influence event experiences, we should interpret and detail these major components with care. Figure 7.2 below highlights the key links between the practical questions to ask with the underpinning structures from experiential theory (Beard and Wilson, 2013).

Schmitt (1999) refers to the need to work with the whole 'being'. The two dimensions of being and belonging in the model are more complex topics, with the events literature offering little guidance in this respect. The Hong Kong case study does however offered interesting creative ideas.

Understanding and applying the model

The discussion so far in this chapter shows that event design is neither straightforward nor an exact science, and that human experiences cannot be reduced to set strategies, formulas or recipes. However the model presented here provides just one approach to help event designers purposefully navigate through the considerably complex human experience dimensions. The fundamental design process involving the model that highlights six core dimensions of the human experience (Figure 7.2) will now be explained by presenting an example from a Sheffield based charity that supports homeless people. This charity regularly hosts an event that involves participants, often donors, sleeping out on the streets for one night with homeless people.

An undergraduate student (Russ, 2014) used the model (Figure 7.2) to understand the experience of the 'sleep out', as it was known. His results suggest that participants in the sleep-out experienced a stronger understanding of homelessness, and a more lasting relationship with the charity. The event consistently provides three key outcomes; emotional connection and differentiation for the charity in a competitive charity marketplace, meaningful experiences for the attendee, and much needed income for the charity. When interviewed the participants commented how the sleep-out really enhanced their fundraising charity experience, and that the memorable nature of the event was very closely linked to the cause.

Participant responses support the notion that the experience should dazzle the senses, touch the heart, and stimulate the mind (Schmitt, 1999). Russ (2014) believes that this link to the cause, and the experiential nature of the event, made it unusual; not many charity events incorporate their cause experience in such an immersive, unconventional way. Russ suggests that charity event design should, if possible, merge the cause and the event in a much more direct way. The following data highlights the six elements of the human experience, starting in the middle of the model with the sensory experience that connects the individual inner world experience with their outer world experience.

The sensory experience

This case example provides insight into how through the design of the event key sensory experiences can be carefully positioned at the heart of the attendee experience. A number of authors highlight the significance of the sensory component of experience design (Lindstrom, 2005; Hulten et al., 2009; Hulten, 2011). Lindstrom talks of 'sensory signatures' associated with products, services and experiences. In the case of an event, there would be an opportunity to develop an event sensory signature through, for example, the lighting impact, the furniture and props used, the smell as you enter the venue, the colour and texture of the food and the music playing. Lindstrom reveals what it is that the world's most successful branding companies do so well, namely the integration of touch, taste, smell, sight, and sound; with startling and measurable results. His underlying research was carried out by a large business research institution, and he drew on countless examples of both product creation and retail experiences. His philosophy is that sensory signatures should be created by appealing to all the senses, not simply sight and sound.

The interview data from the sleep-out event with homeless people evidences the importance of these sensorial experiences, as a key signature of this particular event. The data also highlight the connection to feeling and thinking:

> If I struggled that much for a short period of time then how must somebody deal with this long term… it creates a very visual picture. (Russ, 2014)

> I remember thinking that the trees rustling was quite a nice noise but I wondered what that might be like if you were cold and hungry and, I mean I was in my cosy warm sleeping bag and it made me think what would it be like if it was pissing rain and I was under this tree, you know. Would I be getting wet? Would the leaves be making that noise? Would I be thinking how lovely they are? Would I be looking at the stars thinking gosh, you know. Or would I be stuck in a doorway or whatever so it did make me think about the surroundings that I was in. And I knew that I had people round about me, if I had been on my own I'd have felt incredibly vulnerable." (Russ, 2014)

Such reflections by attendees on their experiences provide event creators with numerous clues to opportunities that exist within the design process for future events to optimise the sensory stimulation felt by attendees. The internal experience of the attendee can now be considered, starting with the emotional dynamics of an event experience.

■ The inner individual emotional experience

Tolle (2006) teaches us how our emotions are in fact reactions to the brain, played out in the theatre of our body. In cultivating experiences that will positively influence future behaviour and affinity with the hosting organisation, event creators must recognise the importance of triggering emotions. Sleep-out data reveals the milieu of emotional experiences:

> And I knew that I had people round about me, if I had been on my own I would have felt incredibly vulnerable." (Russ, 2014)

> The abseiling ones were just terrifying. That's more... I think you kind of do that, and then forget about the charity, not forget about the charity but it doesn't give you the same ties and emotional connection towards the charity as the sleep out did." (Russ, 2014)

Emotions were continuously emerging, for example in going to the soup kitchen before going to get cardboard that would become the bed to sleep on. All these elements of the experience are significant to the design process.

■ The individual experience of knowing

The human capacity to want to learn something is exceptional, and the desire for knowledge and knowing is particularly significant to the event experience. If event designers understand what attendees want to know, then this this can be embedded throughout their experience. During the interviews with sleep-out participants there were many responses that linked to the knowledge dimension. It appears that, in the opinion of participants, to experience the sleep-out is to really know it, and understand it. There was a strong desire to understand the cause, and to learn about the project and the reality of homelessness. The result, for the participants, was a change in perception, and, most certainly an increased awareness of the plight of homeless people. Homeless people were at times concerned that a one night experience might be erroneously interpreted as experiencing homelessness.

This deeper understanding by participants of the sleep-out affected subsequent memories. The telling of stories to significant others, and beyond through for example social media, was commonplace. Data extracts illustrate the significance of knowledge to the sleep-out experience:

> Would I be looking at the stars thinking gosh, you know. Or would I be stuck in a doorway or whatever so it did make me think about the surroundings that I was in
>
> I thought it was little more than a soup kitchen to be honest, I didn't realise how much they were involved with the clients
>
> It just made us more knowledgeable
>
> ….and it just sort of makes you realise how fine the line is between you know, what most of us have and what some others don't
>
> Interviewer: And that's something you wouldn't have thought about without doing the event?
>
> No I don't think so.   (Russ, 2014)

■ The inner individual experience of being

Whilst many texts recommend that event designers work with the conative, affective and cognitive, few consider deeper human psychology such as our sense of being. The more difficult psychological aspects of the deeper human self should be considered in event design, particularly in relation to the sense of identity. If Schmitt (1999) suggests that the event experience should involve our entire being, what then is our sense of being? Participants on the sleep-out project talked of the impact it had on them, and they used words such as stunned which are important outcomes for the charity given their objectives. Such an experience can of course be unsettling; it can shake up our judgement and value system and our views on life and who were are. These issues are at the very heart of our sense of being in the world. Event experiences have the potential to transform us and the following response from one participant highlights the impact of the sleep-out experience when they realised that two very different beings were forging their connection to each other, and their sense of belonging to something bigger, and the unusual juxtaposition of two contrasting identities:

> Here was this laddy, all dishevelled and everything, put his arms around me and gave me a big hug and said "I bloody love you I do" and I said come on then I'll buy you a cup of tea. What amazed me was that here was me in my business outfit and my suit and all the rest of it heading to meetings, posh briefcase, and here was this laddy with his mangy dog giving me a hug in the middle of the street (Russ, 2014)

■ The outer world experience of doing something

The active outer world experience of doing things (the conative) played an important role in the sleep-out event. Participant comments suggest that donating money to the charity has three levels to it, similar to findings from Hover and Mierlo (2006): the basic level of engagement is that of simply giving money, with low experience reality. Then there was an element of active doing, such as the sponsored adventure experiences like abseiling, which were undoubtedly memorable, but seen as low reality experiences with little connection with the cause. However, with high perceived reality of the sleep-out event, the experience was not only memorable but it was potentially transformative, an issue explored below (Hover and Mierlo, 2006). Participants commented on the value of doing something active for the charity rather than passively 'just' donating. Interestingly the sleep out experience also embraced the reversal of the conative: notably the problematic experience of boredom that homelessness can bring, i.e. of not having anything to do.

> I walk past people begging in the subway, every single day and that kind of constantly reinforces that, you know, something needs to be done and that perhaps the Cathedral Archer is a good way of contributing."

> It was more the talk and the tour around the facilities about what they actually do. A bit more detail about all the depth of what they do and the lengths that they go to, to help people

> You see these appeals on telly and pulls at a heart string but then once that adverts gone off and you've donated, it's kind of, it's forgotten because you've just handed some cash over … but when you've actually done something like that and you get a real experience of what one night of their life's like… definitely has a bigger impact than just handing money over

> (Russ, 2014)

■ The experience of belonging and relating

Participant data from the sleep out project reveal the many people and places contributed to their sense of belonging. One person mentioned being a 'doggie person', and that gave a sense of belonging, or relating to Gavin, a homeless person who also had a dog. Participant data also highlighted a sense of belonging with other humans:

> Whether they were on Tracy's staff, volunteers or people who had actually done the sleep out. There was very much a feeling of oneness, you know, all being in it together kind of thing

Belonging also surfaced in relation to specific spaces

> If you were just in town that moment, not in a sleeping bag, not lying on the floor, not under a tree wouldn't bother you at all but it

7

kind of made you have a different kind of awareness of people who were around you

I want to make an impact on my own doorstep and Sheffield is my home now

(Russ, 2014)

The kitchens, the cathedral, the city, the outdoors, and sheltered places were also some of the significant places referred to in the participant data.

Mapping the experience journey

The metaphor of a journey acknowledges the time and space dimensions within event design. Back in the early 1960s, the idea evolved that leisure experiences comprised of several time periods or phases. This phenomenon became known as the multi-phasic dimension of experience (see for example Clawson and Knetsch, 1966). It was argued that, for example, travel to and from the site of the experience were significant and therefore important to embrace within the design process. Their research noted that satisfaction or dissatisfaction changed in each phase of the experience.

Using the notion of a journey, or multiple journeys, with movement, travel, and venturing to and from an event, these phases of the experience are now appreciated as important to the experience design. The touch points or 'stations' along the journey route are also significant, with interactions designed into the changing experience. The pre-event phase often includes understanding anticipation, and excitement, and the sense of starting out on a journey. The post event experiences typically include recollection and reflectiveness, surfacing memories, and the telling of stories, with the experience of ending, reflecting, lasting memories, including other experiences of journeys. There are of course many touch point intersections that can generate interconnectedness within an event experience.

A cartographic approach can be utilised to visually represent this phasic analysis, so that the design of the experiences can be seen, and understood. Figure 7.3 below highlights the stages that can be employed in developing this cartographic event design process. Figure 7.3 below shows the time span along the x-axis, with the six core event experience dimensions teased out along the y-axis.

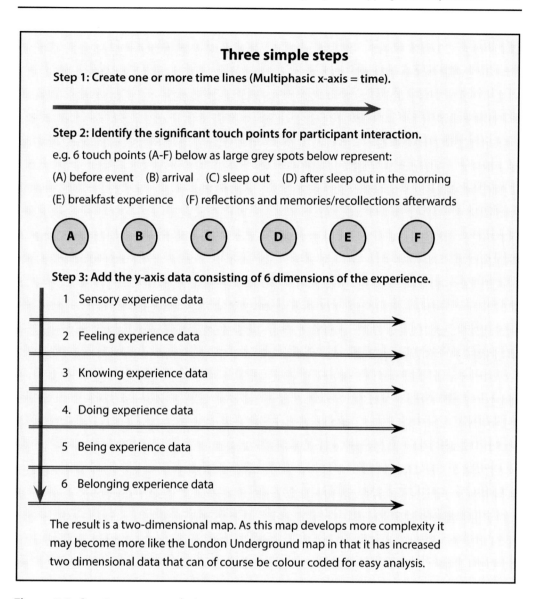

Three simple steps

Step 1: Create one or more time lines (Multiphasic x-axis = time).

Step 2: Identify the significant touch points for participant interaction.

e.g. 6 touch points (A-F) below as large grey spots below represent:

(A) before event   (B) arrival   (C) sleep out   (D) after sleep out in the morning

(E) breakfast experience   (F) reflections and memories/recollections afterwards

A   B   C   D   E   F

Step 3: Add the y-axis data consisting of 6 dimensions of the experience.

1   Sensory experience data

2   Feeling experience data

3   Knowing experience data

4.   Doing experience data

5   Being experience data

6   Belonging experience data

The result is a two-dimensional map. As this map develops more complexity it may become more like the London Underground map in that it has increased two dimensional data that can of course be colour coded for easy analysis.

Figure 7.3: Creating an event design map

Why is an event map helpful? It is no coincidence that in times of war the military planning process took place within a 'war room'. Such a room had large maps adorning both walls and tables. Models of troops, tanks, planes and ships allowed a visual element to the evolving interactive planning process. If we return to the beginnings of the chapter we realise why: human language has severe limitations when complex thee dimensional processes are involved.

Conclusion

This chapter established the complex and contested nature of the event experience: the central debate concerns the extent to which an experience is socially, psychologically, culturally, environmentally or otherwise constructed. Routinely referred to in the literature are the three interrelated aspects of the sensory, cognitive, affective and conative dimensions of the event experience. An integrative model, highlighting six macro dimensions of the human experience was constructed and explored by utilizing data collected from a sleep out event with homeless people.

International case studies from Hong Kong and Malaysia further highlighted creative design principles illustrating both micro and macro aspects of event experiences. Finally a two dimensional mapping techniques was introduced that used a time line to analyse the multi-phasic way in which the experience unfolds, highlighting the benefits gained by teasing out data relating to the six selected dimensions of the event experience.

Study questions

1 In the human experience model what are the six most significant dimensions of the human experience that can be taken into account when designing events?

2 In what way can models, maps and other navigational aids help or hinder event design?

References

Baumeister, R. F. and Leary, M. R. (1995). The need to belong: desire for interpersonal attachments as a fundamental human motivation, *Psychological Bulletin*, **117** (3), 497-525.

Beard, C. (2010). *The Experiential Learning Toolkit: Blending Practice with Concepts*, London, Kogan Page.

Beard, C. and Wilson, J.P. (2013). *Experiential Learning: A Handbook for Education, Training and Coaching*. London: Kogan Page.

Berridge, G. (2012). Designing event experiences, in S. J. Page and J. Connel (eds), *The Routledge Handbook of Events*, Oxford, Taylor Francis Group: pp: 273-288.

Bitner (1992). Servicescapes: The impact of physical surroundings on customers and employees. *Journal of Marketing*, **56**, 57-71.

Burr, V. (2003). *Social Constructionism*, London: Routledge.

Clawson, M. and Knetsch, J. L. (1966). *Economics of Outdoor Recreation*, Baltimore, MD: Johns Hopkins Press.

Holbrook, M. (1999). *Consumer Value*, London: Routledge.

Holbrook, M. B. and Hirschmann, E. C. (1982). The experiential aspects of consumption: consumer fantasies, feelings and fun, *Journal of Consumer Research*, **9**(2): 132-140.

Hover, M., and van Mierlo, J. (2006). Imagine your event: Imagineering for the event industry. Unpublished manuscript. Breda University of Applied Sciences and NHTV Expertise, Netherlands: Event Management Centre.

Hultén, B. (2011). Sensory marketing: the multi-sensory brand-experience concept, *European Business Review*, **23** (3), 256-273.

Hultén, B., Broweus, N. And Dijk, M. (2009). *Sensory Marketing*, Basingstoke. Palgrave Macmillan.

Kull, R (2008). *Solitude: Seeking Wisdom in Extremes*, CA, New World Library.

Lindstrom, M. (2005). *Brand Sense*, London, Kogan Page.

Mannell R. C. (1984). The playful side of laughter. *Journal of Leisurability*, **11**, 4-7

Mannell, R. C. and Kleiber, D. A. (1997). *A Social Psychology of Leisure*, Pittsburgh, PA: Venture Publications.

McIntyre, N and Roggenbuck, J. W. (1998). Nature/person transactions during an outdoor adventure experience; a multi-phasic analysis, *Journal of Leisure Research*, **30**, 401-422.

Mehmetoglu, M. and Engen, M. (2011). Pine and Gilmore's concept of experience economy and its dimensions: an empirical examination in tourism, *Journal of Quality Assurance in Hospitality and Tourism*, **12**, 237–255.

O'Sullivan, E.L and Spangler, K.J. (1999). *Experience Marketing*, State College, PA: Venture Publishing.

Peterson, R. and Getz, D (2009). Event experiences in time and space: a study of visitors to the 2007 World Alpine Ski Championships in Are, Sweden, *Scandinavian Jurnal of Hospitality and Tourism*, **9**(2-3): 308-26.

Pine, J. and Gilmore, B. H. (1999). *The Experience Economy: Work is Theatre and Every Business is a Stage*, Boston: Harvard Business School.

Poon Tip, B. (2013). *Looptail: How One Company Changed the World by Reinventing Business*, New York: Hachette Book Group.

Poulsson, S. H. G. and Kale, S. H. (2004). The experience economy and commercial experiences, *The Marketing Review*, **4**, 267-277.

Rossman, J.R. (2003). *Recreation Programming: Designing Leisure Experiences*, Urbana, II: Sagamore Publishing.

Russ, W. (2014). The significance of experiential events for the charity sector and their impact on attendees through event analysis, Unpublished Undergraduate Project, Sheffield Hallam University, May, 2014.

7

Schmitt, B. H. (1999). *Experiential Marketing: How to get customers to sense, feel, think, act, relate to your company and brands.* New York: The Free Press.

Sheets-Johnstone, M. (2009). *The Corporeal Turn, an interdisciplinary reader,* Exeter: Imprint Academic.

Tolle, E. (2006). *A New Earth: Awakening your life's purpose.* London: Plume.

8 Creating the Eventscape

Jane Tattersall and Richard Cooper

Learning objectives

- To gain an understanding of the importance of creativity in event design.

- To demonstrate how the event environment can be shaped to influence the emotional responses of attendees.

- To demonstrate application of the eventscape model to help design the best experience for stakeholders, attendees and event employees.

Introduction

As human beings, we make judgements based on our emotional responses, be it to products, services, situations and other people; and what they say or do. Emotions, whether we choose to respond to them or not, influence our actions every day and are deeply connected to memory, as explained in the previous chapter. As event creators, we cannot know the intimate psychology of the people who will come to our events. However, we can apply our knowledge of stakeholders' intended event outcomes and, through careful assessment of attendee profiles, design the limitless combinations of interactions that will engage event attendees. This is achieved by focussing upon their senses, to create emotional responses that are memorable and satisfy and exceed expectations. An outcome-oriented approach to Strategic Event Creation must therefore include the goal of evoking emotions to provoke positive memories for event attendees, employees and stakeholders.

We know from the previous chapter, and also Chapter 4, that different people may have different motivations to attend events and that they also experience things differently at the same event, so we cannot 'control' event experience. However, we should be fastidious about meticulously influencing the event environment to create an eventscape that achieves the desired outcomes for both attendees and wider stakeholders. This chapter looks at elements of the physical environment that events take place in, and shows how through clever design and management of spaces and people, this can be achieved.

■ What is the eventscape?

We understand landscape to mean the visible features of an area of land and in our imagination the combination of different physical elements, in different seasons and conditions can seem limitless. A cityscape is the urban equivalent of a landscape, seascape is a coastal interpretation and moonscape conjures up images of our crater marked celestial entity. Back down to earth, 'servicescape' was coined by Booms and Bitner (1981) to mean the physical elements that combine to make an environment which has an important impact on customers' and employees' experiences in the service sector, as initially applied to retail services or the hospitality industry. Mossberg (2007) draws parallels between the concepts of 'servicescape' and 'experiencescape', understanding both to represent a complex mix of environmental features that influence internal responses and behaviour, but she also highlights a distinction between the delivery of services and the consumption of experiences.

Bringing these elements together we therefore define 'eventscape' as:

> A combination of the tangible elements which shape the event environment and therefore influence the emotional responses and experiences of attendees, event staff, and other involved stakeholders.

The combined desired outcomes and objectives of the stakeholders should always drive the creation of an event. Therefore a key skill of the event creator lies in weaving together these elements to directly shape the eventscape of attendees and subsequent perception of success or value by each of the stakeholders. This chapter explores the range and combination of elements and interactions that can be crafted or orchestrated, to achieve a lasting, positive experience from first awareness of an event, the event itself and memories thereafter, for all the stakeholders of all types of events. That is a tall order, but with knowledge, skill and practice, event creators can manipulate their tangible resources imaginatively to surpass event objectives.

Furthermore, we build on previously published knowledge to enable readers to identify, develop and implement a set of competencies to create events that generate customer value and are a source of value and competitive advantage for other stakeholders. The first thing that we explore is creativity, which is strongly emphasised by the industry voice in Chapter 14 and is often an overlooked element of the event manager's toolkit. However, we argue here that it is a skill that is a pre-requisite to a successful event, rather than an 'add on'.

The skilled event creator

Presented with the same brief and resources, it is fairly predictable that different event creators will propose different events, based on their skills, knowledge and prior experience. Proficient event creators use their expertise to create eventscapes that provoke appropriate emotional responses from attendees and facilitate a feeling of connection between the attendees, the event content and the event staff. In this section we discuss some specific knowledge and skills that characterise event creators and differentiate them from 'traditional' event managers. A review of service sector related literature finds that whilst there is plenty of discussion relating to the generic skills required for successful leadership, management, project management and hospitality management, the literature available for specific skills or competencies related to events is more limited.

Existing textbook literature acknowledges key areas of competence that a professional and successful event creator should be proficient in, including technical, sector and industry expertise, project management skills, health and safety knowledge, marketing, site and stage management and the ability to work to tight deadlines, often at short notice and under pressure. Interestingly, the model presented by Bladen et al. (2012, p.44) examines the competencies of an effective event project leader and does include intuition (or gut feelings, just knowing what will work or not work through experience and practice) and emotional resilience (or the all-important 'can-do' attitude), seen by some as the difference between average and spectacular. Figure 8.1 illustrates this successful combination of traits.

This model also adds 'vision and imagination' to the mix, alongside the need for 'strategic perspective', and 'sensitivity'. This is coming closer to the traits that we argue are needed for 'creativity' and 'awareness of emotion', so that event creators can understand and influence people's emotions to create an immersive event experience. There is a need for more research in this area and perhaps the difficulty in quantifying and capturing these traits explains the current absence. However, the skills of relationship management, creativity and innovation are often missing from such literature, along with the skill of avoiding negative emotional responses as well as creating positive ones.

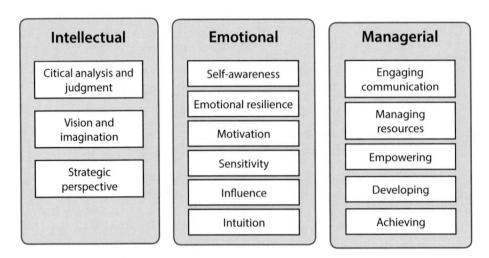

Figure 8.1: The traits of successful event creators. Source: Bladen et al, 2012, p.44

It could be argued that we need to place higher value on creativity within an events creator, to develop new and novel eventscapes that meet the requirements and challenges of the ever-changing environment. Creativity applies not only to the artistic approach we take to the presentation of events, but also to the cognitive skills we can train ourselves to use to generate systematic, planned innovative opportunities and solutions for event creation challenges. Often the challenge lies in finding people with the right skills to work within a creative team, so that collectively, ideas are generated and turned into reality.

Industry voice: Eamonn Hunt, CEO Very Creative Ltd , UK

Early in my career, I worked as a lighting designer in theatre where there is a very clear emphasis on creativity and on a particular show there might also be a desire to challenge the perceived norms around how it is going to be staged. In theatre it is the Director's vision that the technical and creative teams all work to achieve, so it is essential to work collaboratively, and to ensure that all options are considered. No idea is a bad idea; it might just not be the best one today!

Closely associated with taking a creative approach to events is the need for continuous innovation. Innovation involves finding a new and better way of doing something and much of society is based on innovations that have occurred in the past. It can be stated with certainty that innovation provides us with the standard of living we have today.

Besides creating spectacular visual impacts at an event, innovation and creativity can revolutionise many business practices including ideas development, problem solving, managing the events process, use of technology, presentation and facilitation, logistics, site planning, crowd management, staging, catering, managing clients, sales, ticketing, evaluation… in fact any element of an event can be transformed through taking an innovative and creative approach.

Peter Drucker has written about innovation in several books and has outlined seven sources that we can look at to generate new innovations, four from industry and three from the societal environment. Figures 8.2 and 8.3 identify how these concepts can be applied to events to help generate new ideas for products and services.

The Unexpected

An unexpected success or an unexpected failure – such as crowd problems leading to new venue design and entrance procedures.

An unexpected outside event – such as the terrorist attacks in September 2001 and the increase in video conferencing.

This can be a symptom of a unique opportunity.

The Incongruity

A discrepancy between reality and what everyone assumes it to be – such as festival organisers assuming that poorly managed toilet facilities or lengthy entrance queues are acceptable.

A discrepancy between what is and what ought to be – such as the public's assumptions and the reality of the sustainability of events.

Innovation based on a process need

When a weak link is evident in a particular process, but people work around it instead of doing something about it, an opportunity is available to the person or company willing to supply the missing link. For example, the development of hybrid conferences and meetings has meant that high profile speakers who might not previously have been booked due to cost, travel and convenience factors, can now participate due to the development of virtual technology.

Changes to industry or market structure

The opportunity for an innovative product, service or business approach – Hybrid meetings.

This occurs when the underlying foundation of the industry or market shifts such as in recession, legislation or new standards, e.g. sustainability – recent EU austerity measures have meant that meeting and event professionals have been more willing to embrace innovation and technology at a faster pace, possibly due to the need to do more, with less, or due to cultural differences between regions (Pofeldt, 2014).

Figure 8.2: Sources of innovation from industry applied to events, adapted from Drucker (2007)

Demographics

Opportunities are created when there are changes in a population's size, age structure, composition, employment, level of education or level of income.

Changes in perception, mood and meaning

Innovative opportunities can develop when there are changes in a society's general assumptions, attitudes or belief.

New knowledge

Advances in scientific and non-scientific knowledge can create:

- New products
- New markets

Figure 8.3: Sources of innovation from the societal environment, adapted from Drucker (2007).

Industry voice: Eamonn Hunt, CEO Very Creative Ltd, UK

Though we are often asked to cut budgets and save money, we are rarely asked if there is a better way to do that, rather than simply beat down the supplier prices. Our innovation and creativity are often suppressed by our need to get on and get things done.

Being a creative thinker and pursuer of innovation in events inevitably involves a degree of risk taking, be it financial (yours or your client's money), organisational, (credibility, future business, employees) or personal reputation; all depending upon the nature of creativity or innovation you are proposing. Risk is also a personal trait, as different people have different perceptions of risk and risk-taking. This is expanded in events, given the wide variety of event types and the variations of scale and scope and the uncertainty and complexity of events.

When we consider all of the skills and competencies required by an event creator, we highlight the skills of innovation, creativity and risk taking as being integral to the profession. We also show the need to understand people's emotions and then creatively work to enhance the positive feelings we want them to experience at our event, some of which can be achieved through the manipulation of the event's tangible elements – the eventscape. This leads to the sections below which explain where this area of academic research has developed, and how it can be moved forward from atmospherics, through servicescape to eventscape.

Industry voice: David Jamilly, Co-founder, Theme Traders, UK

With rapid recent advancements in technology, the potential for innovation has extended dramatically in terms of planning and delivery. Some of the most ground-breaking events utilise a combination of traditional theatre techniques and highly advanced technology. Getting the blend right requires a broad based skill set including creativity and an understanding of contemporary art and fashion. This needs to be underpinned by the psychological ability to get inside the heads of your potential audience in advance of the design stage.

Atmospherics to servicescape to eventscape

Initially this section looks at the development of the terminology of servicescape and the importance of the sales environment to a consumer, especially that of a service based product. This area of academic research has mainly been derived from retail operations, although the principles of the theories have been applied to other settings such as hospitality. This section demonstrates how research on operations and hospitality constitutes a foundation for event creation. It will show how proficient event creators can build on the theories presented below to design the eventscape, moving the framework forward from operational to strategic.

8

■ Services and atmospherics

The differences between the selling of a tangible product versus the selling of a pure service are highlighted by a range of authors (for example Zeithaml et al 1985; Palmer, 2011) with physical evidence as a 'p' in the marketing mix being added to highlight the way that consumers search for and use tangible clues to assess the quality of the service provided. Rafiq and Ahmed (1995, p.7) develop this, noting that:

> The physical environment itself (i.e. the buildings, decor, furnishings, layout, etc.) is instrumental in customers' assessment of the quality and level of service they can expect, for example in restaurants, hotels, retailing and many other services. In fact, the physical environment is part of the product itself.

If a consumer has a psychological response to a physical environment, then, as Bitner (1992) shows, planning the physical environment can be the difference between business success and failure. However, the manipulation of scale and atmosphere in places of consumption are nothing new in history. For example Kotler (1973) points out that 'magnificent temples' in Ancient Greece and 'soaring cathedrals' in mediaeval times were constructed to elicit a psychological response in people, in this case humbling people by highlighting the power of religion.

Kotler (1973) used the word 'atmosphere' when viewing the importance that the consumer gives to the feel of the place in which the purchase of a product occurs. He then coined the term 'atmospherics' to show the different factors that businesses can intentionally manipulate and control to create an overall atmosphere that consumers respond to positively. As consumers view atmosphere through their senses, sight, sound, scent and touch (see Table 8.1), so the manipulation of atmospherics must appeal to the consumers' senses to elicit a positive response to the atmosphere. The reverse is also true, in that the atmosphere can be manipulated to put off consumers, for instance from entering a retail store for which they are not the target market. Kotler and Levy (1971) called this 'selective de-marketing'. A business will try to create what Kotler (1973) called an 'intended atmosphere', which could be very different from the 'perceived atmosphere' in the mind of the consumer. The perceived atmosphere will also vary from consumer to consumer, as tastes will differ on personal, generational and cultural levels. This creates issues for the designer of the atmosphere, as appealing to an identified target market is a core component of a successful marketing plan with the drive to positively improve customers' opinions and therefore sales.

Senses	Atmosphere dimensions
Sight – Visual	Colour
	Brightness
	Size
	Shapes
Sound – Aural	Volume
	Pitch
Scent – Olfactory	Scent
	Freshness
Touch – Tactile	Softness
	Smoothness
	Temperature

Table 8.1: Atmospherics, adapted from Kotler (1973).

■ Servicescape and consumer behaviour

Booms and Bitner (1981, p.36) coined the term 'servicescape' to describe the "environment in which the service is assembled and in which the seller and customer interact, combined with tangible commodities that facilitate performance or communication of the service". Bitner (1992) developed this further, exploring the psychological impact of atmospherics on a consumer's behaviour. This is similar to Mehrabian and Russell's (1974) theories of environmental psychology which develop the idea of a stimulus-organism response (S-O-R). In this case the stimulus (S) would be the environment, which the consumer will evaluate (O) and cause a response (R). These emotional responses were then classified as pleasure, arousal and dominance. Turley and Milliman (2000) develop this, saying that these emotional responses will lead to two opposing types of behaviour in people, either to 'approach' or 'avoid'. Approach type behaviours are positive behaviours, such as wanting to spend time in the environment, exploring and bonding with others, this leading potentially to consumers purchasing more because they are happy. Avoidance type behaviours mean not wanting to stay in the environment either to explore or spend money and ignoring communication attempts from others, so the environment is causing people to withdraw into themselves.

Kotler's (1973) list of atmospherics (Table 8.1) was amended by Bitner (1992) to develop this link between the environment factors and behaviour.

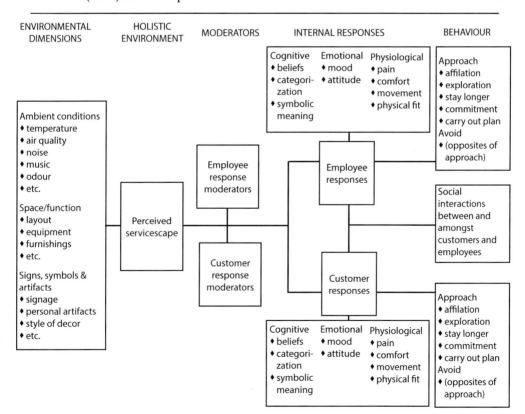

Figure 8.4: Framework for understanding environment-user relationships in service organisations, adapted from Bitner, 1992.

Kotler (1973)	Bitner (1992)	Berman and Evans (1995) / Turley and Milliman (2000)
Sight – Visual Colour Brightness Size Shapes	**Ambient** Temperature Air quality Noise Music Odour	**External v ariables** Exterior signs/displays Entrances Height/size/colour of building Address/location Surroundings Parking/congestion/traffic
Sound – Aural Volume Pitch	**Space/Function** Layout Equipment Furnishings	**Internal variables** Flooring/carpeting Colour schemes/paint/wallpaper Lighting Music/PA Scents Width of aisles Merchandise Temperature Cleanliness
Scent – olfactory Scent Freshness	**Signs, symbols and artefacts** Signage Personal artefacts Style of décor	**Layout and design variables** Space design and allocation Placement/grouping of merchandise Work station placement Placement of equipment/furniture/cash registers/Racks/cases Waiting areas/rooms Traffic flow Waiting queues Dead areas
Touch – tactile Softness Smoothness Temperature		**Point of purchase and decoration variables** Point of purchase displays Signs and cards Wall decorations Pictures/artwork/certificates Product displays Usage instructions Price displays
		Human variables Employee characteristics Employee uniforms Crowding Customer characteristics Privacy

Table 8.2: Atmospheric variables development

Bitner's work also developed the ideas of service quality and the interaction necessary between staff and consumers within this selling environment or servicescape. She argued that the behaviours of both customers and staff are affected by the environment where they meet, so if employees feel uncomfortable in the servicescape where they work they are not going to feel like offering good service to the customer. Also, if the customer or attendee is feeling uncomfortable in the servicescape, then they are not going to interact with the staff in a positive way. It requires both the staff and the customer to feel happy in the environment, creating 'approach type' behaviours in both groups, which allows a conducive experience to take place.

This capacity of the environment to elicit a consumer or staff response, thus shaping their behaviour, highlights the importance of how manipulating and managing the servicescape element can be used to improve business performance. The next section looks at these elements in more detail.

Table 8.2 shows the development of 'atmospheric variables' from Kotler's atmospherics, through to later work by Turley and Milliman (2000), which developed the importance of staff and human interaction within the overall servicescape. The sections below look at these variables, highlighting factors that would create the approach or avoid responses in customers and staff. We develop this later in the chapter in Table 8.3.

8

Atmospheric variables

The sections below highlight some of the results of the research conducted into servicescapes. Please see Mari and Poggesi (2013) for a recent review of the available servicescape literature.

■ External variables

As external variables create first impressions, they are not to be overlooked in importance. Human beings evaluate situations and places in a very short space of time, as a part of our innate 'fight or flight' response, therefore making a good first impression is vital to attract and retain customers. If the outside of the shop, restaurant or other venue is not appealing, then the internal atmosphere might never be seen by consumers. There is also the fact that customers will evaluate not just the actual location of the business, but also the micro and macro areas around that business, before making a decision to go to that location or not.

■ Internal variables

These are variables such as use of colour and texture in furniture and floor/wall coverings, lighting, scents and sounds, and cleanliness. Some of the easiest variables to change are things like music. Obviously this is very target market sensitive, as it must appeal to that target market to make them feel happy. The use of lighting to highlight areas of interest, as well as providing overall safe levels of light, has been utilised in many settings. Colour can be used to shape emotion, but also convey meaning, with colours having significance which varies between cultures. Red, for example, is the colour of danger, passion and romance in Western Culture, but the colour red can symbolise good fortune and happiness in Chinese culture. Smells or odours are another area for consideration. Smell is a very powerful stimulant and memory reminder. Nice smells can create good emotions and memories, but stale or rotten smells can put off a customer faster than any other stimulus (Ward et al., 2003).

■ Layout and design variables

The actual layout of a servicescape can shape peoples' emotions and behaviour. A simple example would be a restaurant where the tables were placed very close together. In this environment, people would feel uncomfortable, and less likely to stay for any length of time. This could be useful for a fast food restaurant, where high turnover is wanted and needed, but for a more upmarket venue this would counteract the need for customers to spend more time at the venue and spend more money.

The same can apply to a retail environment, where the space between racks and shelves must be of a size where people can feel comfortable passing each other. We all have a zone of 'personal space' around us, and if strangers are forced into our personal space due to layout issues, we will feel unconformable in that environment.

■ Point of purchase and decoration variables

These variables look at product display, signage and information, so these are secondary design details to make the internal factors work. Most studies have concentrated on retail environments, with shelf location, product placement and point of purchase displays being prominent in the research. Signage is a key consideration in a service environment. You want staff to be free to serve customers and sell things, not to be there just to act as an expensive sign. It is therefore much more effective to spend money on logical, high quality signage so that customers can find their way around.

■ Human variables

These variables look at the influence of other customers, and the influence of the staff, on the consumer's experience. Turley and Milliman (2000) highlight that crowding is a factor that can be more of a problem for some customers than others, mainly due to the reasons that people are there. Customers who are 'out shopping' may be more relaxed about crowding than those that have a specific shopping task in mind. Crowding can be created through a variety of reasons, from poor layout issues, through to staff being slow to serve, leading to queues. McGrath and Otnes (1995) point out that customers respond to the look and feel of other customers, again using the physical clues to make judgements. Staff appearance is another physical evidence clue for customers. So staff wearing a uniform and cheerily greeting customers will give customers a much higher perception of quality than where neither of those things take place.

From servicescape to eventscape

With the understanding that servicescape gives us, we can utilise this to develop a model applicable to events, called 'eventscape', as defined on page 142. Events differ from retail, hospitality and other service settings, in a variety of ways, notably that a large number of events are one-off creations and the requirement, therefore, is to get it right first time. There are numerous excellent chapters in text books and academic papers that discuss, at length, the component parts, domains or areas of responsibility of events management that need to be considered carefully in the conception, planning and delivery of events (Silvers, 2004; Berridge, 2007; Matthews, 2008; Bowden et al, 2010; O'Toole, 2011; Getz, 2012; Bladen et al, 2012;). If you are reading this chapter, then it is likely that you have also read some of this body of knowledge and if you have not, we recommend that you do. Bowden et al (2011) uses the EMPS phases of the project management of events to comprehensively outline the factors to be managed, and we must remember when creating events that at the heart of each of the individual processes, must be the drive to exceed all of the stakeholders' objectives.

The components of an eventscape comprise: a place or medium (for virtual events); a message or purpose; someone or something to connect with (the participants); and someone to make it happen (the staff). After that, the vast number of combinations of the different elements depend on the size and type of event (Silvers, 2004; Getz, 2005), the complexity and uncertainty (O'Toole, 2011), of the desired outcomes of the event in question for all stakeholders, the resources available, and the imagination, skill and experience of the event creator. Clearly the host objectives will dictate some of component parts of these events, but the specialness of an event is the product of the ingenuity of the event creators. Words associated with 'special' include exceptional, unusual, remarkable, unique and outstanding. We should strive to inspect each element of the eventscape to identify where, using innovative and creative ideas and thinking, we can design elements that will be perceived by the attendees and clients to deliver highly on these terms. However, in Strategic Event Creation, it is important to remember that attendees construct their own experience of an event, based on their perceptions of the various touch points or interactions provided and facilitated by event creators, influenced by their own previous experiences. Therefore, event creators cannot control the individual experiences of customers (Zomerdijk and Voss, 2010), but can design and combine the various elements of the eventscape to facilitate desired outcomes.

■ Elements of the eventscape

Pine and Gilmore (1999) describe a set of 'cues' that form the context in which an experience is created. Previously Carbone and Haeckel (1994) described clues emitted by products, services and the environment, that are orchestrated in the design of experiences. It is crucial to also consider that event attendees and participants will experience these various influencing factors at different times in the event process; before, during and after the staging of the event, in different places and circumstances. They will then interpret the combination of experiences they encounter to form a holistic opinion of their total experience (Zomerdijk and Voss, 2010) and although they may forget or forgive less positive elements because of, perhaps, a spectacular main event, event creators should be wary of sacrificing or settling for one element over another.

Zomerdijk and Voss (2010) suggest six propositions in designing the chain of service encounters that are summarised below.

The design of experience-centric services involves:

1 Designing a series of service encounters and cues

2 Sensory design

3 Requiring frontline employees to engage with customers

4 Paying attention to the dramatic structure of events

5 Managing the presence of fellow customers

6 Closely coupling backstage employees to the front stage experience.

The eventscape model

■ The variables

Bringing together and updating the models discussed previously, there is an opportunity to progress the servicescape concept to develop an eventscape. This is initially through the adaptation of previous models of servicescape by adding variables more pertinent to the events world. These are shown in Table 8.3 and are intended as categories, rather than an exhaustive list.

Eventscape variables

External variables	**Internal variables**	**Human variables**
Exterior signs/displays	Stands/booths/tables	Employee characteristics
Entrances and procedures	Staging	Attendee characteristics
Disabled access	Seating	Employee uniforms
Height/size/colour of building	Catering and consumables	Crowding
Address/location/public transport	Barriers/walkways	Flow and bottlenecks
Surroundings	Flooring/carpeting	Meeting points
Entertainment	Colour schemes/ paint/wallpaper	Privacy (Restroom Catering facilities)
Parking/congestion/traffic	Lighting	Employee-attendee engagement
Security / Stewards	Music/PA/Production	Attendee-attendee interactions
Set design	AV Technology	Quality of speakers and/or entertainment
	Scents	Language and Communication
	Disabled access	
	Merchandise	
	Temperature	
	Cleanliness	
	Washroom facilities	
	Security / stewards	
	Set design	

Layout and design variables	**Event specific design elements**
Space design and allocation	Programme design and content
Placement/grouping of merchandise/props	Signage and event information/interpretation
Reception/work station placement/service or information points/security	Programme/price displays
Placement of equipment/goods for sale/ furniture/lecterns/points of sale	Interactive technology
Waiting areas/green rooms	Drapes
Flow of people and service	Wall/table decorations
Disabled provision	Pictures/artwork/certificates
Waiting queues	Product/organisation
Bottle necks and dead areas	Displays
	Usage instructions
	Point of purchase displays
	Props, gifts, prizes
	Feedback collection
	Set design

Table 8.3: Eventscape variables

These eventscape variables include elements that are generic to events creation but may not necessarily apply to all events. Staging, for example, may be a core requirement for some events, but not all. The wide variety of events clearly means that some variables will be very important at a particular event, but others may be completely unnecessary. The variables detailed below are a toolkit that the event creator has at their disposal. The application of specific elements can only make sense within the strategic event context of any given event situation.

The models of Bitner (1992) and Turley and Milliman (2000) highlight the importance of considering the needs of event employees to ensure their working environment is creating a positive experience for them; not only for their welfare and comfort but also to encourage productivity, safety and engagement with customers or attendees. Of course the level of engagement of different members of staff or employees will depend on their role and expectations thereof. Figure 8.5 is a development of this and illustrates how the eventscape variables in Table 8.3 may be interpreted by individual employees and attendees, depending on their perceptions and situation, to impact on their mood, emotions and ultimate experience.

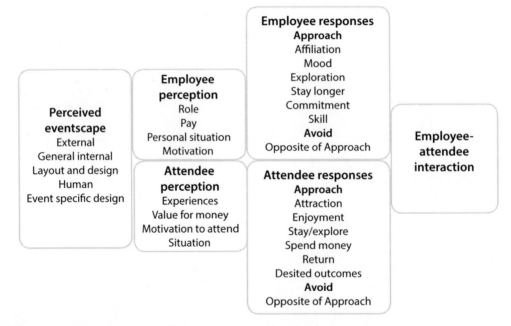

Figure 8.5: Impact of the eventscape for attendees and employees, and their interactions.

Table 8.4 proposes a range of emotions or the 'emotionscape' that should be considered at every stage of the eventscape design process. Every element has the potential to elicit 'approach' or 'avoid' behaviours from attendees and employees alike and the eventscape matrix in Table 8.5 later in the chapter is a useful planning tool to help get this right.

Range of attendee emotions	Range of employee emotions
Ecstasy	Immersion
Surprise	Motivation
Immersion	Engagement
Engagement	Satisfaction
Action	Comfort
Inspiration	Boredom
Motivation	Confusion
Entertainment	Dissatisfaction
Satisfaction	Anger
Comfort	Fear
Boredom	
Confusion	
Dissatisfaction	
Anger	
Fear	

Table 8.4: Potential emotionscape of attendees and staff

Strategically designing the right eventscape

8

■ Eventscape model

We can now apply the principles outlined to help shape the optimum eventscape for any number of events, with the event objectives as the driver. We have previously discussed the cues or clues that will impact on the attendees' experience and emotions and it is important to remember that some of these touch points may occur well before the event; beginning with the initial marketing or invitation, the point of purchase, the build up to the event, the event itself and any post-event evaluation or marketing contact.

Eventscape creation is particularly based upon the outcome obsessed and purposeful design principles outlined in the introductory chapter. Appreciating the strategic context of the events is inherent to event design. This can be facilitated by the ranking of the most important factors; for example the importance of the theme, quality or budget, and are there other stakeholders, such as sponsors, to consider. The relative importance of these factors is dependent on the complexity and type of event.

The next stage is to carefully consider the desired response of the audience; from full participation to passive observation. It is crucial to continuously measure the developing ideas against the original event objective at each stage of the process. Only when these major factors are determined, can the tangible elements of the eventscape be confidently designed and evaluated against each previous set of decisions.

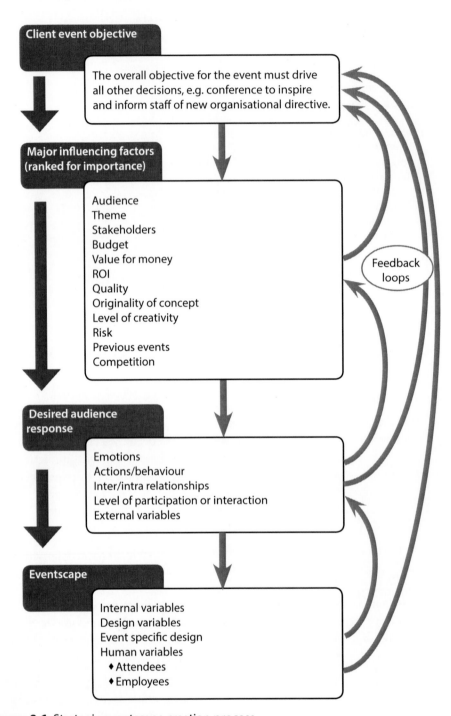

Client event objective

The overall objective for the event must drive all other decisions, e.g. conference to inspire and inform staff of new organisational directive.

Major influencing factors (ranked for importance)

Audience
Theme
Stakeholders
Budget
Value for money
ROI
Quality
Originality of concept
Level of creativity
Risk
Previous events
Competition

Feedback loops

Desired audience response

Emotions
Actions/behaviour
Inter/intra relationships
Level of participation or interaction
External variables

Eventscape

Internal variables
Design variables
Event specific design
Human variables
  ◆ Attendees
  ◆ Employees

Figure 8.6: Strategic eventscape creation process

Industry voice: David Jamilly, Co-Founder, Theme Traders, UK

The essence of any event has to be the fulfilment and enjoyment of the audience and these should be the controlling considerations at all stages of the event cycle. Decisions may be negotiated and renegotiated, creative ideas and operational plans may change many times, attendee numbers alter, budgets increase or decrease, people come and go and ultimately an event may not even proceed, because of any number of internal or external factors.

■ Shaping the eventscape to fit objectives

To facilitate bringing together the best mix of elements to achieve objectives and design decisions, Table 8.5 proposes an eventscape design matrix, which can be adapted for simple or complex events.

The matrix starts with the identification of the variables and eventscape elements that will be used and manipulated to appeal positively to emotions to satisfy client, attendee and employee experiences. Events occur over time (even at a straightforward event, there is a beginning, a middle and an end, requiring operations, programming and content to be delivered in the right order, by the right people at the right time), therefore the matrix provides scope to adapt the table for any event, to analyse each moment in time and inch of space in minute detail or to be used as a broad planning document, cascaded to other departments for development. The matrix encourages consideration of how sensory stimulation can be incorporated at each stage, to further engage with attendees' senses.

Using the matrix, elements that commonly cause dissatisfaction at events (queues, toilets, catering, service, poor management, lack of information, miscommunication) should be considered and those which create satisfaction and delight (surprise, specialness, quality services, quality production, good staff relations, value for money) should be amplified and exploited to create a sustained positive experience. The complexity of the event will also impact on the number of factors to be included in the matrix. .

Each variable may have associated planning documents spread over several pages, or many, many pages, depending on the event and number of phases, spaces, people and content.

8

Variable	Phase/Space	Timeline phase or area of the event / Element	Positive Emotion (Approach) What emotion are you looking at appealing to? (Table 8.4)	Negative Emotion (Avoid) What emotion are you trying to avoid? (Table 8.4)	Importance/Outcome How important is this element, what outcome do we want to stem from that emotion?
External Sensory?	Phase 1 Arrival Outside Venue Sight Sound	e.g. the entrance? Venue People, music?	e.g. curiosity? The entrance gives little away	e.g. the entrance is so hidden people can't find it and feel frustrated.	e.g. Very important first impressions, people are drawn to want to enter, and have a heightened sense of expectation, as they have been given limited, but enough, visual clues as to the event inside.
Internal Variables Sensory?					
Layout and Design Sensory?					
Event Specific Design Elements Sensory?					
Human variables Attendees					
Human variables Employees					

Table 8.5: Eventscape design matrix

Concluding thoughts

At the heart of Strategic Event Creation is the drive to engage with attendees and to achieve the outcomes and objectives of all of the various stakeholders, discarding the notion of 'offering experiences per se' (Zomerdijk and Voss, 2010 p.68). Event creators should move away from trying to guess existing preferences and instead begin to shape them purposefully by 'designing a setting in which the meaning of the experience [event] is created in a favourable way' (Gupta and Vajic, 2000),

The previous chapter outlined the importance of understanding the profile, needs and motivations of attendees, so that events can be purposefully designed to satisfy those needs. What we suggest here is that by building on that knowledge it is possible to use a matrix to carefully plan an eventscape that considers the emotional impacts of the various individual physical elements of an event that make up the whole, and also to elicit positive, memorable associations associated with events so that people (attendees, employees, other stakeholders) feel their expectations are met or exceeded, and consequently events are considered successful from all perspectives.

8

Case study: Theme Traders Ltd. stage the North West Fest. Showcase Event for 70 top industry professionals, July 2014

Brief: To design and deliver a unique must-attend event for highly experienced, successful and discerning industry practitioners.

Object: To create an unforgettable and positive premium experience. To demonstrate top creativity and cutting-edge production techniques with a view to both maintaining pole position in the creative production field and to opening new avenues for future events.

Attendees: Heads of events for major blue chip corporates. Heads of marketing for key media agencies.

Concept: SECRET PARTY. Location to be revealed on the day of the event itself.

Marketing: Superb design hardback luxury invitation, 6 weeks prior, indicating only the area of London, the timings and that food and drink would be provided.

Regular social media teasers were posted throughout the lead-in period building intrigue, for example, asking guests for their shoe sizes. Dedicated website, twitter and facebook.

Design: Guests to experience everything they would have at a normal 2 day festival *but in just 2½ hours through a heightened super-sensory immersive experience.*

(It is important to remember that guests had no idea what the event was until they arrived.)

Meeting Point: (Divulged only on the day): A retro blue camper van in BandQ car park.

On arrival at the camper van, guests were issued with their festival supplies, drinks, sleeping bag, pop up tents and other paraphernalia by our 'hippy' festival folk and a festival map to get to the site itself. They were also changed into UV splattered wellington boots.

They then had to find their own way to the location, a 5-10 minute walk several streets away. Festival stewards in high visibility vests were positioned strategically at street corners and other random characters were planted along the route, including a 'drug dealer' in gold chains and a sheepskin jacket giving out alcoholic sorbets on sticks.

The festival site, which was actually a semi-derelict warehouse complex fluttered with brightly coloured banners and flags. Guests were greeted with loud music and surround sound effects. Bouncers checked them before issuing wristbands for entry.

A large concrete area had been turfed and sectioned off as the campsite complete with random musicians, fragrant falafel van, glitter face painters and a drumming scaffold tower. Guests were encouraged by actors and 'plants' to put up their tents and cook marshmallows over the smoking fire pits and to help graffiti a large white concrete wall. Guests were surprised to encounter already drunken revellers slumped in the portaloos!

Suddenly two rusty shipping containers come to life with loud vibrating drum and base as guests participated in a UV rave inside along with glowing effects (wellingtons, drinks and make-up) and a pumping DJ.

The rave halted and everyone was helped into full white chemical suits and goggles. They then entered a totally white box room with white carpet and hundreds of tubs of coloured powder for the guests to throw. Bhangra beats played as the 'Colour Fest' ensued with high plumes of brightly coloured dust wafting into the air and covering the guests who became technicolour rainbows.

Amid the yelps of fun; thunder and lightning sound effects boom and a small entrance is revealed for everyone to exit and trudge through a boggy mud walkway pit adorned with upside-down umbrellas as a floating ceiling. Water sprays added to the weather effect.

Guests were then helped out of their protective suits and ushered through a tunnel filled with thousands of balloons which needed to be popped in order to gain access to an amazing chill-out room.

Psychedelic projections on all walls and roof, clusters of funky soft furnishings, aroma machines and relaxing mood music all helped to create a feeling of serenity and calmness after all the excitement and activity so far. Drinks and vivacity flowed with ease as guests settled into a mood of comfort and recall of their adventures getting to this point. A giant mushroom character walks through handing out munchies! Hippy chanting, dry ice cocktail stirrers and live Arabic drumming all added to the experience.

Once again, the loud volumes start pumping and curiosity is aroused as confetti, glitter and penny toys seem to be appearing on top of the ceiling. The room although with the appearance of a solid structure is actually totally made of paper. As a live band is heard doing sound checks and the main stage lights shine through the paper, guests spontaneously (sparked by actors) blast through the paper walls, ripping the room down and showering themselves in glitter and confetti. They then found themselves in front of centre festival stage as an amazing band started to play a fusion of folk and hip-hop. They scream for 'more' as the band launches into a last number.

At the end of the last number, all house lights abruptly come on as festival ushers come in and start the clean-up, sweeping and clearing and directing guests back up to the entrance where transport awaits to take them to the local stations.

There were many reports of dazed people wandering around London in festival paraphernalia; mud splattered wellington boots, glittered faces and powdered clothing!

Study questions

1 Using the examples given in Figure 8.2, consider the societal sources of event innovation identified in Figure 8.3 and generate potential new ideas for capitalising on these circumstances.

2 Apply the eventscape model and matrix to the case study example, identifying the objectives, primary outcomes, variables and their emotional and physical impacts. Remember to include the sensory elements and impacts and importance of staff interaction considerations.

3 Clearly innovation and creativity were inherent in the development of the case study event. Discuss the innovations that Theme Traders implemented and their likely impact on the emotional responses of the guests.

References

Berman, B. and Evans, J. R. (1995). *Retail Management: A strategic Approach, 6th Edition*, Prentice-Hall, Inc., Englewood Cliffs, NJ.

Berridge, G., (2007). *Events Design and Experience*. Elsevier, Oxford

Bitner, M. J. (1992). Servicescapes: The impact of physical surroundings on customers and employees. *Journal of Marketing*. **56**(2), pp. 57–71.

Bladen, C., Kennell, J., Abson, E. and Wilde, N. (2012). *Events management: An Introduction*. Routledge

Booms, B.H. and Bitner, M.J. (1981). Marketing strategies and organization structures for service firms, in Donnelly, J.H.and George, W.R. (Eds), *Marketing of Services*, American Marketing Association, Chicago, IL, pp. 47-51

Bowden, G., Allen, J., O'Toole, W., Harris, R. and McDonnell, I. (2010). *Events Management*. 3rd ed. Oxford: Elsevier

Carbone, L. P., and Haeckel, S. H. (1994). Engineering Customer Experiences. *Journal of Marketing Management*, **3** (3), 8-19

Drucker, P. (2007). *Innovation and Entrepreneurship*. Routledge

Getz, D (2005). *Event Management and Event Tourism*. New York: Cognizant

Getz, D. (2012). Event Studies: Discourses and Future Directions. *Event Management*, **16**, 171-187.

Gupta, S. and Vajic, M. (2000). The Contextual and Dialectical Nature of Experiences in Fitzsimmons J.A and Fizsimmons M.J, eds *New Service Development: Creating Memorable Experiences*. Thousand Oaks, CA Sage pp. 35-51

Kotler, P. (1973). Atmospherics as a marketing tool. *Journal of Retailing*. **4**, 48–64.

Kotler, P and Levy, S (1971). Demarketing, yes, demarketing, *Harvard Business Review*, November – December, pp. 74 – 80

Mari, M and Poggesi, S (2013). Servicescape cues and customer behavior: a systematic literature review and research agenda, *The Service Industries Journal*, **33** (2), 171-199,

McGrath, M A. and Otnes, C (1995). Unacquainted influencers:when strangers interact in the retail setting, *Journal of Business Research*, **32** (3), 261–72

Mehrabian, A, and Russell, J A. (1974). *An Approach to Environmental Psychology*, MIT Press, Cambridge, MA.

Mossberg, L. (2007). A marketing approach to the tourist experience. *Scandinavian Journal of Hospitality and Tourism*, **7** (1), 59–74

O'Toole, W. (2011). *Events Feasibility and Development. From Strategy to Operations*. Elsevier Ltd.

Palmer, A. (2011). *Principles of Services Marketing*. McGraw-Hill Higher Education; 6th edition

Pine, J.B. and Gilmore J. H. (1999). *The Experience Economy: Work is Theatre and Every Business a Stage*. Boston: Harvard Business School Press.

Pofeldt, E. (2014). Mastering Meeting Tech. *Conference News* July/August

Rafiq, M. and Ahmed, P. K. (1995). Using the 7Ps as a generic marketing mix: an exploratory survey of UK and European marketing academics, *Marketing Intelligence and Planning*, **13** (9), 4 - 15

Silvers J.R. (2004). *Professional Event Coordination*. John Wiley and Sons, New York

Turley, L. W. and Milliman, R. E. (2000). atmospheric effects on shopping behavior: a review of the experimental evidence, *Journal of Business Research* **49** 193–211

Ward, P., Davies, B. J. and Kooijman, D. (2003) .Ambient smell and the retail environment: relating olfaction research to consumer behavior, *Journal of Business and Management*, **9** (3)

Zeithaml, V. A., Parasuraman, A. and Berry, L. L. (1985). Problems and strategies in services marketing, *Journal of Marketing*, **49** (2) 33-46

Zomerdijk, L.G. and Voss, C. A. (2010). Service Design for Experience-Centric Services. *Journal of Service Research.*

.

8

9 Food and Function

Liz Sharples

Learning objectives

■ Explore the role and significance of the food and drink offer at a range of events.

■ Discuss how the food service element can support and echo the strategic objectives of the event.

■ Provide examples of how the menu experience can be used to enhance the overall event experience.

Introduction

It has long been acknowledged that food and drink plays a vital part in the success of nearly every event, whatever its scale, purpose or significance. An investigation into historical accounts of feasts and festivals held throughout the ages, and in communities around world, emphasizes the importance of food as a central part of religious, political, social and cultural ceremony and celebration. (Tannahill,1988; Kiple and Kriemhild, 2000; Anderson, 2005; Civitello, 2011; amongst others)

For example, early historical accounts of Eleanor de Montfort, Countess of Leicester, reveal the role of the communal meal in political communication in aristocratic households in thirteenth century England (Kjaer, 2011). Eleanor gained a reputation for excellent hospitality wherever she travelled with one account reporting that:

> During the evening here Eleanor richly entertained the citizens
> of Winchelsea, with a meal including 2 oxen, 8 sheep and a
> vast quantity of geese, capons and other fowl; plates were also
> purchased. The 20s.4d. disbursed on bread would have bought
> enough loaves for 356 diners. (Kjaer, 2011).

Food at this event clearly played a key role in providing nourishment and sustenance for Eleanor's retinue and the invited townsfolk. However, perhaps more importantly, the lavish nature of the meal successfully reinforced the host's position and influence within court and wider society. In modern society we witness a similar scenario when a president or member of a royal family entertains visiting dignitaries to their home country with an extravagant banquet which sends clear messages associated with power, position and status.

Food continues to play a key role in the twenty-first century event experience. The budgets, production methods, types of menu, service methods and consumer expectations have changed over the centuries, and there are a myriad of food experiences offered at events around the globe, but many of the core values associated with the giving and receiving of hospitality remain the same. Regardless of the size, purpose or nature of the event, participants have an expectation that they will receive some level of hospitality at nearly every event they attend. Imagine the reaction of guests attending a family wedding where no wedding cake or champagne is served, that spectators would feel when arriving at an open air music festival with no food concession stands available or of delegates travelling to a business meeting to find that there are no refreshments provided.

Quite simply, food is a crucial element of nearly every event and it could be argued that it has the potential to make or break an event experience. Participants rarely comment on food served at an event when it is competent but are quick to criticise if the food is poor. It is essential that the operational aspects of the food and beverage delivery are given full consideration (health and safety, food production/service method, timing of meals and so on) but how do we ensure that the food on offer is also in line with the strategic objectives of the event and will complement and enhance the entire event experience?

Note: (for 'food' read 'food and drink' throughout the chapter)

The academic study of food and events

If we consider the academic progression of an events management student it could be argued that it is not essential for a graduate to have an *in-depth* understanding of the food and hospitality aspect in order to produce a highly successful event. This argument appears to be supported by the academic community as, despite the central role that food plays in many events, the majority of degree level *events* courses in the UK, and indeed in other universities around the world, make little reference to this area of study in their curriculum.

An examination of current event management literature also reveals little about the importance or relevance of food to events, with few food related articles being published in the key events management journals over the last five years. Discussion in the majority of events text books is also limited. For those who wish to find out more about the strategic relevance and importance of food and hospitality to the event experience, it is important to widen the literature search. The following section provides a few signposts for the reader.

As a starting point it is important to recognise that the study of food is complex and attracts scholars from a wide variety of backgrounds. Academic literature is plentiful, with books/journals providing an insight into many fascinating areas of study. Food can be viewed through a variety of lenses including sensory and organoleptic qualities (see *The Journal of Sensory Studies*); social, anthropological and cultural dimensions (see *Food, Culture and Society: An International Journal of Multidisciplinary Research*); food and the environment (see *The Journal of Agricultural Sustainability*) and consumer and nutritional issues (see *The British Food Journal*). There are many others.

The study of hospitality has also become well established as an academic subject over the last forty years, in a number of countries, and this literature provides interesting reading for the events student and professional, in relation to the innovative production/service of food and wine at events and the field of gastronomy. As we will read later in the chapter, in order for an events professional to have an informed conversation with a caterer or hospitality provider, when designing the food element of an event, it is vital to have some appreciation of up to date trends in this area. (See *The International Journal of Hospitality Management*, *International Journal of Contemporary Hospitality Management*, *Gastronomica* amongst others).

The area of literature concerned with experience and emotion, as related to events management, is discussed comprehensively in other chapters (see Chapters 4, 7 and 8) but how this body of knowledge then resonates with the eating/dining provision is important. The linkages that exist between food/hospitality provision and the notion of experience and emotion are well understood in both the academic and business community. The simple act of eating is one that arouses the human senses through taste, texture, sight and smell and chefs and restaurateurs through the ages have become masters of presenting food in a way that excites these senses and creates memories. The phrase 'menu experience', in the hospitality context, has been discussed by a wealth of authors including Wigger (1997) and Stierand and Wood (2012). There is also a mature understanding of how the design/ ambience of a restaurant/eating space (colour schemes, lighting, furniture, table settings and so on) and the style of food service can influence the overall dining experience (see Carvalho de Rezende and Silva, 2014; Chua, et al., 2014). The fascinating relationship between food service and theatre is another rich seam of literature for students to explore (Gardner and Wood, 1991) and see section later in the chapter on food for novelty.

Food and event strategy

Chapter 1 clearly discusses the five guiding principles which should under-pin the thinking which takes place by the event host, the event creator and the stakeholders when co-creating an event. It is therefore important that the food component of any event should not be seen as an afterthought (which too often happens) but instead forms a key part of the master-plan and eventscape (Chapter 8). This must be relevant, and of the right quality, to echo the strategic event objectives.

It is imperative to consider the needs of the various partners and stake-holders to ensure that the food on offer, at the event, is in line with their own personal or organisational objectives. Consider, for example, the chal-lenge if you were tasked with planning an evening party on behalf of the Department of Business, Innovation and Skills (one of the UK Government departments) at the Heal's shop in London, which is well known as a hub for cutting edge design, (see http://www.heals.co.uk), with an objective to bring together and celebrate British design and trade. The event host then informs you that the headline sponsor of this event will be the Dyson company, another global company well known for its invention and cutting edge tech-nology, (see http://www.dyson.co.uk), and the owner, James Dyson, will be the keynote speaker. This scenario presents many challenges with regards to the food package for this event, most importantly the need to serve dishes which are stylish and innovative to reflect the mission of celebrating good design, but as this event is concerned with promoting Britishness the food must also reflect this aim, perhaps by using local food suppliers from the London hinterland.

To further understand how food can be used as part of a strategic plan it is useful to consider the different *roles* that food can play at an event. The following categories are not exhaustive but provide some useful thinking about food, and its function, at events. It is important to acknowledge that the food offer at many events fulfills more than one strategic role; for exam-ple it may have a primary function as *fuel* but also be *sustainably sourced*.

■ Food for fuel and health

Our bodies work at their best if they are provided with the right amount of calories and the right balance of nutrients on a daily basis. An understand-ing of what constitutes a healthy diet is well established, although increas-ing numbers of the population, in developed countries such as the UK and developing countries such as India, choose to ignore this information and the rise of obesity and other weight related diseases such as coronary heart disease and diabetes is of concern to the World Health Organisation (World Health Organisation, 2014).

This poses an interesting question. How much responsibility should event creators take to ensure that a high quality balanced diet is on offer at their event and should this motive be a key part of the overall event strategy? At some events, for example a major sporting event such as the Olympics, this aim is obviously vital to the success of the event and carefully selected caterers will be fully briefed to ensure that all athletes/competitors are receiving the correct nutrition that they need. (See discussion on catering for the Commonwealth Games later in this chapter).

However, increasingly, event creators are acknowledging the fact that good nutrition, provided through the refreshments served at other types of events, such as meetings and conferences, can help in achieving long term health benefits for participants whilst also resulting in better performance/attention at the actual event. Suggestions include: the balancing of carbohydrate and protein throughout the day; limiting portion sizes to ensure that delegates are not overloaded; providing caffeine at key times as a stimulant; offering super/brain foods such as blueberries and oily fish; serving healthy snacks such as fresh fruit and nuts/seeds and making adequate provision for guests with special diets/ allergies/intolerances. At a recent event held by the Law Society in London (Law Society, 2014) the event planning team used a low G.I. (glycemic index) menu and commented:

> Recently a client set us a culinary challenge for their conference that was to be held in the Common Room and Strand, Fleet and Bell Suite. In order to keep their delegates awake, alert and full of creativity, as well as setting a good dietary example, they requested that we create a special, low G.I. diet for the event. The chef team started with some simple substitutions: arrival biscuits were exchanged for yoghurt and granola shots, mid-morning biscuits exchanged for cereal bars and mid-afternoon biscuits were swapped for fruit skewers. For lunch the team tackled the low G.I. challenge by creating a special menu of skinless roasted Norfolk chicken breast with olive oil and rosemary dressed sweet potatoes; line caught mackerel with saffron marinated shaved fennel; cucumber ribbons and new potatoes in a lemon vinaigrette; warm feta cheese, egg and bulgar wheat salad with mixed seeds, red pepper, green beans and olives; mixed green salad leaves with olive and balsamic dressing; warm wholemeal pitta strips and homemade raspberry and lemon cheesecake.

A number of interesting Industry articles (for example Porcellini, 2014 and MPI, 2012) provide useful information about how to cater strategically for delegates with health in mind.

■ Food for prestige and status

Food choice and eating patterns are dictated by a number of factors including gender, background, ethnicity, economic status, and lifestyle (Keane and Willetts, 1994). It could be argued that as twenty-first century consumers we have become increasingly sophisticated and cosmopolitan having the ability to select from a wide range of food opportunities and experiences, both in supermarkets and in restaurants throughout the world (Warde, 1997). Dining out is seen as a regular leisure activity for many people in the developed world and some consumer sectors have become accustomed to purchasing specialist food products (Wycherley, A. et al, 2008) and sparkling wines, like Prosecco, as part of their weekly shop (Business Wire, 2014).

This results in a challenge for both event creators and event caterers. Event participants and delegates are no longer satisfied with simple meal options, such as a ham and cheese sandwich lunch and a simple 'meat and two veg' dinner. If the event host has stated that one of the primary event objectives is about creating a sense of luxury, status and prestige at the event then the food and drink on offer must match this aspiration.

Consider, for example, the staging of the third American Express World Luxury Expo to be held in the Riyadh Kingdom of Saudi Arabia in 2015. The event website states that the exhibition will "showcase the world's leading luxury brands, to an ultra-affluent and highly discerning target audience" (American Express World Luxury Expo, 2014). Guests are carefully selected from a number of databases such as elite associations, luxury shops and private banks. Typical visitor profiles include members of the royal family, international business decision-makers and leaders of key member associations. This exclusive event of three thousand guests facilitates networking with suppliers of fine art, private banking, antiques, gems, yachts, fashion, real estate and private aviation over three days. Event partners include American Express, the Saudi Investment Bank, *Bespoke*, a luxury lifestyle publication and *Sayidaty*, a Pan Arab women's magazine.

How does the event creator meet the hospitality and food needs of this demanding audience? Their solution is to stage the event at the five starred Ritz Carlton Hotel, originally envisioned as a guest palace for visiting dignitaries and heads of state. The selection of this venue immediately gives the event host, creator and partners a feeling of confidence. The hotel is home to six world class restaurants and a brigade of highly experienced chefs, more than capable of providing an extensive range of event menus to meet the complex needs of these delegates (http://www.ritzcarlton.com/en/Properties/Riyadh/Meetings/Culinary.htm).

9

The following case study reinforces the importance of selecting the right venue and level of catering provision when wanting to provide food for a prestigious group of guests.

Case study: The World Economic Forum

The World Economic Forum (WEF) is an international not-for-profit foundation, established in 1971, with its headquarters in Geneva, Switzerland. It is independent and impartial and is committed to improving the state of the world through public-private co-operation. The WEF works closely with many major international bodies and engages business, political, academic and other society leaders in an effort to shape future global and regional agendas. It works in a 'spirit of global citizenship' (World Economic Forum, 2014) with 'moral and intellectual integrity' (World Economic Forum, 2014) at the heart of its decision making.

The Forum holds its annual event in Davos-Klosters, Switzerland which is a 'mash-up' (Manuel, 2014) of business, political, celebrity and charity guests. In 2014 the theme was 'The Reshaping of the World: Consequences for Society, Politics and Business' and its three day programme included 250 speakers including David Cameron (UK Prime Minister), Anshu Jain (CEO Deutsche Bank, Germany) and Matt Damon (Actor and Water. Org, USA).

The WEF event has a serious mission and facilitates important discussion but the event hosts are also keen to simply get people to talk and network, regardless of their background.

'Jimmy Wales, the co-founder of Wikipedia, tells of a dance floor encounter at Davos a couple of years ago when he was dancing to Maroon 5's 'Moves Like Jagger' and turned around to find the real Mick Jagger, of the Rolling Stones, dancing next to him 'The thing about Davos', he says, 'is that everyone comes eventually' (Manuel, 2014).

Catering for this unique group of people presents an interesting challenge, with many private parties being hosted around the town, as well as the official receptions. In the main hotel, the Belvedere, over 320 parties took place over five days in 2014 generating 35% of the hotel's annual revenue, (Young, 2014) with staff serving:

- 1,594 bottles of Champagne and Prosecco
- 3,088 bottles of red and white wine
- 3,807 cups of coffee and tea
- 80kg of salmon
- 16,805 canapes
- 1,565 mini pizzas
- 1,350 chocolate-covered strawberries

Meticulous planning goes on throughout the year with key staff from the WEF but also with representatives of the following year's delegates, who may wish to hold their own party. The expert kitchen brigade needs to be totally flexible with Maik Baatsch, Sous Chef, reporting of having 20 minutes to arrange an unexpected party for 50 people at a previous forum. 'We had 40 chefs in the kitchen, each of them made a dish for five, and that was that' (Young, 2014). He spent the Tuesday night with 20 Korean chefs preparing for the Korean party, which included the country's president, top Samsung executives and the international pop-star Psy (Young, 2014).

Inevitably when catering for an international, diverse, prestigious and demanding clientele there are challenges; providing food of an exceptional quality whilst meeting complex ethnic and dietary requirements. Kosher, halal, vegetarian, vegan, gluten-free, lactose-free menus are all in a day's work for the catering team and if special ingredients are needed they will be sourced regardless of cost.

■ Food for community, celebration and symbolism

Food, for thousands of years, has been closely intertwined with the concept of socialisation and celebration amongst families, friends, colleagues and communities. The majority of people are familiar with the notion of gathering around a table, or in a communal space such as a church, a village hall or a local hotel, with people whom they know well (and sometimes new people too), with an aim to create strong bonds and/or to celebrate a special occasion. Food at many events plays a powerful social role and can range from a simple Harvest supper, to celebrate a specific point in the agricultural calendar, (still marked in many rural communities around the world), to an elaborate wedding feast with extended family and invited guests. Mennel et. al, (1992) and others comment on this practice highlighting the importance of *commensality* – the forging of friendship and mutual obligation through the act of eating and drinking together. Many twenty first century event hosts and creators embrace this concept and carefully design their food offer to strategically support socialisation, communication and networking at their events. A number of specialised event companies take this idea one step further, offering bespoke corporate team-building days which use food activities as their focus (see www.foodatwork.co.uk).

The symbolic coming together around a table, or in a venue, to share food is usually pleasurable but there has always been an understanding that the organisation of refreshments at social events can sometimes be challenged by the power structures of family, gender and social status (see Nugent and Clark, 2010). Think about the difficult situations that can arise when planning a family wedding! The event creators therefore need to be sensitive to such considerations in their event design.

9

At some social occasions, such as those attached to national and religious holidays (Easter and Christmas for example), *specific* foods are highly symbolic and deeply embedded in the rituals of that event. Consider, for example, the different types of traditional cakes made in communities around the world, such as *bolo rei* in Portugal, *stollen* in Germany and *panforte* in Italy to mark the Christmas season. Many of these incorporate dried/glacé fruit and spices, and it is interesting to note that even the smell of these ingredients can evoke strong memories of family and childhood connected to this festival. Other events are strongly linked to key points in our lives, such as the birth of a child, the coming of age or the joining of two people in marriage. Food at these events is rooted in tradition and an examination of foods served at wedding feasts around the word makes interesting reading. Chudova (2011) reports on the wedding rituals of the Komi/Zyrian people, an ethnic group whose homeland is in the north-east of European Russia:

> In the context of wedding rituals, food serves as an integrating symbol which aims to unite the parties of the bride and the groom, creating a new group of relatives. The fertility and wealth of the young couple is modelled with the help of the culinary code. The bread and salt of the wedding feast act as a symbol of wealth and love, and perform a protective function. Fowl and eggs in wedding rituals act as specific markers of mythological time.

In the twenty first century despite the fact that many of us live in urban settings, enjoying a technologically driven 24/7 lifestyle which is far removed from the natural rhythms associated with the growing of crops, or the changing of the seasons, we still take pride in punctuating our lives with celebratory events. Sometimes the food offering stays true to its historical and cultural roots but inevitably the commodification and globalisation of food has led to some interesting developments. Wedding cakes still retain their symbolic significance at the heart of a wedding celebration but are now styled and themed to fit the overall wedding concept, as event design becomes ever more sophisticated (Choccywoccydoodah, 2014 and Jane Asher, 2014). Another interesting adaptation is the moon cake, a sweet filled pastry product, traditionally given to family and friends to commemorate the Mid-Autumn Festival in China (Zhongqiujie). This traditional product has assumed a more commercial role with elaborate, branded pastries, made by Haagen Daaz and Starbucks, assuming the new norm amongst younger consumers who present boxed mooncakes to work colleagues and important clients (Branigan, 2012).

■ Food for sustainability

Over the last forty years the relationship between global food production and the environment has been at the crux of many discussions by governments, academics, the agricultural community and environmental lobbying groups. Their focus is simple; how do we ensure that we can feed a rising global population in a fair and sustainable way? (Earth Summit, 2012). This debate is complex, and highly political, but there is no doubt that this is a hot topic for individuals and also amongst the business community. A number of UK food scares, such as the BSE/CJD crisis in the 1980s, (Food Standards Agency, 2014) and the Foot and Mouth outbreaks in 2001 and 2007 (DEFRA, 2008) have challenged our understanding of how food is grown/produced/manufactured and the publication of the landmark *Food Miles* report (Paxton, 1994), sharpened consumer focus about the global transportation of food.

The outcome of this growing awareness of the relationship between food and the environment has created a demand, amongst some consumers, for food that is produced in a more sustainable way and, in particular, for locally/regionally sourced food with clear provenance. There has also been a growth in demand for organic (Soil Association, 2014) and Fairtrade produce (Fairtrade, 2013). In 2009 WWF-UK launched its One Planet Food programme, with an aim to reduce the environmental and social impacts of food consumption in the UK. They work across the food chain to reduce greenhouse gas emissions (GHGEs), protect biodiversity and reduce the impact of food on finite water resources. The aim is to move towards sustainable food choices which support global agriculture and biodiversity. Their 2011 report (WWF, 2011) provides a good overview. Restaurateurs and caterers have chosen to capture this growing interest in the environment, and responsible sourcing, and many now create menus that reflect their locality. This mission has been championed by a number of celebrity chefs including Hugh Fearnley-Whittingstall at River Cottage (http://www.rivercottage.net) and Rick Stein in Padstow (www.rickstein.com).

9

It is therefore fitting that if an event host and creator have a requirement to promote good environmental practice, as a key part of an overarching event strategy, it is appropriate that the food element reinforces, and dovetails with, this message. This drive towards sustainable food provision is also in line with new event industry environmental standards which have been showcased at a number of recent major events. For example, the *Food Vision* document created for London 2012 served as a blueprint for the contract caterers and food suppliers involved with the event (London, 2012) and for other events that followed.

Smaller, regional events are also reaping the rewards of providing local, fresh food with clear traceability. The Freedom Festival held in Hull, UK, is one of Yorkshire's largest and most prolific arts events, attracting 80,000 visitors in 2013. The following statement from their website (http://www.freedomfestival.co.uk) outlines their food mission and lays down strict sustainability criteria for caterers who wish to get involved:

Freedom Festival Ltd is offering a number of catering spaces to reflect the theme associated with the festival. Traders will be selected on the basis of quality and integrity of produce. Quality is understood in terms of taste and authenticity, and integrity extends to environmental and social responsibility. We look to promote the best food and drink that does not harm our environment, food producers, animal welfare and human health.

Priority will be given to providers of innovative cuisine, representing local, national and international flavours, utilising fresh, locally sourced, fair trade produce and sustainable packaging, and it is a requirement that all ingredients fit the following minimum standards:

☐   Meat – Red Tractor/RSPCA Freedom Food assured

☐   Fish – derived from sustainable sources (MSC/organic certified)

☐   All caterers must be able to document the production and traceability of their product.

■ Food for authenticity

The idea of achieving an authentic dimension, with regards to the food served at an event, is associated with a drive to showcase the 'true' or 'real' origins/cultural dimensions linked to certain foods and cuisines. An extensive number of studies have examined the construct of food and authenticity, from a number of different standpoints, and themes including provenance, ethnicity, place, time and uniqueness have emerged (Kuzenof et al.,1997; Bessiere, 1998; Beer, 2008; Sims, 2009; amongst others). As event creators in a competitive marketplace, who seek to differentiate and provide enhanced experiences, a focus on authenticity in the food offer could be appealing and appropriate at some events.

In practice it is interesting to see how authenticity is played out in a modern real life setting. For example, when a restaurant describes its offer as serving 'authentic Italian food' what does this mean? Is the menu styled on a peasant diet as consumed in a rural region of Italy two hundred years ago, or are guests likely to be served a freshly made calzone pizza served with a glass of Pinot Grigio? This area of study includes some fascinating debates as regional and national cuisines have changed and flexed significantly over the centuries and it is sometimes challenging to distinguish fact from fiction (Taylor, 2012).

The discussion of how the notion of authenticity can be used in a strategic plan to create distinct and memorable food service experiences, for example, at heritage/cultural events, has received limited attention in the literature.

However, a study by Robinson and Clifford (2011) which discusses how the foodservice experience, created at a Medieval festival in Australia, had successfully augmented specific aspects of event authenticity, and prompted repeat visits, is useful. This study and others report that although catering is sometimes seen as a secondary activity, at many heritage/cultural events, an appropriate innovative food service offer, directly linked to the event objectives, has the potential to "intimately engage and submerse consumers into various cultural, spiritual, spatial and temporal places" (Sims, 2009). In reality this may be the smell of a simple game stew cooking in a large cauldron over an open fire at a historical re-enactment event, the visual impact of a hog roast served at a Medieval fair or the pouring of a foaming glass of apple juice which has just been pressed in a traditional wooden press, in front of the visitors using apples from the local orchard.

In this section it is also important to note that food or drink can sometimes be the *primary* activity of a cultural/heritage event rather than the supporting activity. There has been a significant growth of highly successful food, beer and wine festivals around the world and this is well documented by a number of authors. (for example, Hall and Sharples, 2008).

An example of this is the staging of a number of events at the World Heritage site of Hadrian's Wall to commemorate its 2000 year history. The following description demonstrates how the food experience can sit right at the heart of a family orientated event;

> Almost 2000 years on and amazingly Hadrian's Wall is still 'here'. English Heritage is celebrating the 72-mile long World Heritage Site that dips and winds through two counties in a week long programme of events. During May half-term, join us for a week-long celebration of all things Roman. Birdoswald Roman Fort will become a centre of Roman food and cooking; enjoy samples of food you never knew existed and be surprised by traditions that stem from our Roman ancestors. Tantalize your taste buds and see our Roman potter demonstrate his craft in this one-off surprising event. (English Heritage, 2014).

■ Food for novelty

As mentioned earlier in this chapter, the relationship that exists between food service at restaurants or banquets, and the theatre is long established. When we enter a restaurant, or fine dining experience at an event, we become part of the set with the waiting staff as actors performing around us, as they stylishly present our food from the opening scene, through to the closing of the stage curtains as we leave.

We also know that a fine line has existed for many years between haute cuisine and art. A glimpse into magnificent illustrations of cakes and puddings appearing in early cookery books (for example, *Mrs Beeton's Book of Household Management*, first published 1861) confirms that food at this level is more than basic fuel, with eye appeal being of equal importance.

Well known chefs in the nineteenth and early twentieth centuries, including Careme (1784–1833) and Escoffier (1846–1935) set the standard in Europe, creating modes of practice for kitchen/restaurant operations, which established the notion of serving dishes sequentially (away from the Medieval banquet where all the food was placed on the table at once), and starting to catalogue the classic repertoire of dishes which have become the backbone of chef's training over the last two hundred years.

In the 1960s however there was a shift in thinking and chefs, including Paul Bocuse and Alain Chapel in France, 'began to rebel against the rigid rules of cuisine classique' (Abrams, 2013b). By the early 1970s the term Nouvelle Cuisine was born. One of the key transitions was a trend towards lighter food and the individual plating of each course for each diner in order to achieve maximum visual effect (Gayot, 2014).

The blending of food and art gets ever closer as modern chefs such as Heston Blumenthal at the Fat Duck, UK (http://www.thefatduck.co.uk) and the Roca brothers at El Cellar de Can Roca, Spain (http://cellercanroca.com/index.htm) continue to push culinary boundaries, designing dishes with unique flavour combinations and using new types of technology to prepare, cook and serve food with huge flair and originality. This direction of travel has been adopted by many event caterers and there is now an understanding that food, carefully planned, is capable of providing novelty, excitement and surprise as part of the strategic design of an event. For example, the use of liquid nitrogen allows event caterers to 'magically' conjure up ice cream in seconds, in front of their guests, and new developments with ice production allows the event creator to introduce drama into cocktail/bar service (Abrams, 2013a) producing sculptural drinks that are edible works of art.

The aim to introduce novelty in the food on offer at events is not restricted however to haute cuisine. At the California State Fair, thousands of visitors queue to buy food from one of 125 food vendors where novelty is the buzz word:

> side-show dishes are the attention-grabbers…created by
> concessionaires who spend their off-time in mad-scientist mode,
> obsessed with research and development. It's almost a competition
> or a matter of pride to see who can come up with the most startling
> dishes, and the public is always game to try them….daring diners
> sample the likes of alligator tail and fudge-covered scorpions….

cheeseburgers topped with deep-fried ice cream, hot beef sundaes and deep-fried beer. ..last year's top novelty was the Big Rib, 2 pounds of smoked USDA prime beef attached to a 17-inch-long cow rib bone, giving new dimension to the 'on a stick' template (Pierleoini, 2014).

From strategic creation to concept development

Having considered the strategic role that food can play at events, how can we ensure that our objectives can be successfully delivered by the catering team, a key stakeholder, who will interpret our ideas and put them into practice?

The scale and complexity of food delivery at events varies greatly from a simple 'fuel-stop' lunch served in a company board room, to a multi-concession operation serving thousands of visitors attending Chelsea Flower Show. In-house catering teams successfully deliver high quality food experiences at many events, held in venues around the world, for example the 5 starred hotel which was discussed earlier in the chapter. In this scenario chefs can safely rely on well-equipped storage, production, and service facilities. Many events, however, use an external specialist who is contracted to deliver a bespoke food experience with food being prepared on or off-site. Each outside caterer has its own specialism and capability. (See Sodexho at www.sodexoprestige.co.uk, Rhubarb at www.rhubarb.net/events/corporate-events and The Admirable Crichton at www.admirable-crichton.co.uk). Catering technologies, such as sous-vide and cook-chill, play a major part in modern event catering ensuring large quantities of food can be served safely, efficiently and with excellent plate appeal.

As event managers it is easy to assume that this aspect of our event will be looked after by specialist outside caterers, or food and beverage departments in venues, who are far more knowledgeable about this area than we are? Although we may not be experts in food production/service, the relationship and communication channel that we establish with partners, such as caterers, and the detailed brief that we produce together as co-creators, will be key to an event's success.

So what is the starting point for an event creator who is keen to ensure that the food on offer at their event is a good reflection of the strategic event objectives? To conclude this chapter we look at the highly successful process that was adopted when preparing for one recent major event.

9

Case study: The 2014 Commonwealth Games

The following excerpts are taken from documentation prepared for the 2014 Commonwealth Games in Glasgow and clearly show the progression of ideas from the development of the general mission and sustainability statements (A) to the development of a statement which outlines the key objectives of the Catering Operation (B) to the establishment of their Food Charter (C) and finally the advert for attracting contractors (D). You will clearly see here that several strategic messages are maintained throughout the documentation to ensure that all stakeholders have a clear message of what they intend to co-create.

A. From the Introductory section of the 2013 Business Plan and Sustainability Plan

'The Commonwealth Games in 2014 will be a spectacular display of **world-class sporting talent**. But success won't just be measured in medals. It'll be measured in **jobs and the development of our businesses.** And it'll be measured in the **number of people getting active** and making use of the facilities available in our communities

'The team at Glasgow 2014 comprises everyone who has a role in delivering the Games, which includes **contractors, suppliers, stakeholders and volunteers**. We are a **diverse and inclusive organisation** in which everyone plays a significant role. We have one common goal – to deliver an outstanding and memorable Commonwealth Games. **Our people** are key to making this happen'.

'Crucial to this vision is staging a Games which set a **high benchmark with regards to sustainability**. This benchmark has been clearly set out in the OC's Environmental and Sustainability Policy. The OC are committed to **sourcing sustainably**, ensuring that all required goods and services are procured to an end that demonstrates, wherever feasible, **ethical, social, environmental and economic benefits'**

(Glasgow2014 - 2013 Business Plan, 2014)

(Glasgow2014 Sustainability, 2014)

B. From the 2013 Business Plan which discusses Catering Provision for the Games

'The team's aim throughout 2013 will be to finalise and execute in excess of 60 contractual agreements with specialist services companies to deliver **efficient, timely, consistent, sustainable and friendly levels of service**. Following contract awards, Catering, Cleaning and Waste will manage selected companies to achieve project timelines that guarantee Games readiness. This includes the anticipated recruitment, training and accreditation of a more than 6,000-strong skilled workforce of chefs, food and drink services attendants, management, cleaners, waste collection and waste processing personnel. **The team will work with a group of past and present Commonwealth athletes in a food focus group to generate feedback regarding Athletes' Village**

dining, and the 1,000-plus food items required to **help all competitors perform at their best, while providing a taste of home.**

The Commonwealth Games Food Charter will be developed **with the advice of stakeholders** and will provide **defined ethical standards** to catering service contract companies'.

(Glasgow2014 - 2013 Business Plan, 2014)

C. The Commonwealth Games 2014 Food Charter

'The **legacy** of the Food Charter will act as a **blueprint** for major sporting and cultural events held in Scotland beyond the Games. As well as showcasing the Scottish larder, it outlines a commitment to the **ethical, safe, and healthy-living** standards for all food served across the Games, including **traceability**. The **provenance** of food, **where it comes from and how it has been produced**, is central to the Charter which will establish Games-time **food sourcing standards**. Glasgow 2014 seeks to **showcase Scottish produce** to help contribute to the **wider industry ambition to grow the value of the sector** and develop **Scotland's reputation as a Land of Food and Drink**. The Food Charter has been developed with advice from a range of stakeholders, including government agencies, educators, health agencies, Non-Governmental Organisations:

Scottish Government Food and Drink Industry Division; Scotland Food and Drink (and related industry stakeholders including Quality MeatScotland; Seafood Scotland; Scottish Bakers and Soil Association Scotland); Scottish Enterprise; Glasgow City Council; Food Standards Agency – Scotland; British Hospitality Association; Glasgow Restaurant Association

One of Glasgow's obligations is to stage a Games with **responsible environmental and sustainability** standards. It aims to minimise its impact on the environment and seek opportunities that will enhance the environment. Glasgow 2014 also aims to **promote healthy living**, and will do this via the provision of a variety of **authentic foods, including healthier options**. The Food Charter will contribute to a key objective of both Glasgow 2014 and the Scottish Government's Legacy 2014 programme: to **improve the health of Scotland's population**, with a particular focus on the prevention of obesity. Glasgow 2014's challenge is to deliver a catering programme that **meets the needs of many stakeholders** while remaining **on time and on budget**; and within **space, security and supplier constraints**.

It will strive for **best value** and encourage **open and transparent procurement** of catering services and food supplies from businesses in Scotland, the EU and beyond. Glasgow 2014 will publicise its successes, knowledge and good practice to emphasise the message that its Food Charter demonstrates commitment to sustainable procurement and to achieving **good outcomes for athletes, for people working or attending the Games, and for food suppliers.**

(Glasgow2014 Food Charter, 2014)

D. The Advert for Contract Caterers

'We are looking for Catering Service companies with the proven ability to consistently deliver throughout the Glasgow 2014 Commonwealth Games Villages and Venues a variety of food and drink products and services that are **inclusive, creative, healthy, value for money, of dependable quality and served in a friendly, efficient and timely manner**.'

(Glasgow2014.com/media, 2014)

The following statements (Glasgow2014 Commonwealth Games, 2014) made by a number of key stakeholders/partners associated with the event provide valuable feedback for the event host and creator and allow them to see the key strategic role that food has played in the event ensuring its strong legacy:

> Scotland's food and drink is among the world's finest, so it's fitting that Glasgow 2014's Food Charter should set a new benchmark for the country's major events.... this Charter is the result of a great partnership between the Games and Scotland's food and drink industry and demonstrates our shared ambitions for the highest standards in the sourcing of produce consumed during Glasgow 2014 by everyone from athletes to spectators… the Commonwealth Games is an opportunity to showcase Scotland's outstanding produce and the values behind it to our visitors from across the globe.

> *David Grevemberg, Glasgow 2014 Chief Executive.*

> Next year, Scotland's rich natural larder will be sampled by visitors from all over the world, particularly during the 2014 Commonwealth Games in Glasgow … throughout the Games, the Athletes' Village and all the Games venues will benefit from this innovative Food Charter; a promise to proudly serve Scottish food of the highest quality and traceable provenance. Glasgow 2014 anticipates serving over two million meals, with the finest home-grown produce providing the backbone of this huge catering operation

> *James Withers, Chief Executive, Scotland Food and Drink*

> It is important that all competing athletes eat the best possible range and standard of food to fuel their performance levels during the Glasgow 2014 Commonwealth Games… through the Food Focus Group, the Athletes' Advisory Committee have been involved in discussions to help ensure happens at Glasgow 2014 and we welcome today's Food… I look forward to seeing the principles and standards set out in the Commonwealth Games Food Charter used as a basis for a wider Food and Drink Charter for Events in Scotland. This will present a great opportunity for Scottish food and drink businesses to supply good quality, healthy, authentic food and drink at local, national and international events across the country starting in our second Year of Food and Drink in 2015.'

> *Rhona Simpson, Chair of the Glasgow 2014 Athletes' Advisory Committee*

Study questions

1 Consider a local event that you are familiar with. Using the framework provided in the chapter (which proposes a number of strategic roles that food can assume) write a 500-750 word proposal which you could use when tendering for a contract caterer(s) for the event.

2 Consider your own knowledge of food and beverage management as part of Strategic Event Creation. Having read this chapter produce a reflective personal audit and development plan for yourself to improve your understanding of this key area.

References

Abrams, J. (2013a). On performing the ephemeral; on ice cream and the theatre, *Performance Research*, **18** (6), 112 -121

Abrams, J. (2013b). Mise en Plate, the scenographic imagination and the contemporary restaurant, *Performance Research*, **18** (3), 7-14

American Express World Luxury Expo, (2014). worldluxuryexpo-riyadh.com, accessed 08/09/2014

Anderson, E.N. (2005). *Everyone Eats: Understanding Food and Culture*, New York University Press, New York

Beer, S. (2008). Authenticity and food experience: Commercial and academic perspectives, *Journal of Foodservice*, **19**, 153-163

Bessiere, J. (1998). Local development and heritage: traditional food and cuisine as tourist attractions in rural areas, *Sociologia Ruralis*, 38(1), 21-34

Branigan, T. (2012). Mooncakes, China's traditional festive gift, are getting a makeover, The Guardian 27 Sept. www.theguardian.com/world/ 2012sep/27/ mooncakes-china-traditional-festive-gift, accessed 22/07/2014

Business Wire, (2014). Research and Markets UK Wine Market update. www. researchandmarkets.com/research/9k6hvh/wine-market, accessed 20/08/14

Carvalho de Rezende, D. and Silva, M. A. R. (2014). Eating out and experiential consumption: a typology of experience providers, *British Food Journal*, **116** (1)

Choccywoccydoodah, (2014). www.choccywoccydoodah.com/bespoke-cakes.html, accessed 10/07/2014

Chua, B., Jin, N., Lee, S. and Goh, B. (2014). Influence of mechanic, functional and humanic clues on customers experiential values and behavioural intentions in full service restaurants, *Foodservice Business Research*, **17** (2), 67- 84

Chudova, T.I. (2011). Food symbolism in the connect of Komi (Zyrians) wedding rituals, *Archaeology, Ethnology and Anthropology of Eurasia*, **39** (3)

9

Civitello, L. (2011). *Cuisine and Culture, A History of Food and People,* 3rd edition, Wiley, New Jersey

DEFRA, (2008). Foot and mouth disease 2007: a review and lessons learned. www.gov.uk/government/publications/foot-and-mouth-disease-2007-a-review-and-lessons-learned, accessed 10/08/2014

Earth Summit, (2012). www.earthsummit2012.org/about-us/previous-summits, accessed 10/08/2014

English Heritage, (2014). Hadrian's Wall Festival, Roman Food and Cooking, www.english-heritage.org.uk/daysout/events/hadrians-wall-festival-roman-food--cooking-Bir-24-05-2014, accessed 20/07/2014

Fairtrade, (2013). Annual Report, www.fairtrade.org.uk/en/whatisfairtrade/socialannualreports, accessed 15/08/2014

Food Standards Agency (2014). food.gov.uk/business-industry/farmingfood/bse, accessed 10/08/2014.

Gardner, K. and Wood, R.C. (1991). Theatricality in food service work, *International Journal of Hospitality Management,* **10** (3), 267-278

Gayot, A. (2014), The true story of this French culinary revolution, www.gayot.com/restaurants/features/nouvellecuisine.html, accessed 30/08/2014

Glasgow2014 - 2013 Business Plan (2014). www.glasgow2014.com/document/annual-business-plan-2013, accessed 20/08/14

Glasgow2014.com/media, (2014) Glasgow 2014 has a taste for games time catering services at venues and villages. www.glasgow2014.com/media-centre/press-releases/glasgow-2014-has-taste-games-time-catering-services-venues-and-villages, accessed 20/08/14

Glasgow2014 Commonwealth Games (2014). www.glasgow2014.com/media-centre/press-releases/glasgow-2014-places-food-charter-top-menu-commonwealth-games, accessed 20/08/14

Glasgow2014 Food Charter (2014). legacy2014.co.uk/news/glasgow-2014-food-charter, accessed 20/08/14

Glasgow2014 Sustainability (2014). www.glasgow2014.com/procurement-sustainability-policy, accessed 20/08/14

Hall, C.M. and Sharples, L. (2008). *Food and Wine Festivals around the World,* Elsevier, Oxford

Heston Blumenthal (2012). www.telegraph.co.uk/news/uknews/9586987/Hestons-orange-Christmas-puddings-already-on-eBay.html, accessed 01/08/2014

Jane Asher (2014). www.janeasher.com/celebration-cakes, accessed 08/07/2014

Keane, A and Willetts, A (1994). Factors that affect food choice, *Nutrition and Food Science,* **94** (4)

Kjaer, L. (2011). Food, drink and ritualised communication in the household of Eleanor de Montfort, February to August 1265, *Journal of Medieval History*, **37**(1), 75–89

Kiple, K.F. and Kriemhild, C.O. (2000). *The Cambridge World History of Food*, Vol. 1, Cambridge University Press, Cambridge.

Kuzenof, S., Tregear, A., and Moxey, A. (1997). Regional foods: A consumer perspective. *British Food Journal*, **99**, 199-206

Law Society (2014). www.113chancerylane.co.uk/latest-news/keep-your-delegates-creative, accessed 08/07/2014

London 2012 (2012). www.sustainweb.org/resources/files/reports/London_2012_Food_Vision.pdf, accessed 08/08/14.

Manuel, G. (2014). www.efinancialnews.com/story/2014-01-20/davos-preview-who-is-who-at-the-world-economic-forum?ea9c8a2de0ee111045601ab04d673622, accessed 22/08/14

Mennel, S., Murcott, A., van Otterloo, A. (1992). Commensality and Society, *Current Sociology*, **40** (2).

MPI (2012). www.mpiweb.org/Magazine/MPINews/20120201/Food_for_Thought, accessed 08/08/2014

Nugent, J. and Clark, M. (2010). A loaded plate, food symbolism and the early modern Scottish household, *Scottish Historical Studies*, **30** (1)

Paxton, A. (1994). The Food Miles Report: The dangers of long-distance food transport, SAFE Alliance, London, UK. www.sustainweb.org/publications/?id=191, accessed 10/01/2014

Pierleoni, A. (2014). Dining at the State Fair is all about novelty food. www.sacbee.com/2014/07/06/6532472/dining-at-the-state-fair-is-all.html, accessed 20/08/2014

Porcellini, T. (2014). Use food as fuel for conference meals and breaks. www.connectyourmeetings.com/how-to-use-food-as-fuel-for-conference-meals, accessed 08/07/2014

Robinson, N.S. and Clifford, C. (2011). Authenticity and festival foodservice experiences, *Annals of Tourism Research*, **39** (2), 571- 600

Sims, R. (2009). Food, place and authenticity: Local food and the sustainable tourism experience, *Journal of Sustainable Tourism*, **17**(3), 321-336.

Soil Association, (2014). Organic Market Report at www.soilassociation.org/marketreport, accessed 10/08/2014

Stierand, M. and Wood, R.C. (2012). Reconceptualising the commercial meal experience in the hospitality industry, *Hospitality and Tourism Management*, **19**, 118 -123

Tannahill, R. (1998). *Food in History*, 2nd edition, Penguin, London.

Taylor, A.L. (2012). www.bbc.co.uk/food/0/19648820, accessed 05/08/2014

Warde, A. (1997). *Consumption, food and taste: culinary antinomies and commodity culture*, Sage, London

9

Wigger, G.E. (1997). *Themes, dreams and schemes: banquet menu ideas, concepts and thematic experiences*, Wiley, New York.

World Economic Forum (2014). www.weforum.org, accessed 14/08/2014.

World Health Organisation (2014). www.who.int/research/en, accessed 01/08/2104.

WWF (2011). Live well: a balance of healthy and sustainable food choices, WWF UK in collaboration with Rowett Institute of Nutrition and Health, University of Aberdeen. www.assets.wwf.org.uk/downloads/livewell_report_Jan11.pdf, accessed 28/08/2014

Wycherley, A., McCarthy, M., Cowan, C. (2008). Speciality food orientation of food related lifestyle (FRL) segments in Great Britain, *Food Quality Preference*, **19** (5).

Young, E. (2014). Davos 2014: Hosting the rich and famous. www.bbc.co.uk/news/business-25843923, accessed 20/08/2014

10 Marketing Events:
Three perspectives to support Strategic Event Creation

Craig Hirst and Richard Tressider

Learning objectives

- Recognise and distinguish between the three broad perspectives that underlie event marketing thought and practice.

- Hold a broader view of the roles that event participants play in constructing their experiences and value during their interactions at events, and the implications that this holds for event marketing practice.

- Recognise how a more strategic approach could benefit event creators.

Introduction

This chapter presents three perspectives of marketing to aid Strategic Event Creation and to facilitate the shaping and co-creation of valuable and meaningful event participant experiences. Specifically we draw on a framework which suggests that successful event marketing should encompass a broad and deep understanding of three distinct yet interrelated points of view (Tresidder and Hirst, 2012). In essence this framework is aligned with a consumer marketing perspective, but a range of the ideas could be applied to business to business contexts, in the sense that the underlying themes facilitate a greater understanding of how value and meanings are created and produced through the marketing and event design process.

This chapter is strategic in its focus as it takes a holistic view of marketing by exploring the overarching logic that guides its implementation and practice, rather than adopting a focus on specific tactics and marketing principles. Indeed these latter approaches can be reviewed elsewhere in a rich strand of literature that spans decades, and in view of this they do not warrant further discussion here. Accordingly the chapter aligns well with the specific focus and rationale for the book, which is to capture the essence of events in all their forms as strategically created and facilitated projects, rather than 'bolt on' operational activities that are delivered in support of some others' goals or strategic intent. However, in light of some of the arguments presented later, this chapter should ideally alert the strategic event creator to the creative and productive roles of their attendees, and that value creation and meaning production is both a fluid process and shared activity, taking place between producers and consumers rather than an activity only carried out by event creators. In this case, these arguments, and this perspective, more generally fully relate to Crowther's assertions in Chapter 1 of this book, that 'event creators are architects of experience journeys for their attendees and facilitators of outcomes' and that practitioners should be mindful of the fact that 'the creator's role is restricted to the purposeful crafting of settings in which the groups and individuals can attain their experiences, as experience is unavoidably derived rather than delivered'.

■ The exchange perspective of events marketing

The first perspective we will cover is known as the *exchange perspective of marketing* (e.g. Bagozzi, 1975). From the point of view of the literature, this is the most common perspective and the one that most marketing frameworks and theories originate from. This is not a perspective that we are recommending the event creator to adopt, but it is useful to consider it if only to reveal its limitations. Importantly, the underlying feature of this perspective, which distinguishes it from the others, is how it conceives of the roles and differences between event marketers and their attendees. Following the broad logic of economic theory and how this presents the differences between producers and consumers, the exchange perspective holds that customers seek out and purchase events to experience the *value* that is built and stored in them, for either immediate or future consumption. Event marketers are therefore instrumental in producing, communicating and delivering the value that is perceived and ultimately consumed. The money and/or advocacy that a participant supplies in return to the company for the experience of attending an event are what complete the exchange. Broadly speaking, this view simply holds that event marketing operates at the intersection of production and consumption and serves the marketplace by mediating supply and demand.

In effect, the key issue at play here is the concept of value, broadly defined (see Holbrook, 1999 for a thorough examination), and how it is experienced. This perspective of events marketing embraces the view that marketing centres on the production and exchange of *value*, and it is the differences between who is active in its production and consumption that are central to its logic.

To summarise, in the words of Schau et al. (2009, p.30):

'Modern marketing logic, as derived from economics, advance[s] a view of the firm and the customer as separate and discrete; the customer is exogenous to the firm and is the passive recipient of the firm's active value creation efforts'

As such, the exchange perspective is the closest approximation to the essence of marketing as defined by both the CIM (Chartered Institute of Marketing) and AMA (American Marketing Association) and mostly underlies the definitions found in most general marketing and events text books. This perspective thus structures most thinking around the event marketing process whereby event creators are tasked with:

1 Identifying and segmenting their markets.

2 Profiling attendees based upon need states and their potential to provide reciprocal value.

3 Efficiently allocating marketing resources in a competitive event context to position their products and meet the identified needs of their potential attendees.

4 Engaging in review activity to determine the success of their efforts and activity as well as the value that they have created for both themselves and their attendees.

Accordingly, the exchange perspective places the events creator in the privileged role of value creator and experience manager. And from this point of view, we are forced to accept the notion that events should be conceived as bundles of benefits, or containers of value and experiences, that participants can access simply through attendance (Holt, 1995). This perspective also makes the large assumption that event creators are instrumental in constructing and delivering these valuable experiences to their audiences, and relatedly, that attendees are mere recipients. However, as this chapter progresses we will see that recently this perspective and its associated theory are running into trouble from both an academic and practical point of view. This is because this perspective broadly overdetermines the importance of the event creator's role in value creation and experience design. A growing body of evidence from a number of schools of marketing thought are identifying and mapping out a different point of view (e.g. Vargo and Lusch, 2004, Lusch and Vargo, 2008; Arnould and Thompson, 2005; Holt, 1995), which when combined, suggest that it is the event participants who create their experiences rather than the other way around. Instead of being central to the process of value creation event creators are now placed in a lesser but no less important role as practitioners who shape the context through which valuable experiences can be created and realised. Accordingly we are simultaneously seeing the balance of power shift from

10

the creator to the user, but not a diminished role or set of responsibilities for the event creator themselves. In fact, in view of the new perspectives of event marketing that we are about to discuss, we are arguably witnessing the opposite; that is to say the event creators role becomes more nuanced, strategic and involving. To explore this thinking in more detail and what it means for practice we will now examine our next perspective.

Events marketing as facilitator of service and interaction

Over the last decade a new direction in marketing has arisen that challenges the underlying logic of the exchange perspective. This emerging perspective similarly holds the concept of value as central to its logic, however it is in the focus around who creates value that it fundamentally differs. Rather than holding the assumption that event creators produce, and attendees consume value, this view suggests that value creation is a shared and fluid process, and that value is dynamically produced through the activities and interactions between event marketers and their audiences.

While there is a lot of debate about the origin of this perspective (e.g. Levy, 2006), most literature cites a paper by Vargo and Lusch (2004) as a key moment in this turn in marketing thought. In fact this paper itself is called 'Evolving to a New Dominant Logic of Marketing'. While this and later papers flesh out the orientating propositions of this perspective, which number between eight and ten in total (see Vargo and Lusch, 2004, Lusch and Vargo 2008), the key concepts through which we ground our arguments are *service, interaction, consumer resources and consumption practices, and co-creation*. We will discuss each in turn, but must point out at the start that there is significant overlap and co-dependency between these concepts (also see Crowther and Donlan, 2011).

■ Service

This concept acknowledges the fact that consumers put products into service to meet their own specific goals, as evidenced by the discussion in Chapter 4 of this book about the many and varied event attendee motivations and expectations. In this respect, in acknowledgment of the fact that different consumers may pursue different goals from other consumers, or that a consumer may pursue different goals when consuming the same product on different occasions or in different contexts, it implies that the experience and outcome of consumption is relativistic (Holbrook, 1999). That is to say, the experience and outcome of consumption is relative to:

1   The individual or people involved in consumption

2   The context, time or situation in which consumption unfolds

3   The manifold consumer goals that frame and direct consumption (Holbrook, 1999)

4   The resources (Arnould et al., 2006) and consumption practices (Holt, 1995; 1997) that consumers bring to bear in their consumption.

To flesh out some of these points we can consider the motivations for attending the F1 Monaco Grand Prix. For some, a burning passion for the sport may drive and direct their consumption, while others may be just paying a visit to witness the spectacle on the off chance that they were in Monaco at the time. On the other hand a consumer who is driven by status could attend purely to accumulate the kudos that they perceive will result from being present at this 'hallmark' event. Another may be there just to accompany their partner or friend and therefore may spend more time soaking up the atmosphere or chatting with others than getting involved with the race itself. Finally, a person could attend in the capacity of work, and as a result be using this prestigious context to network and maintain relationships with key clients and to create leads.

Accordingly, while these people are sharing in the same basic experience, they are each using the occasion for different reasons and in turn creating unique experiences and forms of value; they are producing the experience of the Grand Prix on their own terms. In respect of practice, this implies that event creators must begin to account for the multi-dimensional nature of their events and the experiences that they potentially provide, and to not become fixated on one particular form of value or set of experiences. What is more, in designing their events, the event creator's role is to shape the context (or 'eventscape' – see Chapter 8) to accommodate the flexibility for attendee-led value creation. They must be mindful of the ways in which they can mediate or constrain damaging forms of attendee behaviours that may negatively impact upon and devalue attendee experiences more broadly.

■ Interaction

In light of this discussion we can see that contrary to the exchange perspective, which infers that value is stored within the event itself, the service logic posits that value is only experienced and realised in use. In this respect rather than being activities that contain value, events are better conceived as designed experiences with potential for value and which allow for significant variation in interpretation and use (Holt, 1997). Furthermore, following Holbrook's (1999, p.5) assertion that consumer value is best conceived as an 'interactive relativistic preference experience', we concur that the experiences derived by attendees from events are dependent upon interaction. To be exact, it is only when a consumer interacts with an event and its marketing that perceptions and judgements of value are brought into being.

10

Importantly, in relation to the temporal scope of events, interaction becomes more significant. This is because attendee interactions at events can be broad, deep and wide ranging, or light touch, superficial, and fleeting, and anything in between. Generally speaking, people spend a lot of time at events. On top of this, as Chapter 7 shows, an attendee may interact with the natural environment, other attendees, the eventscape, staff, marketing materials, amongst many other experiential touch points during their experience. Therefore, the potential for directing or curating the experience of attendees and the value that they perceive becomes increasingly complex and problematic. The difference that inclement weather may make on the experiences of revellers at Glastonbury or spectators on the roadside watching the Tour de France, is but one example of the many factors that event organisers have to consider, which marketers of manufactured products would never have to.

Consumer resources and consumption practices

The service logic of marketing also illuminates a different but complementary way of thinking about event attendees from that of the exchange perspective. Rather than solely profiling the market in terms of broad customer characteristics as market segmentation theory suggests (e.g. McDonalds and Dunbar 2012), that is by demographic, socio-economic, or psychographic variables, service logic requires a shift in orientation to a focus on *consumer resources*, (e.g. Arnould et al., 2006) and *consumption practices* (Holt, 1995). This switch is premised upon the changing nature of value creation and debates about who is involved in its production. On the one hand, if we accept that value is produced purely by event creators as per exchange theory, then it is reasonable to accept that we can make valuable use of market segmentation principles and practice. This is the case because we would be subscribing to a view that we can match the value embedded in our events with a group of customers whose needs or wants and financial resources match our positioning in the market. On the other hand, when we begin to think about event attendees as value creators themselves, we need a refreshed way of thinking.

Put simply, the argument suggests that value is created only when attendees integrate their own resources (see the next paragraph) with those offered by the event creator, during the process of consuming the event itself. This line of thinking is obviously at odds with market segmentation theory which broadly accepts the assumptions about value drawn from the exchange perspective, in the sense that an event can be conceived as a bundle of benefits or container of value that a person can access simply through attendance (Holt, 1995). Given this shift in thought, rather than merely profiling our attendees prior to consumption as we would when engaging segmentation studies, this approach calls for greater consideration of the process of event consumption itself. To be precise, in addition to segmenting their audiences, event creators must also study the resources and consumption practices that attendees deploy when shaping their experiences, and creating value. This approach will in turn supply rich consumer insight that can be leveraged to improve event designs and marketing activity.

But what do we mean by resources and practices? On the one hand, we define attendee resources as the range of personal assets and capabilities that people utilise when interacting with events, such as their time, effort, knowledge, skills, imagination, creativity and money etc., (see Arnould et al., 2006 for detailed review) and on the other, following Holt, (1995, p.1) we simply define consumption practices as 'what people do when they consume'. In Richardson's and Turely's (2008) work into football fandom for example, we are shown how a range of consumer resources and practices are "used… [at football matches and through other peer to peer interactions]… to maintain social distinctions between 'real' fans and 'day-trippers' and as a means by which 'in' group membership is achieved and awarded to others." In this respect, it is what fans do, and it is the resources they deploy during attendance at matches and related consumption activity that creates the value they desire, which in turn allows them to achieve their goals of being identified as 'proper supporters' and to accrue elite status. This logic can be similarly applied to other event contexts.

In these instances, the value being pursued is not purely based upon how well a match is organised and staged, by an event creator, or how well the team performs on match day or during the season more generally. In this context, value is produced in a number of fan-induced ways. Fans accrue status through *practices* related to frugality and service (Ibid). To achieve their goals, 'real fans', are expected to attend all matches no matter what, and in doing so, are forced into spending lots of money and time. Furthermore, by virtue of their status, 'real fans' are classified by their encyclopaedic knowledge of their team's history, players and current form, as well as the passion through which they sing their teams songs. This implies that supporters have to expend lots of time and effort developing this knowledge and acquainting themselves with their team's specific match rituals. Having acquired both the knowledge and attended the matches, supporters are then able to accrue more status through the stories and experiences that they can share with others about the great sacrifices that they endure following their team. In addition, armed with a range of mobile devices these supporters may then leverage their social networks, such as Facebook, Twitter or YouTube to share their stories and experiences on a broader scale.

10

In relation to the theory, we can clearly see from this example how important the *resources* of time, money and knowledge are to these consumers in achieving their goals. The collective experiences of these fans, which can then be conveyed as stories, are also valuable *consumer resources* in this context as are the social media platforms and the devices through which they could be shared. We can also see how fundamental the *practices* of budgeting, personal sacrifice, continuous learning, and the ritual acts of singing and storytelling are in value creation in this context, in the sense that these are leveraged to create and cement their identities as 'real fans'.

This insight, which shows how value is crafted through consumption, demonstrates how vitally important it is for event creators to account for the resources that attendees bring to bear when interacting with their marketing materials and the experiences they offer. Or as Vargo and Lusch (2004), Holt, (1995), and Arnould e al., (2006) suggest, we need to think about the resources and practices that our attendees integrate with those that we supply through our events as they produce their experiences. Importantly this means that the event creator needs to focus much more on what takes place through a customer's journey during selection, acquisition, consumption and withdrawal from an event; not only on figuring out who their customers are prior to their attendance.

The two following case studies ground these arguments further.

Case study: The Burning Man Festival

In Kozinets' (2002) study of the Burning Man festival (also see http://www.burningman. com/whatisburningman), we are shown how festival participants engage in a range of de-commodification *practices* to facilitate their goals of escaping the market and consumerism. In particular they: (1) employ gift giving and barter to sidestep monetary exchange and economic transactions; (2) attempt to subvert their everyday roles as customers by engaging in performance art and making offers to the wider Burning Man community in the form of artworks and installations; and (3) they mask or disguise any significant markers of the marketplace such as brand logos and trademarks etc. In performing these *practices* 'Burners' engage a range of *resources* such as their creative imaginations, interpersonal skills and resourcefulness. Moreover, in order to survive the harsh conditions of the Nevada Desert where the festival takes place, Burners take along sufficient supplies and draw upon a range of material *resources*, such as water, sunglasses, and suncream etc. In advance of embarking on their journey to the desert, Burners may also seek to develop their knowledge and survival skills by reading books or consulting websites or magazines. The Burning Man website itself offers a range of *resources* and guidelines for this specific purpose (see http://survival.burningman.com).

Adapted from Kozinets, 2002

Case study: The Whitby Goth Festival

Goulding and Saren's (2009) study of the Whitby Goth Festival (also see http://www.whitbygothweekend.co.uk), describes in detail how participants engage a range of *resources* and *consumption practices* to achieve a range of consumption goals. Motivated by gender politics, and frustrations with contemporary media representations of the female body and beauty ideals, the Whitby Goths from this study seek to 'put the curves back into the feminine', 'blur the boundaries' between the genders, and pursue 'gender as fantasy' through a range of *consumption practices* (Ibid, p.27) In doing this they draw on a combination of *resources*.

Goulding and Saren (2009) claim that the vampire myth is central to the Goth's experiences and *consumption practices* at the festival. This they argue is because the mythology of the vampire subverts traditional notions of sexuality, with vampires being represented as androgynous and sexually ambiguous in much of the literature and media. To quote the paper:

> 'the vampire violates the norms of femininity and masculinity. There is no desire for marriage and procreation. Rather, in their search for blood, they can find physical intimacy with a person regardless of age, gender, race or social class. Sex is transmuted into an exchange of bodily fluids (known as the "dark gift," or the transfusion of the vampire's blood into the victim in order to create a new vampire) where reproduction, if it occurs at all consists of the gift of eternal life' (Ibid, p.29).

Thus, knowledge of the myth and the media which disseminates it, such as Bram Stoker's Dracula become fundamental *resources* through which consumption at the festival is practiced. Furthermore, the context of the event is a vitally important *resource* itself, as Whitby 'represents a spiritual home for Goths', due to its central role in vampire mythology, being both where Dracula first set foot on English soil, and where Stoker found his inspiration for his novel and the Dracula character in the first place (ibid, p.30). In view of this we can thus see how important the wider cultural context and media representations are in framing the experiences of Goths at this event, and how these *resources* are integral to the consumption practices and interpretive strategies of attendees (Kozinets, 2001). Importantly, this research parallels other studies of events which show how the media and myth pattern the experiences of participants and the ways in which cultural narratives and historical context become *resources* that are selectively used in consumption (See Belk and Costa, 1998; Peñaloza, 2001).

Furthermore, this research shows that Goths fashion their identities at the festival through clothing choices, and cosmetic use. Their identities are produced and expressed through a combination of material *resources* and related *consumption practices*. In their bid 'to put the curves back into the feminine' for example, some participants of the study accentuate and mould their bodies through wearing corsets and other elaborate costume. Alternatively, those who seek to 'blur the boundaries' of sexuality, perfect their

10

androgynous look in similar ways, by mixing male and female fashion codes and costumes, while attendees who pursue 'gender as fantasy' explicitly reference the vampire
in their choice of clothing, even to the point of having fangs permanently fitted. Those
who take this mythical form of expression to the extreme even sleep in coffins and travel
by hearse during their time at the festival. Finally, this research shows that chronological
time is also a key *resource*, for the Goths as it is reported that participants spend "up to
three hours to complete [their] 'look'" (Goulding and Saren, 2009, p.32).

Adapted from Goulding and Saren, 2009

To draw this section to a close, we can see that this approach, by necessity, advocates a more microscopic and nuanced view of the consumer and
consumption, which is implicit in the strategic precepts of stakeholder cen-
tricity and purposeful event design introduced and reviewed in Chapter 1.
Alongside the traditional approach to market segmentation, the contemporary events practitioner, as argued in Chapter 4, benefits greatly from getting
much closer to their attendees in order to gain awareness and knowledge of
the consumption practices, and consumer resources that are undoubtedly
integral to the creation of customer value and their experiences in general.
It also demonstrates that the event creator is not the only one who is sup-
plying the valuable *resource*s that their attendees interact with in forging
their experiences and realising their outcomes. This perspective demands a
closer reading of an attendee's consumption, and to reveal this insight, event
practitioners must go much further than merely surveying their customers' experiences and satisfaction levels through questionnaires, etc. They
need to be in the field with them instead, and in doing so engage a range of
interpretive and interactive investigative approaches such as observation,
in-depth interviews and market orientated ethnography (see, Arnould and
Price, 2006 and also Chapters 12 and 13). In doing so, event designers will
not only achieve more for their customers by being able to offer more of
the resources that are integral to their projects; such insight also affords the
opportunity to build deeper and more meaningful relationships with them
more generally. In consequence event creators will be equipped to make
more informed marketing decisions and (co)produce more valuable event
experiences.

◼ Co-creation

We now turn to the final root concept of this perspective, which is co-
creation. In view of the discussion above, it should be clear that the most
significant departure from the exchange perspective of marketing is the
keen focus upon how value is created for event attendees. Rather than
the creation of value being seen as the sole preserve of event creators, we
now see that consumers play a fundamental, if not central role. In this

respect the literature now acknowledges the notion of value co-creation or co-production whereby both organisations and consumers are viewed as value creators with shared roles in the value creation process. In light of this, the perspective therefore has significant implications for how events are created and the ways in which we practice marketing more specifically. To draw upon the lexicon of consumer resource theory (Arnould et al., 2006), we now see that event organisations offer but one resource amongst the gamut of resources that attendees bring to bear in their value creating activities. While event creators still play a key role in defining their unique selling points and value propositions through their marketing and event design activities, they must be flexible and comfortable in the fact that their consumers perform a similarly active role. Consequently, by embracing the ideas of co-creation, event creators have a much better opportunity for facilitating the value creation of event attendees. The emphasis on facilitator rather than producer is key. To use a popular analogy, 'beauty is in the eye of the beholder'; we must acknowledge that experience and value is created and perceived by event attendees rather than packaged and supplied by event creators.

Events marketing as a socio-cultural process and practice

Our final perspective builds upon the preceding two perspectives, but expands upon them by introducing the notions of meaning and values. That is to say, the marketing and consumption of events not only creates value, it also mediates, produces and distributes socio-cultural meaning and values and this understanding is important for event creators in fully interpreting the marketing challenge they have. Hence this perspective more fully explains the motivations for attending the Whitby Goth Festival and the ways in which participants produce gender identities, and the ways in which fans of football accrue social status amongst their peers by attending all of a season's matches and cup games. This perspective also reinforces the view of consumers that is advocated by the service perspective of marketing, as much of the theory that supports this in turn highlights the central role that consumers play in both meaning production and in creating cultural and social value. Put simply, as evidenced by Burners and Goths, consumers utilise supplied *resources* from the event creators in the form of events and marketing materials, as well as their own, to construct their own meanings and create their own forms of cultural value (Arnould et al., 2006). Or to utilise the language of the service perspective of Arnould (2007, p.58), events in their broadest sense 'provide the service of identity provision and communication'.

10

In this respect we draw upon a broad body of theory and research to illustrate:

1   The symbolic nature of events and how they relate to attendee identities

2   The roles that events and their consumption play in community formation and sociality

3   The learning we can derive from this for event marketing thought and practice.

Event symbolism and attendee identity

A central theme of this approach is the notion that events carry symbolic or semiotic significance and value, which in turn become valuable resources for attendees. In the words of Levy (1959, p.118), *'people buy things not only for what they can do, but also for what they mean'*. Furthermore, studies show that consumers find these meanings valuable and useful for all manner of reasons (e.g. Arnould and Thompson, 2005; Holt 1997) and that events in their broadest sense, and the consumption practices that they facilitate, are used as markers of social status and standing, expressions of personality and lifestyle, and sub-group or brand community affiliation. Consider, for example how Royal Ascot or the Glyndebourne festival (see http://glyndebourne.com/) differ from each other and also differ in relation to Glastonbury or a League One football match in terms of cultural meaning and social significance. These and many other forms of events clearly carry and denote deep associations that have developed dynamically over time and in so doing act to classify their attendees. To quote Levy (1959):

> a symbol is appropriate (and the product will be used and enjoyed) when it joins with, meshes with, adds to, or reinforces the way the consumer thinks about himself...[and]... Most goods say something about the social world of the people who consume them. The things they buy are chosen partly to attest to their social positions.

Moreover event creators play a significant role in shaping these meanings and communicating them to their audiences through their practices, and therefore must take heed of what this means for their roles as cultural intermediaries. To draw on the ideas of McCracken (1996), in effect, marketing and event curation becomes a conduit through which meanings in the 'culturally constituted world' pass through events to attendees. In respect of practice, this means that event designers must purposefully select symbols, images, and materials, as well as use language that convey meanings that are considered important to their attendees when designing their events and producing marketing materials. For example Goths would appear to respond well to images and stories from vampire mythology as well as gothic architecture and scripts more generally. On the other hand,

Burners would value communications that revoked the primary status of the marketplace and devalued the role of brands and commercial activity. Additionally, following widespread media reports about unsavoury behaviour at Ascot (Kupfermann, 2014) most attendees would welcome a return to the traditional and prestigious values that underscored this event, and as such appreciate the dress code that the event creators now supply for attendees and the ways in which they ensure that it is followed (see http://www.ascot.co.uk/dress-code).

In light of this insight, it is vital that event creators fully understand the relationship between what their events stand for, to a range of stakeholders, and in what ways these meanings hold value for their attendees. They must also become accustomed to the cultural scripts and symbols that give life to these meanings. To be precise, event creators must think strategically about the symbolic significance and value of the materials, people and other resources that they draw upon in creating their events in their entirety - from purposefully designed collateral such as advertisements and flyers through to basic requirements like toilets and wash facilities. In view of the latter revellers at Glastonbury will have very different expectations than audiences of opera.

■ Event consumption and community

Another significant aspect of the socio-cultural approach to events marketing is how it illuminates the social aspects of event consumption. Social-cultural changes are, amongst other things, leading to the breakdown of traditional communities and to individuals feeling more isolated, and as a result, research has found that people are looking for new ways in which to forge friendships and experience community. Research shows that consumption in general and attending events in particular, are primary vehicles through which to realise these goals (McAlexander et al., 2002). Events are profoundly communal and offer a way in which to link with others and engage in shared experiences; they thereby offer significant social value (Belk and Costa, 1998).

A growing body of research has thus started to map the ways in which brands and events link people together (Cova, 1997; Cova and Cova, 2002) and forge community (Muñiz Jr. et al., 2001), as well as providing insight into the nature and anatomy of consumption practices within these communities, and how these in turn create value for their members (Schau, et al., 2009). Moreover, much of this work has strong ties to events, brandfests, raves or festivals. Importantly, research has also demonstrated that these communities are often made up of relatively heterogeneous groups of people who bear little in common other than an interest or passion for the product or experience (Thomas et al., 2012; Cova, 1997). For event creators,

10

the learning here is obvious, as this finding alone significantly challenges market segmentation theory which is broadly dependent upon event attendees sharing one or more personal, characteristics with each other such as their age, income, or values. Instead the criterion of commonality through which we may be able to successfully define a valuable segment from this perspective is based upon commonality of interest or event patronage. Another valuable 'take-away' for event marketers from these ideas is that "work on... consumption communities emphasises that part of what companies... [really]... end-up selling is access to like-minded consumers" (Arnould, 2007, p.63). The consequence of this is that event marketers ultimately become relational partners and facilitators of community practices and experiences, rather than purveyors of extraordinary and entertaining experiences per se. And in accordance with this, event creators must have the capacity to develop the tools, skills and competencies for community service and maintenance. To be precise, event creators must seek ways in which they can facilitate and enhance their attendee's peer2peer interactions and communication, as this will not only augment their experiences, but will allow them to offer more value in general. These types of interventions will also help to keep their events alive in the minds of their attendees and stakeholders over time.

New technology for example, in the form of Web 2.0 and mobile, is providing new ways for event participants to come together, and share their experiences. The organisers of the Burning Man festival, for instance, offer a number of platforms for Burners and prospects to interact both on and offline. Their online forum 'ePLaya' has over 52,000 members and presently carries 95,631 individual posts around 48,260 topic themes (see https://eplaya.burningman.com). Their website also hosts thousands of images, from participant photographers, that document the experience of the festival over time. In the off line context, the Burning Man Project also supports a Global Regional Network made up of affiliates who co-ordinate and facilitate community activity. According to their website, these actors organise mini events and activities and use technology to leverage 'dialog, collaboration and inspiration' to keep the Burning Man spirit alive (see http://regionals.burningman.com/main/about-the-regional-network).

This insight is crucial for event creators because it demonstrates how attendees are taking their experiences outside of the managed event context and sharing them in rich detail with others, in a multitude of online and offline mediated environments, both pre, during and post event. And this is happening whether it takes place through the sponsored platforms or facilitation of the event creator or otherwise. In this sense, event experiences transcend both time and space, and are increasingly self-organising and directed, and the emphasis shifts to the attendee. On the one hand, space is transcended as attendee's experiences and interactions, in the form of photos, videos and the written word, are moving beyond the confines of the physical event itself, into virtual spaces and mobile platforms such as Twitter, Facebook, YouTube and WhatsApp. In this respect, these experiences then transcend time, as these communications leave virtual footprints between attendees, leaving evidence of their experiences in virtual space for others to view or comment upon at their leisure. Not only does this show how experiences can be improved by community interaction, it also provides a cautionary note as well as a number of marketing opportunities for event designers more generally. In terms of the opportunities for event creators, these behaviours and the platforms and contexts in which they unfold provide new places and media in which to interact with their audiences, and to facilitate peer to peer communications. They also offer a platform for marketing research whereby event creators can account for their attendees' preferences and record their gripes, as well as map the ways in which their attendees create their own experiences and values (see Kozinets, 2010). In this respect these communities afford opportunities for both product development and service recovery in equal measure, as well as a chance to augment the experiences of attendees by bringing them closer together.

Conclusion

This chapter has introduced the reader to three perspectives that frame event marketing thought and practice, and represents a different approach through which to consider marketing and events. In particular we have demonstrated how the received view of marketing in the field, which is the exchange perspective, is being dislodged and challenged by two emerging approaches.

These more recent approaches draw attention to the productive and creative roles of their audience and attendees, and accordingly illustrate how the privileged role of the event creator in value creation and meaning production is being undermined. Importantly we can see from this perspective how important the concepts of interaction and attendee resources and consumption practices are to both value creation and realised experiences. In this respect we advocate an approach to marketing, which brings the event creator closer to their attendees, and one which is much more interactive, and sensitive to their goals and experiences. A plentiful supply of insight is waiting to be found on the ground and in the contexts through which events are co-created and experienced.

In drawing attention to the cultural approach to event marketing, we show how important meanings and values and notions of identity and community are to event design and attendance. As well as the ways in which the wider cultural context and media support attendees' experiences and facilitate the achievement of their goals. People do not just go to festivals to create value and seek entertainment. Amongst other things, they attend in the hope of shaping and realising identities and to forge community and kinship. Accordingly, event creators must begin to accept their role as cultural intermediaries and guardians and facilitators of community practices. In so doing they will realise the significant value and potential that these roles offer to practice. Not only will they be able to design more compelling and meaningful events, and create more expressive marketing materials, they will also be able to develop more lasting and durable relationships with their audiences and attendees.

Study questions

1   In what fundamental way does the exchange perspective of event marketing differ from the service and interaction perspective?

2   Identify and select an online community that is formed around an event or festival and analyse the ways in which this 'resource' is used by its members

References

Arnould, E. J. (2007). Service-dominant logic and consumer culture theory: Natural allies in an emerging paradigm. *Research in Consumer Behavior*, **11**, 57-76.

Arnould, E. J., Price, L.L. and Malshe, A. (2006). Toward a cultural resource-based theory of the consumer. In: Lusch, Robert F., and Vargo, Stephen L. (eds.). *The Service-Dominant Logic of Marketing: Dialog, Debate, and Directions*. 91-104.

Arnould, E.J. and Price.L. (2006). Market-oriented ethnography revisited. *Journal of Advertising Research*, **46** (3), 251-262.

Arnould, E.J. and Thompson, C. J. (2005). Consumer culture theory (CCT): Twenty years of research. *Journal of Consumer Research*, **31** (4), 868-882.

Bagozzi R. P. (1975). Marketing as exchange. *The Journal of Marketing*, **39**(4), 32-39.

Belk, R.W. and Costa, J. A. (1998). The mountain man myth: A contemporary consuming fantasy. *The Journal Of Consumer Research*, **25** (3), 218-240.

Cova, B. (1997). Community and consumption: Towards a definition of the "linking value" of product or services. *European Journal of Marketing*, **31**(3/4), 297-316.

Cova, B. and Cova, V. (2002). Tribal marketing: the tribalisation of society and its impact on the conduct of marketing. *European Journal Of Marketing*, **36**(5/6), 595-620.

Crowther, P., and Donlan, L. (2011). Value-creation space: The role of events in a service-dominant marketing paradigm. *Journal of Marketing Management*, **27**(13-14), 1444-1463.

Goulding, C., and Saren, M. (2009). Performing identity: an analysis of gender expressions at the Whitby goth festival. *Consumption, Markets and Culture*, **12**(1), 27-46.

Holbrook, M.B. (1999). *Consumer Value: A Framework For Analysis And Research*. London, Routledge.

Holt, D.B. (1995). How consumers consume: A typology of consumption practices. *Journal of Consumer Research*, **22** (1), 1–16.

Holt, D. B. (1997). Poststructuralist lifestyle analysis: Conceptualizing the social patterning of consumption in postmodernity. *Journal of Consumer Research*, **23** (4), 326-350.

Kozinets, R. V. (2002). Can consumers escape the market? Emancipatory illuminations from burning man. *Journal of Consumer Research*, **29**(1), 20-38.

Kozinets, R.V. (2010). *Netnography; Doing Ethnographic Research Online*, Sage

Kozinets, V. (2001). Utopian enterprise: Articulating the meanings of Star Trek's culture of consumption. *Journal of Consumer Research*, **28**(1), 67-88.

Kupfermann, J. (2014). 'Bawdiness, booze and the women who have turned my beloved Ascot into... CHAVSCOT, by a traditional lady race fan', *Mail Online*, 19th June. www.dailymail.co.uk/femail/article-2663179/Bawdiness-booze-women-turned-beloved-Ascot-CHAVSCOT.html#ixzz3B8XIyTg5, accessed 22/08/2014

Levy, S.J. (1959). Symbols for sale. *Harvard Business Review*, **37** (4), 117-124.

Levy, S.J. (2006). How New, How Dominant? in R.F. Lusch,. and S.L. Vargo (Eds.), *The Service-Dominant Logic Of Marketing: Dialog, Debate, and Directions. (p. 57-65).* Armonk, N.Y, M.E. Sharpe.

Lusch, R.F. and Vargo, S.L. (2008). Service-dominant logic: Continuing the evolution. *Journal of the Academy of Marketing Science*, **36** (1), 1-10.

McAlexander, J. H., Schouten, J. W. and Koenig, H. F. (2002). Building brand community. *Journal of Marketing*, **66**(1), 38-54.

McCracken, G.(1986). Culture and consumption: A theoretical account of the structure: A theoretical account of the structure and movement of the cultural meaning of consumer goods. *Journal of Consumer Research*, **13** (1), 71-84.

McDonald, M. and Dunbar, I. (2012). *Market Segmentation: How to Do it and How to Profit from it, revised 4th edition*, Wiley.

Muniz Jr, A. M., and O'Guinn, T. C. (2001). Brand community. *Journal of Consumer Research*, **27**(4), 412-432.

10

Penaloza, L. (2001). Consuming the American West: Animating cultural meaning and memory at a stock show and rodeo. *Journal of Consumer Research*, **28**(3), 369-398.

Richardson, B. and Turley, D. (2008). It's far more important than that: Football fandom and cultural capital. *European Advances in Consumer Research*, **8** , 33-38.

Schau, H. J., Muniz Jr, A. M. and Arnould, E. J. (2009). How brand community practices create value. *Journal of Marketing*, **73**(5), 30-51.

Thomas, T. C., Price, L. L. and Schau, H. J. (2013). When differences unite: Resource dependence in heterogeneous consumption communities. *Journal of Consumer Research*, **39**(5), 1010-1033.

Tresidder, R. and Hirst, C (2012). *Marketing In Food, Hospitality, Tourism and Events: A Critical Approach.* Oxford, Goodfellow Publishers.

Vargo, S. L. and Lusch, R.F. (2004). Evolving to a new dominant logic for marketing. *The Journal of Marketing*, **68** (1), 1-17.

11 Realising a Legacy

Stewart Hilland

Learning objectives

- Appreciate the growing importance of creating event legacies and how this phenomenon stems from the expectations related to large scale, high profile public events.

- Examine the strategic approach that can be taken in leveraging event legacy.

- Explore the application of event portfolios across all sectors as a method of achieving legacies.

Introduction

Although some events may be seen as ends in themselves, to be enjoyed for their intrinsic merits alone, many who design, plan and deliver events are interested in generating enduring outcomes that go far beyond the time frame of the event itself. This long term perspective is common in the public sector, where policy makers in national governments, local authorities and cities have turned to events because of the economic, social and other benefits that they are believed to bring. In this context, events are seen as agents of renewal, regeneration and redevelopment that offer wide-ranging legacy opportunities linked to the building of new facilities, infrastructure improvements, employment programmes, housing developments and so on. The utilisation of events for this purpose is generally associated with large-scale, peripatetic, sporting competitions like the Olympic Games, FIFA World Cup and Commonwealth Games, that are staged at great cost to the host, and therefore require strong return on investment (ROI) to justify an expenditure that is largely funded out of the public purse. The assessment of these events, and others that are smaller in scale, but nevertheless important in terms of investment and consequence, has been the focus in academic literature, so the chapter will begin by considering aspects of this research as a route into a much broader examination of the public, not-for-profit and private sectors. The discussion will turn from high profile and high impact single public spectacles to significant but less ambitious on-going events that are part of a more subtle, integrated and managed approach. The individual events in these situations may not command the same degree of attention that is accorded to their mega cousins but collectively, often as a portfolio, they have the capacity to be leveraged for substantial and far reaching gains.

Legacy - a definition

Legacy has become something of a buzz word over the past decade or so and is now frequently used indiscriminately (and incorrectly) to refer to any form of beneficial outcome in any situation. So what is the correct usage of legacy in the context of an event and how does legacy differ from other terms, like event impacts and event outcomes, which appear in event management literature? A thorough analysis and discussion of event legacy is provided by Thompson et al. (2013), who unpick a concept that researchers have described as multifaceted (Chalip, 2002), elusive (Cashman, 2006) and still evolving (Gold and Gold, 2008). Based on the cross-checking of the terminology and its interpretation by writers in the field of sports events, five key considerations emerged in the thematic review:

1   The use of 'legacy' rather than another word like 'impact' or 'outcome'

2   If legacy is bestowed or planned

3   The temporal nature of legacy, so whether or not legacy has to be permanent/lasting or if it can be described as short term/long term

4   The need to think about legacy from both positive and negative viewpoints

5   The setting of legacy from local to global

Event situations are certainly complex and the finer details of the way that legacy is interpreted can be set out case by case, but the pervasive use of the word means that a general, overarching definition of event legacy would be helpful. It is beyond the scope of this chapter to enter into a thorough discourse on this subject but reflecting on the findings of Thomson et al. (2013) and their five key considerations, a simple interpretation is offered that places legacy in the context of event effects. The term 'effects' is chosen because all events have effects; in a sense, the effect is the raison d'être of the event. Legacy is then seen as the long term or permanent effects that take shape before as well as after an event and they are effects that need to be specifically planned in order to avoid negative consequences.

Long term effects: public sector event legacy

The rhetoric surrounding legacy is due in large part to the long term outcomes that are predicted from the investment in major international sporting competitions: notably the Olympic Games, FIFA World Cup and Commonwealth Games. These events may be short in duration but they are high in expectations and the pressure on hosts to devise something distinctive and memorable frequently leads to a hefty commitment of public money. The most expensive price tag belongs to the Olympic Games: the 'basic' delivery cost is weighty in itself but the scale of funding jumps appreciably when the expenditure for major Olympic infrastructure and other projects is added on. In staging the London 2012 Games, for example, the operational, day-to-day costs for running the event amounted to £3 billion (DCMS, 2012a) and this was largely met from sponsorship, ticket sales, merchandise and funds provided by the International Olympic Committee (IOC). However, the total bill rocketed when outlay by the Olympic Delivery Authority on construction and transport developments, a figure of over £6.7 billion, was added on (DCMS, 2012a). In addition, public money is widely used to finance many other, secondary, schemes. These projects may not get off the ground without the push provided by the event and they usually require a funding involvement that extends well after the event. Turning to London again, the legacy story 'Beyond London 2012' produced in the wake of the Games (DCMS, 2012b) identifies a raft of legacy goals under the headings of 'Sport', 'Growth', 'People' and 'City', including many programmes that fit into this secondary category.

The scale of legacy ambitions connected with London 2012 is not unprecedented, as demonstrated by Leopkey and Parent (2012) in their detailed study of Olympic bid documents and final reports. The content analysis undertaken by these authors points to the growing significance attached to legacy goals in recent decades; a trend that is certainly influenced by the expectations of the IOC and also the need for Olympic hopefuls and eventual hosts to divert attention from the financial investment required for the long term rewards that the investment can generate. Although extensive infrastructure developments linked to the event generally receive the most attention and publicity, the types of legacy benefits go much further. They encompass cultural, economic, environmental, image, education, nostalgia, the Olympic movement, political, psychological, social, sport and sustainability themes, some of which have only an indirect or even tenuous connection with the event itself.

Part of the challenge with legacies is to define them precisely and be transparent about how they are to be realised. Often, legacy objectives become overly complex, as in the case of the Olympic Games where the

11

legacy themes 'have become progressively interconnected over time and, as such, are not distinct from each other and exist with significant overlap' (Leopold and Parent, 2012 p.935). Multifarious, interconnected and ambitious projects require careful orchestration if they are to succeed and whilst legacy is certainly on the agenda these days, it is frequently low down on the to-do list compared with other elements of the event planning process. Indeed, some host nations still view legacies as a bolt-on, in that they secure the event first because it offers legacy possibilities and identify specific projects later that can be accomplished by using the event as the driver. Legacies may even be added on as a knee jerk response to doubts over the achievement of expected effects: if they are unlikely to be met in the way intended, tag on extra legacy goals in the hope of gaining some longer term benefits and thereby demonstrating ROI. There are cases where legacy planning has been left until the event is over, like the well documented usage plan for the Athens 2004 Olympic facilities. This is a prime example of tardy practice that resulted in lost opportunities and revenues (Kissoudi, 2008).

Industry voice: Helen Rowbotham, Director of Consulting at CSM Strategic (formerly PMP Legacy) , UK

It is amazing that it has taken so long for legacy planning to become common practice and be considered early in the strategic planning process. In the past, many hosts thought that the facilities were the legacy and that building them was all that was necessary. However, cities appreciate now that with all of the resources needed to host events, the opportunities to provide a broader legacy are far greater than the sports infrastructure. On the big projects, the investment is so significant and there is such a long lead-in time that the legacy planning needs to begin at the feasibility stage. This is still quite rare but it is how it happened with Glasgow 2014...we had a feasibility team made up of the Scottish Executive, Commonwealth Games Scotland, Glasgow City Council and Event Scotland. We worked together to explore legacy opportunities and challenges, using a cost/benefit approach. This is how it should be...a strategic approach to legacy planning right at the start, ensuring early ownership and a legacy focussed approach to event planning.

The proactive manner in which Glasgow 2014 embraced legacy is evident from the dedicated website and the extensive documentation assembled in the years leading up to the event: see, for example, *A Games Legacy For Scotland* (Scottish Government, 2009), which follows on from the bid documents (see Glasgow 2014, 2009). This example demonstrates that with some events, legacy is now being considered at a much earlier stage in the planning process. But is this early enough and are decision makers linking their event planning to a discernible legacy strategy: one where the event is seen as an opportunity to take advantage of what the host has to offer in order to achieve what the host would like to gain from the experience? Bringing forward the starting point of legacy planning does give greater scope to contemplate how the event can be used as a lever, purposefully and deliberately, to maximise clear-cut, intentional and lasting effects.

Leveraging a legacy

Public organisations rarely assume a benevolent role as event hosts (perhaps London did to a certain extent in staging the post war Olympics of 1948) and automatic ROI through capital project impacts is the expected norm. However, this traditional, impact driven, ex-post view is disputed by O'Brien and Chalip (2007, p.297), who favour an ex-ante, forward thinking strategy to leverage greater benefits, which make the most of the event. In earlier work, Chalip (2004, p.245) states that "...it is no longer suitable merely to host an event in the hope that desired outcomes will be achieved; it is necessary to form and implement strategies and tactics that capitalise fully on the opportunities each event affords." Put simply and pragmatically, hosts should be asking the question: What can this event accomplish for us, given our current situation and future needs and how do we set about fully exploiting it?

Bringing the leveraging of the event to the forefront of the planning process does throw a spotlight on the challenges related to managing legacy initiatives that are often complex and intertwined, as referred to previously. If they are to be disentangled and tackled strategically using the event as a lever, stakeholders who can follow through and action that leverage must be designated. Currently, with the largest public events this is rarely the case. Projects, especially the most expensive, are usually allocated to temporary organising committees that have been assembled to deliver the event. These groups lack the longevity to take the long range view that is needed for successful leverage. Their priority is managing resources short term so that the event is produced on time and on budget. On this subject, Chalip (2014, p7) feels that effective leverage should not be in the hands of event organisers but those who are tasked with "economic development, social development and/or environmental stewardship at the host destination. These include local business associations, government agencies and service organisations."

The procedure for deciding who is involved in leveraging should be undertaken by those who have an extended brief and will be the key custodians of the legacy. They should:

☐   Examine the leveraging potential of events and determine the most viable projects

11

☐   Define the nature and scope of leveraging and the overall strategic approach to be applied

☐   Assign the projects early on in the event life cycle to management groups that have the resources and funding required to match up to the task *and* have a stake in seeing the leverage strategy pursued through to a successful conclusion

Industry voice: Helen Rowbotham, Director of Consulting at CSM Strategic, UK

Getting the right stakeholders around the table at a very early stage and knowing who has responsibility for what is very important in terms of strategic legacy planning… and this means being very clear early on about what you want to achieve and having robust action plans with key performance indicators to measure long term success. Early stakeholder engagement is critical because you can use and build on the energy and momentum that is created around the event. If stakeholder groups feel that they have a voice and are contributing to the early thinking and planning of the outcomes, they are also more likely to be actively engaged in the delivery of the legacy programmes and want to see them through to a successful conclusion.

Effecting productive engagement of this kind seems reasonable on paper. However, issues relating to cohesion of vision and coordination of approach are almost inevitable, which means that oversight and leadership are essential if a diverse set of stakeholder groups with different interests and motivations are to work together successfully. As Chalip (2014, p.9) cautions, there are some 'clear impediments' in terms of alliances and, noting previous studies (Chalip and Leyns, 2002; Taks et al., 2013) he draws attention to a few of them. First, the problems to overcome when competitor commercial businesses have to unite on leveraging initiatives, and second, the concerns that might arise from event organisers/owners who perceive that those tasked with leveraging programmes are pursuing a type of ambush marketing. In addition, he emphasises the necessity for organisations to develop the skills and resources to leverage effectively, and perhaps this is the crux of the matter as 'more work is needed to flesh out the techniques for leverage' (Chalip, 2014 p.10) if those charged with the task are to have the tools necessary to deal with it. Leveraging many faceted, one-off major sports events is complicated but the value of taking a leveraging approach towards the legacy of public events should not be questioned because it is difficult to apply it to the largest of event types (see Smith, 2014, for an interesting perspective on the leveraging of sport mega events using an event-led and event-themed differentiation). Leveraging also has relevance if we adopt what could be referred to as an umbrella view of all public sector events.

These days, national, regional and local governments are responsible for a wide spectrum of events that fulfil many purposes. Some may be one-off, but many are repeated and, as such, have greater sustainability credentials; additionally, they are likely to be designed to meet local needs and resources competently. These events are generators of many effects associated with tourism, sport engagement, culture, community development/cohesion and so on that would not look out of place under the Olympic legacy themes mentioned earlier. Similarly, these events can have long term consequences. Although smaller scale public events are usually localised and, therefore, do not have the capability to engender extensive outcomes that go beyond their immediate environment, their long term effects can still be viewed as legacies. In the most enlightened cases, the authorities regard these events as a portfolio (Getz, 2013; Richards and Palmer, 2010) and they are managed strategically to bring enhanced effects. Chalip (2014, p.7) points out that as most individual events take place over a short time, bringing them together as a portfolio can improve the overall reach with different demographic and psychographic market segments and increase the frequency with which these markets are exposed to the events. Thus, it reflects better practice to take an expansive view of public events, in which the focus shifts from single events and their success or failure in legacy terms, to the strategic management of a portfolio of events that can be leveraged in various ways to generate legacies.

Public sector portfolios

A public sector event portfolio is more than a list of miscellaneous events that belong to the same body. And it is not simply an administrative means of making the best use of resources by adding events where necessary to fill gaps in the calendar or to fill up vacant room nights in local accommodation (Chalip, 2014). According to Ziakas (2014, p.329), a portfolio is an "assemblage of a series of interrelated events" and he borrows from his previous work to explain that the events in the portfolio should complement one another, for example, in the way that together they can engage in knowledge transfer, share physical and human resources, develop common markets and so on.

A portfolio allows event leveraging to go much further, as it is possible to cross leverage events in a manner that can benefit them all and produce enhanced effects for the host. Cross leveraging may well facilitate long term benefits or legacies to be realised optimally and sustainably, as all events within the portfolio can be developed and managed in a holistic manner to complement or reinforce the benefits bestowed by other events (Ziakas, 2014; Ziakas and Coster, 2011). The level and success of cross leveraging

11

hinges on the make-up of the portfolio and whilst Getz (2013) suggests a distinctly financial/business-like structure that can bring enhanced ROI, Richards and Palmer (2010 p.458-9) feel that it should be composed of events that are not "purely assessed in economic terms but also in terms of cultural and social values as well". To produce the desired synergy between the events, they should be "analysed in relation to one another in order to examine their points of relatedness and complementarities" (Ziakas and Costa, 2011 p.410). Therefore, successful portfolio leveraging requires the careful shaping of the portfolio to ensure that it contains a variety of events that offer the host the best opportunities in terms of content, scale, community focus, timing and so on.

Clearly, judicious strategic planning is at the heart of effective portfolio management and one of the principal challenges to be faced, again, is bringing together multiple stakeholders – this time from within and between events – to work collaboratively with a common goal in mind. This may be especially taxing when the usual collection of events is augmented by a wider range of event types or previously separate event categories (like sport and culture) are brought together in the portfolio. Whatever the particular circumstances, Ziakas (2014) underscores the importance of appropriate institutional structures to facilitate the strategic process; the value of informal social networks and interaction amongst those involved, to foster understanding and a shared sense of purpose; a bank of strong local resources and an interest in local and non-local markets that can offer the right audiences.

There are cities that have risen to this challenge successfully and gained positive cross leveraging effects and legacies through inter-organisational stakeholder cooperation. Edinburgh is a prime example and it has made great strides in its pursuit of a cohesive events strategy that brings event organisations and stakeholders together to create a coordinated festival city programme (see Edinburgh Festivals: 'Inspiring Events Strategy' at www.eventsedinburgh.org.uk). For many years, Edinburgh's festivals operated independently and only linked up occasionally: for example, their tactical cooperation on the first joint festivals gateway website in the late 90s. However, the creation of Festivals Edinburgh in 2006 has brought the festivals together, as a portfolio, and led to a strategic framework with greater cohesion across the many partnerships that they have in common (refer to www.festivalsedinburgh.com). Unlike Edinburgh, where the portfolio is distinctly cultural in composition, Manchester has built on its prowess in sports events and the assets (infrastructure, human resources and expertise) that are a legacy of the 2002 Commonwealth Games, to branch out and develop a more comprehensive portfolio of events. This example illustrates the development of synergies between sport, culture, business and other events (see Strategic Aim 2 of the '2014-20 Greater Manchester Strategy for the Visitor Economy' at www.marketingmanchester.com, as well as 'Reframing Manchester's Cultural Strategy' at http://www.manchestercul-turalpartnership.org).

In the current discourse on public sector event portfolios, Ziakas (2014) cautions about the need for further conceptual elaboration and empirical testing of portfolio frameworks. However, there is already evidence from other sectors to suggest that well managed and cleverly leveraged event portfolios are the way forward in terms of lasting benefits or legacies.

Not-for-profit and private sector event legacy

Academic literature on the subject of event legacy is devoted almost exclu-sively to the public sector and, so far, this chapter has followed the same path. However, if event legacy is tackled from a leverage standpoint, then the not-for-profit (NFP) and private sectors have something to offer in terms of good practice, since charity and commercial organisations follow a clear strategy in the utilisation of events and, significantly, this strategy may well be applied to a portfolio of events that can bring about lasting effects.

For most charity organisations, events are seen as one element of a multi-pronged programme that is designed to meet the overriding goal of supporting a specific cause. Charity events can take many forms and it is this variety that empowers charities to utilise events in a multitude of ways. Generating income for the charity is the most widely appreciated use of events because so many people either participate actively in fundrais-ing events or they support those that do, indirectly, through sponsorship. However, charities also employ events extensively to build awareness of the organisation, and its mission, educate the public about the cause that the charity supports, engage with communities, develop and reinforce stakeholder relationships and so on. Having so much scope and potential in the deployment of events means that charity organisations need to choose and use events wisely and this requires a strategy that is applied not just to each of the individual events but to the full portfolio. In this manner, a diverse collection of events, with different objectives and targeting different segments can be brought together holistically and leveraged successfully to meet the needs of the charity and produce expected outcomes, in the manner suggested by Ziakas, Chalip and others for public events. The application of event portfolios in the NFP sector and the way that they can be managed to bring about long term effects or legacies will be demonstrated through an examination of two leading UK charities: The British Heart Foundation (BHF) and Cancer Research UK (CRUK). Each demonstrates a clear strategic focus that drives the use of events and unites those who are employed in the process.

11

The vision of the BHF is "a world in which people do not die prematurely or suffer from cardiovascular disease" (British Heart Foundation, 2014). The charity is involved in a wide range of events, both in the UK and overseas, and these events fit into a number of categories that match seven key themes of the organisation (see Table 11.1).

Table 11.1: British Heart Foundation themes and associated events

Strategic Theme	Examples of events that support the theme
Research	BHF works with the British Cardiovascular Society Conference to bring together clinicians, researchers and health care professionals to disseminate the latest advances, learning and information
Prevention	Outreach initiatives are developed to target vulnerable groups or communities and events like No Smoking Day to mobilise people to action
Survival	Events that bring together people, staff and volunteers to learn lifesaving skills like CPR
Support	BHF runs a series of annual events to bring young people with cardiac conditions together
Listen, Engage, Influence	Campaigning activity includes people gathering to demonstrate for better cardiac care, or participating in e-advocacy events (such as lobbying MPs by email), and other campaign initiatives
Growing Income	Fundraising events include the London to Brighton Bike Ride (the biggest single event of the BHF year) which brings together over 36,000 people. The BHF portfolio has hundreds of events (including running, swimming, cycling, hiking, challenges and sky dives) and themed events like 'Ramp Up The Red'
World class	BHF holds a series of annual supporter conferences to engage and celebrate supporters and volunteers

Industry voice: Dr. Charmaine Griffiths, Director of Strategy and Performance at the British Heart Foundation

At the BHF it is our mission to win the fight against cardiovascular disease (CVD), so we are in it for the long game. Growing a business operating model that sustains our work for the long term is crucial, and engagement and events have been an essential part of our work for over 40 years. We have a broad church of events that reflects the breadth of what we do as a charity and the diversity of people involved in our fight against CVD. We don't view the BHF events in isolation from one another. We see the hundreds of events we run each year across all themes as connected parts of our customer journey. And, as we are in it for the long term, our engagement strategy with people across the UK must be too. We recognise that this is how you get the most valuable and meaningful relationships, and build a groundswell of support for our fight to save lives. It's very rare that a one hit wonder event will give you a meaningful and lasting return.

In terms of an approach, we know that by listening and engaging with people we can always improve what we do. Some of this certainly challenges the organisation...but it's key to our success. The new strategy to 2020 has engagement at the heart of it, and recognises that achieving real change needs all of our stakeholders and supporters to play a role. This means we need to accept internally that the BHF can't know everything, or create a perfectly robust concrete plan that can't be shaken. Being responsive to trends in the environment or market, and innovative in approach are key. We respond to trends like the current interest in digital events rather than physical...and are experimenting with interactive mass participation events that help us raise vital funds in a way that people find easy and fun to do.

Over recent years our events strategy has successfully focused on delivering fewer events, bigger and better, whilst maintaining a year-round programme of ways in which people can get involved with the BHF. Strategically we are making decisions to specialise in some areas where we know we've got a unique place in the market and build on the strength of our experience and skills, for example as a leader in cycling events within the charity sector. We have run the largest cycling event in Europe, the BHF London to Brighton Bike Ride, for nearly 40 years and are capitalising on this legacy by growing a series of popular off road, international or overnight cycling events. This makes the most of what we know that we're good at – developing brilliant and popular fundraising activities that raise vital funds for research that fights CVD. Cycling is clearly also brilliant for keeping fit and healthy (and great fun), and therefore it links closely to what we are aiming to do at the BHF. We are also growing mass participation events – building on our February National Heart Month – as well as events that are more focused on our special strengths but, that said, it is important that we have the all-year-round, fabulous portfolio of events that have become our trademark.

11

The classification of the BHF events indicates that the organisation understands how to exploit a wide range of events to meet the various needs of the charity. What is also important in the context of this chapter, however, is that the BHF views the events as a portfolio and manages them strategically (in conjunction with the other strands of its work) to enable the charity to match up to its vision. Individually, the events would be far less effective than they are together, so they are conceived, developed and leveraged to contribute collectively to the achievements of the charity. It is noteworthy, given previous comments on public sector stakeholders, that unifying leadership guides the direction and management of the BHF portfolio. Although the vision for CRUK is, of course, different from the BHF (see the CRUK case study in this section), the organisations have much in common in their use of events. For the BHF and CRUK there is a strong, overriding mission to realise a lasting legacy in support of the charity cause and the place of events in this process is clear. Whilst certain high profile events, like 'The London to Brighton Bike Ride' and 'Race for Life', offer

y positive, long term effects of their own that can have a big influence
n how each charity engages with its public, all strands of the charity's
work are contributing to what is a very impressive legacy. In the charities
examined, this is improving the health and welfare of society.

stry voice: Richard Taylor, Executive Director draising and Marketing, Cancer Research UK

Cancer Research UK (CRUK) is the world's leading cancer charity and its vision is "to bring forward the day when all cancers are cured". The strategy that CRUK adopts has four main strands: working to help prevent cancer, diagnosing it early, developing new treatments and optimising current treatments.

Part of the legacy of CRUK events is enabling people to have a better understanding of who we are as an organisation, what we achieve and the impact that we have. So, for example, on the stage before an event like 'Shine', a walking marathon, or one of the 'Race for Life' events, we regularly have a scientist or a cancer patient testifying to the value of our work. It is very engaging and a powerful way to spread our message and garner long term support and loyalty for the charity. As a scientific organisation, we are at risk of being perceived as remote, distant and simply in a lab. Without events people might not understand us or relate to us in the way that they do.

CRUK employs a portfolio approach to managing its events strategy. This means that the performance of constituent events and how they fit together with other events in the portfolio (and, of course, match up to the needs of the charity) are regularly appraised. Changes are made when necessary to optimise use of resources and improve the effectiveness of the portfolio. The three key considerations with events are: firstly, profitability...the money raised after costs for the charity; secondly, lifetime value, and by this I mean how it helps us move participants through and keep them involved with the charity; and finally, the way that the event supports and builds the brand, enhances our reputation and allows us to achieve our overall goals. We undertake market research and have a Portfolio Board meeting where we look at all of our products and evaluate their performance. So events and other products have to compete with one another for resources and investment, and where they sit in the calendar. The portfolio team then determines whether an event stays, develops or goes...and it is critical that we kill off things as well as start them.

We take a year by year approach to this process and ask questions like...which events are doing well around the country? Where do we get the best responses and returns? Should we grow the events further or do we need to be more innovative and more creative with them? Take 'Race for Life' for example. Participation was declining so we rebranded in 2012 and extended the proposition with an evening version called Twilight. This wasn't about running 5k in the day time – it took place in the evening and aimed to be accessible for all the family, broadening the target segment from women only. Unfortunately, it wasn't as successful as we had hoped so is no longer part of our portfolio, However, this year we've tried another extension of 'Race for Life' and we've called it 'Pretty Muddy'. We've added a bit of fun with a fairly easy assault course (slides, hay bales, ropes and so on), so rather than just running around a park. It's fun and they get really messy...and it stretches them a bit more. We are finding that this has scope in offering women a different challenge that will take them on from 'Race for Life' and it has exceeded all our expectations for sign-ups.

Private sector event strategies

The leveraging value of events is also recognised in the private sector, where events are increasingly utilised in marketing, to connect consumers with the brand and to develop strong relationships with customers over time (Wood, 2009). Whilst many of these events are designed to have powerful short-term, individual impact, the evidence from many companies points to the use of events as part of a co-ordinated, long term strategy that can result in positive outcomes for the brand. Events are developed and delivered to capture the interest of consumers and involve them in a distinctive and special experience. Because of this, some of these events are one-off and are not extended or repeated as this would reduce their impact. However, this is just one category of event and companies need to generate a series of different events in order to have a lasting influence on consumers. Red Bull is a company that does this impressively by inventing and sponsoring innovative events to raise brand awareness, reinforce its brand positioning and build a strong brand ethos amongst consumers, many of whom have become advocates for the brand. The company's link-up with Felix Baumgartner for his Stratos Jump was a spectacular one-off example of event marketing. However, the marketing literature is full of examples from Red Bull's successful campaigns based on its own spectator events like Red Bull X-Fighters, Red Bull Air Race and Red Bull Cliff Diving World Series, alongside experiential opportunities that actively involve consumers with the brand as in Red Bull Flugtag. It takes time to build brand values successfully through the use of events that reinforce a distinct lifestyle and there is no question that Red Bull has an enviable track record in this respect with its own events, its sponsorships and endorsements (See www.redbull.com/en/uk/events to appreciate the company's extensive, brand reinforcing investment in staging and supporting high adrenalin, extreme and fast-paced sport events and performers/teams...as well as cool music festivals, music academy happenings and high tech gaming events... that all fit with a drink that is branded to revitalise the mind and body and 'give you wings'). And Red Bull is certainly not alone; increasingly, the most successful brands are

11

turning to the leveraging of events because of the influential effects that they can generate.

Whilst private sector companies may operate a portfolio of events that can be leveraged in various ways to meet the needs of the company, the question to pose here is whether or not a series of private sector event outcomes can lead to a distinctive legacy for the company. It is clear that one of the characteristics of an event legacy is that it should be a lasting outcome. On this basis, therefore, the simple answer to the question would be 'no', since brands cannot rest on their laurels and think 'job done' and legacy nailed or they would not last long in a competitive, commercial environment. The process is evolutionary so they need to develop and adapt to situations when necessary in order to remain successful. This is not to say that private sector event portfolios do not play an important part in the achievement of company goals; just that these achievements may not endure and are most unlikely to be permanent. Although an event portfolio may not be the route to a lasting legacy in the private sector, there are other ways in which commercial companies can accomplish discernible long term event effects and one of the most interesting in this context is through partnerships with the public sector. Link-ups between the private and public sectors are not new but there have been some developments in this symbiosis; in particular, the type of results expected. Some of this is due to the weighting attached to event legacy in the public sector and the increased importance of demonstrating non-commercial effects through the alliance. This can be illustrated by the official partnership of Virgin Media, a leading UK communications and entertainment company, with the Glasgow 2014 Commonwealth Games. The collaboration clearly benefited the event organisers in the digital promotion services that Virgin Media could provide and, of course, the relationship gave an appreciable boost to Virgin Media's brand presence in the period during and around the Games, so permitting a win-win arrangement for both parties. However, the expectations for Virgin Media went beyond this conventional partnership and offered opportunities that could well enable the company to contribute towards a lasting Games legacy.

Industry voice: Luke Southern, Virgin Media Marketing and Strategy Director, Glasgow 2014 Commonwealth Games

There are a number of reasons why we thought Glasgow 2014 was the right thing for Virgin Media. It is a great chance for us to push our brand out there in a positive way and associate it with something that everybody is going to be talking about in the summer, so elevating our brand. So it will also be a great opportunity to engage with the people that we care about...our customers and our staff...and drive advocacy. It will also elevate the brand through association with the Games and, of course, underlying all of this is a commercial imperative...and we see the Games as a platform to drive the growth of our business. By activating the brand with a live event like Glasgow 2014, it allows people a kind of live experience of the brand and makes the brand more tangible.

As well as bringing the whole of the UK on a broadband journey and educating them with basic digital skills we are, off the back of the Games, leading a number of projects in Scotland that we hope will have very positive long term consequences. It enables us to take responsibility and give something back. For example, a number of senior people from our organisation are going into SMEs to help them to become more digitally literate so that they understand the role that technology can play in their business, and why technology is important for innovation and growth. Some of these organisations are working with disadvantaged or at-risk individuals and we have the weight of the brand, the clout and collateral to try and affect a positive change socially as well as technologically. These are important community legacy benefits.

Interview recorded before the event.

So what we have here is a private sector company that is working with a public sector event to create community enhancements. Virgin Media's association with Glasgow 2014 was not announced until a year before the event so any legacy from the partnership will be, in a sense, a bonus that fits the legacy objectives but was not part of the original plan. The scale of the community benefits that Virgin can accomplish in this case is also modest when balanced against the other legacy ambitions for Glasgow 2014. However, the coming together of public and private sectors in the achievement of specific legacies, rather than conventional sponsorship rewards, is an interesting trend that can be seen with other public sector events. A notable example is the link-up between Sky, one of the leading entertainment and communications providers in the UK, and British Cycling. As principal partner of British Cycling, Sky invests in every level of cycling from the "elite team of World, Olympic and Paralympic cyclists to British Cycling's talent development programmes and grassroots initiatives in schools and local communities. The partnership covers all forms of the competitive sport from BMX to track cycling and road racing, with the aim of bringing on the elite teams and accelerating the development of emerging talent" (British Cycling, 2014). The successes of British Cycling at an elite level in international competitions have been transformational for the sport and, on the back of this success, community level involvement with cycling has developed exponentially. In 2014 there are very few local authorities that have not built cycling objectives into their transport and healthy living programmes (see www.yorkshire.com for 'Cycle Yorkshire' and 'Le Grand Depart Legacy' examples). Clearly, this is a legacy that Sky can lay claim to, in part.

11

Concluding remarks

Event legacy has become something of a hot topic in relation to one-off, large scale public events and is rarely out of the news in popular broadcast and print media. Much of the interest in legacy centres on the understated costs and exaggerated outcomes of these events and when the associated legacy plans are scrutinised, there are often short-comings to report. It may help if events, whatever their size, are managed as part of a portfolio, rather than individually. They can then be leveraged strategically, in a holistic way that will maximise effects, including long-term legacies. The public sector has a lot to learn in this respect from many NFP and commercial organisations that coordinate a portfolio of diverse events with great success and, particularly in the case of NFP, realise notable legacies.

Study questions

1   Compare the legacy ambitions of London 2012 with Glasgow 2014: in what ways are they similar and different? Critically assess the strategic approach taken by the two hosts in delivering the legacies.

2   Investigate the events offered by a city that is not mentioned in this chapter. What evidence is there to show that these events constitute a portfolio rather than a simple collection/calendar of events?

3   Identify further examples of link-ups between public and private sector organisations that are intended to generate long term effects. Consider the reasons for these partnerships and assess the likelihood of them resulting in legacies.

References

British Cycling (2014) Principal partner - Sky. www.britishcycling.org.uk/about/article/bc20120312-about-bc-static-Principle-Partner ---Sky-0, accessed 02/07/2014

British Heart Foundation (2014) British Heart Foundation Strategy 2014. www.bhf.org.uk/publications/view-publication.aspx?ps=1002480, accessed 01/05/2014

Cashman, R. (2006) *The Bitter Sweet Awakening: The Legacy of the Sydney 2000 Olympic Games*, Sydney: Walla Walla Press.

Chalip, L. (2002) Tourism and the Olympic Games, paper presented at the international symposium Legacy of the Olympic Games 1984-2000, 14-16 November, Lausanne.

Chalip, L. (2004). Beyond impact: a general model for sport event leverage, in B.W.Richie and D. Adair (eds.), *Sport Tourism: Interrelationships, Impacts and Issues*, Clevedon: Channel View Publications, pp. 226-252.

Chalip, L. (2014). From legacy to leverage, in J. Grix (ed.), *Leveraging Legacies from Sports Mega-Events*, Basingstoke: Palgrave Macmillan, pp. 2-12.

Chalip, L. and Leyns, A. (2002). Local business leveraging of a sport event: managing an event for economic benefit, *Journal of Sport Management*, **16**, 133-159.

DCMS (2012a). London 2012 forecast to come in almost £400 million under budget. www.gov.uk/government/news/london-2012-forecast-to-come-in-almost-400m-under-budget, accessed 01/03/2014

DCMS (2012b). Beyond 2012: The London 2012 Legacy Story. www.gov.uk/government/uploads/system/uploads/attachment_data/file/77993/DCMS_Beyond_2012_Legacy_Story, accessed 01/05/2014

Getz, D. (2013). *Event Tourism: Concepts, International Case Studies and Research*, New York: Cognizant Communication.

Glasgow 2014 (2009). People, Place, Passion: Glasgow 2014 Commonwealth Games Candidate City File, Volumes 1, 2 and 3. www.thecgf.com/media/games/2014/G2014_CCF_Vol1-3, accessed 01/05/2014

Gold, J.R. and Gold, M.M. (2008). Olympic cities: regeneration, city rebranding and changing urban agendas, *Geography Compass*, **2** (1), 300-318.

Kissoudi, P. (2008). The Athens Olympics: optimistic legacies – post-Olympic assets and their struggle for realisation, *International Journal of the History of Sport*, **25** (14), 1972-1990.

Leopkey, B. and Parent, M. M. (2012). Olympic Games legacy: from general benefits to sustainable long-term legacy, *International Journal of the History of Sport*, **29** (6), 924-943.

O'Brien, D. and Chalip, L. (2007). Executive training exercise in sport event leverage, *International Journal of Culture, Tourism and Hospitality Research*, **1** (4), 296-304.

Richards G. and Palmer, R. (2010). *Eventful Cities: Cultural Management and Urban Revitalisation*, Oxford: Elsevier.

Scottish Government (2009). A Games legacy for Scotland. www.scotland.gov.uk/Resource/Doc/282449/00854055, accessed 01/05/2014

Smith, A. (2014). Leveraging sport mega-events: new model or convenient justification?, *Journal of Policy Research in Tourism, Leisure and Events*, **6** (1), 15-30.

Taks, M., Misener, L., Chalip, L. and Green, B.C. (2013). Leveraging sport events for participation, *Canadian Journal for Social Research*, **3**, 12-23.

Thompson, A., Schlenker, K. and Schlenkorf, N. (2013). Conceptualizing sport event legacy. *Event Management*, **17**, 111-122.

Wood, E.H. (2009). Evaluating event marketing: experience or outcome?, *Journal of Promotion Management*, **15** (1-2), 247-268.

11

Ziakas, V. (2014) Planning and leveraging event portfolios: towards a holistic theory, *Journal of Hospitality Marketing and Management*, **23** (3), 327-356.

Ziakas, V. and Costa, C.C. (2011) Event portfolio and multi-purpose development: Establishing the conceptual grounds, *Sport Management Review*, **14** 409-423.

Part IV
Reflective
Approach

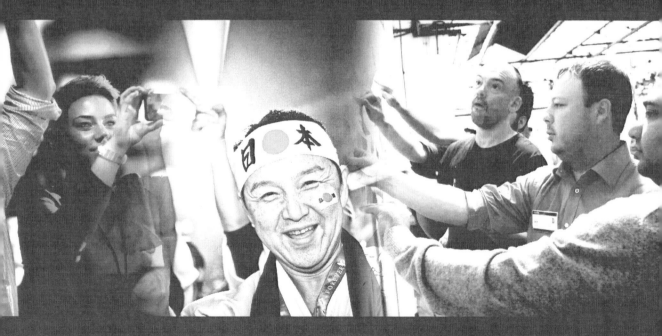

12 Strategic Event Evaluation

Katrin Stefansdottir and Anjalina Pradhan

Learning objectives

- Understand the strategic stakeholder centric approach to event evaluation.
- To realise the importance of on-going event evaluation.
- Realise the barriers to evaluation, how they can and should be overcome.

Introduction

This book has repeatedly encouraged an outcome focussed approach to event creation which is specifically discussed in the early chapters. Indeed a key characteristic of planned events is that they produce many and varied outcomes and impacts, which represent the consequences of an event, and their evaluation is to some degree required. Part Two of the book reviews the diversity of stakeholder objectives and concerns that underpin any event. The outcome based approach is however undermined if event creators do not sufficiently and proficiently embed evaluation throughout the process. Clearly evaluation is scalable and should be determined by the specific event context; stakeholders, size, future plans, and so forth are determining factors. A failure to do this has many adverse effects for both the current and any future events, and also stakeholder relationships. Nonetheless often evaluation is deficient, hence the contention is for practitioners to invest in evaluation in order to become more reflective in their approach.

A key challenge for event professionals is for evaluation to become 'what we do' rather than 'something else we have to do' and this chapter will provide readers with some of the key arguments and approaches to make evaluation an effective and a manageable aspect of event creation.

The next chapter builds upon this by considering much more specifically the methods that can be applied. Often when considering event evaluation, the conversation shifts quickly to the measurement of post event outcomes. While this is integral, a major contribution of this chapter is to identify the three pillars of event evaluation. The three purposes of evaluation, from an event creator's perspective are:

1 To aid decisions relating to the effective design and operations of the current event

2 To identify, explore, capture and communicate important outcomes to share with current and future stakeholders

3 To acquire learning and insight to benefit future event creation

Each of these factors has the potential to make a significant difference to the success of the current event, future events, and the general success for all stakeholders involved, not least the event creators themselves whose careers will be enhanced. Before progressing the discussion about how evaluation can be achieved, it is useful to reflect upon why evaluation in events does not always receive the same intensity of focus as it should. Each of the following reasons, many identified by research (MPI, 2011), represent legitimate explanations as to why evaluation remains an aspect of event creation where, as an industry, we must do better:

☐ Short-lived nature of both events and event teams limits the time available

☐ Difficulties in capturing intangible / soft outcomes increases the perceived complexity

☐ Wide variety of interests and experiences occurring through an event broadens the scope

☐ Future oriented nature of outcomes means evaluation cannot be isolated to the event itself

☐ Isolating event specific outcomes from wider influencing factors makes the results seem less reliable

☐ Potential cost of evaluation, both financially and in time, makes it less appealing than investing these resources in content or marketing

Although each of these points is understandable and certainly add to the evaluation challenge, collectively they must be considered as necessary hurdles to overcome rather than justifications to avoid, reduce, or generally downgrade evaluation. By adopting a proficient evaluation approach that is carefully integrated with the events design, each of the above loses their threat and can be ably managed. A key, and recurring, message in this and the next chapter is that the evaluation approach, to any given event, should be designed and embedded at an early stage as identified by Vladimir Vodalov.

Industry voice: Vladimir Vodalov, Director, EXIT Festival, Serbia

Evaluation is at least a few months of intensive work. But we have to constantly evaluate our work, economy, sustainability, programme, security, safety, visual identity, main message, where we are, where we wish to go. Without evaluation there is no change and without change there is no continuity. Evaluation of one's work is essential for success.

To achieve the three pillars of event creation, detailed above, event creators must collect information pre, during, and post event. This is in stark contrast to the view that sometimes prevails in events whereby evaluation is a bolt-on at the end.

The importance of event evaluation

It is useful to further explore this topic which was introduced above, and identified concisely in the three pillars. For event creators there are many persuasive reasons why evaluation should be considered important. First and foremost that success can be evidenced and showcased and that, equally, underperformance can be analysed. Events include many aspects, therefore successes and failures cannot be easily generalised and are often triggered by specific aspects of the event project and design. The overall success of an event is unlikely to be because every aspect of it is extremely effective. Successful events may contain faulty aspects and underachieving events very probably contain some effective aspects. Therefore well designed evaluation, which identifies the influential factors on the success of the event and provides the depth of insight required, is crucial. The identification of outcomes is hence closely linked to an understanding of how and why those outcomes were achieved. This learning is vital in enabling event creators to learn about which elements of their design works, therefore benefitting future event creation.

There are many other specific rationale for evaluation, some of which are considered below. Chapter 6 discusses the community and the environment, which increasingly is emerging as a vital consideration for event creators. The ability to capture these less immediate or obvious impacts, whether positive or negative, is extremely important in ensuring a positive relationship with this important stakeholder group (as Chapter 2 argues). Attendees are obviously a key stakeholder, as discussed in Chapter 4, and by evaluating carefully with this group an appreciation of their experience can be gathered. If designed effectively, this can also be a co-creative opportunity to engage with participants and benefit from their feed-forward to

12

influence the design of future events. These examples support the need for evaluation to be viewed and carried out on a longer-term basis and not as a one-off exercise, and also indicate the more holistic nature of evaluation. By doing this, both a formative evaluation is carried out during the event in order to improve it, and a summative evaluation is conducted post event (Stufflebeam and Shinkfield, 2007), providing the stakeholders with a judgement of the event's value (Worthen and Sanders, 1987). Although much of the data may only need to be collected once during the event process, its collation and interpretation will have wider and longer term implications, as it is used to inform analysis and presentation relating to the current event, and much more significantly to support and inform future activity.

Regular research by the industry association MPI (Meeting Professionals International) has demonstrated that if business events are evaluated and results reported to key stakeholders, their budgets are more likely to increase or at least stay the same than with those who do not evaluate (see their current reports Meetings Outlook, previous publications are Business Barometer and EventView). It would seem logical to suggest this can be generalised beyond this sector as the process of evidencing outcomes has the potential to enhance relationships and increase trust. To some degree, effectual evaluation and the communication process beyond that is a very useful form of marketing towards future events. Sponsors who receive insightful evaluation relating to their desired ROI (Return on Investment) would seem more likely to wish to continue their relationship with that event. It should be noted that evaluations are also sometimes seen as threats to stakeholders as they are afraid of negative outcomes (MPI, 2011). Therefore, the development of collaborative evaluation approaches to break down these concerns is advisable.

Evaluation provides event creators, and other stakeholders, with powerful and rich information that is not easily identifiable from simply participating in the event. The scale of the evaluation undertaken will necessarily vary depending upon the size and context of the event. A key principle is therefore that evaluation should be proportionate to the event, so a larger event with more resources would seek to interrogate many more aspects and on a larger scale. By applying this logic the commonly perceived obstacles listed in the introduction, such as high costs, time and complexity, are reduced. The emphasis in this book is upon feasible evaluation approaches that are often relatively inexpensive in their resource intensity. See also some of the evaluation tools and methods discussed in the next chapter.

Meaningful event evaluation

Evaluation is an umbrella term that comprises a wide variety of aspects knitted throughout the event life cycle. The focus should not be preoccupied only with more direct and tangible (hard) factors such as attendance, revenue, media exposure, costs incurred, but importantly also upon less tangible (softer) and sometimes less direct factors as argued by Dwyer et al. (2000) and Wood (2009), amongst others. Experience of attendees and wider stakeholders, changed perceptions/intentions, other stakeholders' reactions, new relationships and opportunities triggered, and also wider economic impacts that have occurred as a result of the event are examples of less tangible factors. It is therefore advisable to carry out a valid evaluation using both intangible and tangible aspects, as this provides a deeper and more holistic understanding of the event outcomes. It also delivers a depth of information that provides feed-forward which means event creators can move forward on a more assured footing. The example below from Steve Bather demonstrates how a quantitative approach can be altered with a more qualitative question to reveal a deeper and more meaningful appreciation. Such information and intelligence provides event creators with insight to be able to more assuredly debrief stakeholders and to better inform their own learning and planning for future events.

Industry voice: Steve Bather, CEO, MeetingSphere, Washington, USA

Instead of asking the general quantitative question 'How do you rate the overall value of the meeting to you?' The alternative and more precise phrasing of this question could be in terms of 'How many other things have you thought about that you should have done which would have been of more value to you than sitting here for two days?' or 'What is the value of now understanding and feeling part of the strategic development for the organisation?' or 'How will the knowledge that you now have of the strategy enable you to do your job better?'

12

These questions have been rephrased to much more deeply gain insight into the attendees' thinking. A similar approach can be pursued with other stakeholders and in other contexts, for example by interpreting sponsors' and partners' return on investment evaluation questions, and approaches can be devised to ensure they can be provided with meaningful information. It could be argued that the first stage of evaluation comes at the very inception of the event, and is the interpretation of stakeholder aspirations and concerns. This early evaluation provides the insight necessary to design the evaluation approach. Event creators design their approach to evaluation by understanding the event's strategic context, including stakeholder ambitions and concerns, type and size of the event, resources available, etc. The evaluation methods, each with its limitations and qualities, are then considered and chosen with these aspects in mind. Resource constraints often limit the possible scale of evaluation and rightly so as evaluation, while integral, is one cost within the larger event scenario. Therefore while we argue for more of an evaluation focus, clearly judgements need to be continually made as to what is proportionate and achievable.

A resounding message of this chapter is that whatever the scale and mix of evaluation approaches used, they must be consistent with the strategic event context and provide information that is meaningful to the event creators and stakeholders.

Evaluation considerations

This section examines a variety of issues, tensions, and decisions that event creators must consider in designing and executing evaluation. The considerations discussed below reflect the many issues that surround evaluation, and emphasise the importance for event creators of considering these in a proactive and planned manner to devise their approach.

■ Different outcomes for different stakeholders

A key competence of event creators is to interpret and then 'juggle' the variety of objectives that stakeholders hold, sometimes aligned and complimentary, sometimes opposing. Typically a variety of objectives and aspirations from funders, attendees, communities, and so forth, many of which are explained in detail in Part Two of this book, inform an event and the event creator must ensure the delivery of these, but also the evidencing and communication of that achievement (Bowdin et al., 2011; Getz, 2012). Different events therefore require altered evaluation approaches; consider the variances between a commercial entertainment event, a community flower show, and a political convention. As discussed in Chapters 2 and 3, stakeholders and outcomes differ with events. Many events are held primarily to achieve short term financial return with longer term outcomes very distantly in the mind of funders. Other events are much more strategic with the short term (event specific) outcomes of less consequence and the focus being much more about longer term, maybe softer, outcomes related to awareness generation or changed behaviour. Judgements are therefore consistently made through the event design decisions as to where the priorities are and, in the case of evaluation, what will be focussed upon. Where stakeholders feel their objectives have not been met, or adequately focussed upon, they may express dissatisfaction or feel ignored, therefore the communication process, underpinned by evaluated evidence, is integral to the management of key relationships.

■ Event owner and wider stakeholder outcomes

It is important to achieve alignment by proactively seeking synergy between host and wider stakeholder objectives. For example when soliciting for sponsors and partners, focus should be given to identifying those who share the same general vision for the event, which makes event design and evaluation decisions much more straightforward. Alternatively, the event owner's core objectives might be to some degree competing with those of other stakeholders as discussed in Chapters 2 and 3. Third sector organisations are often good examples of this as they rely on funding from various commercial and non-commercial benefactors and there becomes a risk that their own core mission can become marginal as they seek to please others. Event creators need to make judgements on a priority basis to decide what needs to be evaluated, otherwise the scale will become unmanageable and by trying to achieve too much breadth of outcome, the quality of the evaluation outcome will be reduced. This is a consistent risk that event creators face and the message that comes from this chapter is to do less evaluation, but do it effectively, rather than trying to do more evaluation that will be of limited use. Therefore the priority outcome and impact areas must also be the focus of the evaluation if they are to be adequately managed and evidenced. These conflicts are reflected in Maurice Fleming's thoughts.

Industry voice: Maurice Fleming, Managing Director, Shelton Fleming Associates Ltd, UK

Each client has different focus on indicators for success (Key Performance Indicators). These can be identified by analysing where their concerns were raised during the pitch and implementation phase of the project. So typically, in the event industry, the evaluation phase does not easily follow a fixed set of steps to deliver an evaluation. Instead it is an organic learning process, built throughout the duration of the project where, by observing the client and their areas of concern, you can learn where they will want to see justification and evidence of success. The delivery of an event evaluation must address the areas of concern raised and valued by the client and clearly justify the reasons behind decisions made outside of the initial brief.

12

■ Tangible and intangible outcomes

Required outcomes will sometimes be tangible, such as direct revenues generated or media coverage gained, and as such can be more straightforwardly evaluated through more traditional approaches. Even when tangible, the outcomes may not be so direct; consider secondary spend within a community as a result of a country fair. Very often the important outcomes will be related to intangible (or less tangible) measures, for example community pride or even friendship (Foley et al., 2014), and may need to be recorded in a more qualitative, or narrative form (Getz, 2012). One of many approaches to capture these outcomes is outlined by eventIMPACTS (UK Sport, 2014). The intangible factors are often more challenging to capture, but they are important outcomes, particularly in being able to interpret the 'why' in addition to the 'what'. The hard fact of a 68% satisfaction rate is only of real value to the event creators if they are able to interpret what lies beneath that figure. The depth of information provided by exploring softer factors is of high value and can be extremely influential in explaining issues and making future event design decisions.

■ Motivational factors

Different attendees, similarly to different funders, sponsors, and partners, have different motivations for attending an event. Understanding these motivational elements is part of an event creator's evaluation and may come early in the event cycle, as they will determine event design decisions. If you are, for instance, hosting a conference, in order to address how the motivational levels can be enhanced you would need to interpret the range, and respective importance, of motivations for prospective attendees. As an example, the creators of the annual FRESH conference in Copenhagen (Meeting Support Institute, 2014) effectively evaluate their event from an early stage by engaging potential attendees to suggest topics for sessions and therefore offering a co-creation of the event and better understanding of attendees' motivational factors. Additional approaches may include examination of previous conference evaluation, secondary research, or direct evaluation with the target market. During a conference, the evaluation can be carried out through informal interviews, observation of attendees' participation and enthusiasm during sessions, and by more formal means such as focus groups and questionnaires. Following the conference participants can be encouraged to continue interaction and networking online.

■ Experience-based attendee outcomes

Attendees may have predetermined goals or objectives for attending the event, and how they react or feel towards the overall event or towards specific elements of it, determine positive and negative outcomes. As elucidated in Chapter 4, they may experience a change in perception, attitude or behaviour as they journey through the event and an evaluation needs to capture this change. In a broader perspective, individuals who may not have attended the event may also have been impacted by the event indirectly

(Getz, 2012), and that may all add up to form an overall event experience, with a positive or negative experience-outcome. Therefore evaluation may need to be devised to capture both evolving experiences over time, and also wider outcomes beyond the physical audience.

■ Socio-cultural and political outcomes

Sometimes events have future-oriented outcomes with their impacts going beyond the physical attendees, event host, and sponsors, and associated with the community and society at large. This manifests itself in various ways, including; community pride and involvement (in the form of volunteering, policy development, and government bodies involvement); effects on public facilities, environment; preservation and refreshment of culture and traditions; health considerations and hazards; tourism influx (Bowdin et al., 2011; Getz, 2012). These outcomes can only be captured through evaluation approaches that transcend the time and space parameters of the event. We therefore see much more strategic approaches to evaluation such as that discussed below in relation to the triple bottom line methodology and the portfolio approach discussed in detail in Chapter 11.

■ Environmental outcomes

Growing in importance is the consideration of the environment particularly in considering ways of minimising negative environmental outcomes. All events, particularly large outdoor events, can have negative impacts on the host community because of pollution (sound, visual, air, land), wastage, effects on the ecosystem, energy consumption and carbon release, crowding, and venue construction (Bowdin et al., 2011; Getz, 2012). This has encouraged event creators to invest in sustainable and greener practices in the design of their events but such developments also trigger a shift for event evaluation which must also now incorporate better, and more regular, focus upon environmental impacts such as the event's carbon footprint (Bladen et al., 2012).

12

■ Economic outcomes

There are many economic related outcomes, both direct and indirect, that understandably preoccupy the thoughts of event stakeholders such as trade relations, money inflow through direct tourists (business and leisure) and building social capital, urban economic development and employment opportunities, and income and wealth through sponsorships, grants and funds (Bowdin et al., 2011; Getz, 2012; Bladen et al., 2012). It is important, as Getz (2012) suggests, to evaluate these factors and others related to them. Such economic outcomes have often been deemed more valuable and important than other outcomes as they are more easily demonstrated through evaluation methodologies using financial, quantifiable and measurable information as feedback.

How to evaluate

The design of the evaluation process starts, as indicated previously, with an identification of important outcomes. For example a small art event may have priorities around selling art and attendees' experience and interaction with the art, therefore they design their evaluation to get data from exhibitors of how much art they sold, and adopt observation to determine attendees' experience which is augmented by interviewing a small number of people. This more modest approach is in contrast with large sporting events which may have the necessity and resource to employ research consultants to carry out wide-reaching evaluations including visitor, economic, and social impacts.

Event creators have the opportunity to design the first evaluation of an event on a smaller and very manageable scale, and thereby reduce its cost, complexity and needed manpower. This can then progress over time as the event creators become more confident with what can be achieved and also the plethora of tools available. As previously stated it is better to invest in activity that enables the reporting of focussed, or small-scale results which only address one objective area, than not being able to demonstrate outcomes through any valid data at all. The experience and learning from the evaluation can then be used to build on for future events as is demonstrated in the case study of the Iceland Airwaves music festival evaluation.

Case study: Iceland Airwaves music festival, Reykjavik – Learning from evaluation

Iceland Airwaves is a music festival hosted annually in Reykjavik, the capital of Iceland, in October/November. The first event was held in an airplane hangar in 1999 and has grown into an internationally recognised festival showcasing new music in multiple venues attracting over 9,000 attendees. In addition to the anticipated outcome of increased awareness of Icelandic musicians the event was created to boost tourism in Reykjavik during low-season. In order to demonstrate the value and importance of the event to Reykjavik's economy during the event an evaluation of the turnover by the festival's foreign guests within the city has been carried out since 2010.

The evaluation design has evolved and continuously improved over time as event creators have gained more experience and data to compare. The data collection has been carried out through a face-to-face questionnaire by students at the University of

Iceland approaching international festival attendees. In the first year three students col-lected data which proved not to be sufficient and therefore 10 students have since been recruited on a voluntary basis to do so in exchange for a festival ticket. The evaluation has therefore provided an opportunity for volunteers to participate in the event and invited collaboration with the local university, as their lecturers not only assisted with contacting potential volunteers but also consulted on the design of the questionnaire. The evaluation has always been undertaken by Iceland Music Export (IMX) in close col-laboration with Iceland Airwaves and in the first two years tourism bureaus participated in the evaluation as they also have a large stake in the outcome. Since the first evalua-tion, the questionnaire has been shortened in response to feedback from interviewers and respondents, in order to increase the possibilities of greater response rate.

The evaluation has demonstrated a substantial turnover by the foreign guests and a yearly increase since there are more international guests every year and they spend more money on a daily basis within Reykjavik during the festival. These figures are con-sistent with information provided by Statistics Iceland on foreign tourist expenditure (2011). In addition, the evaluation shows that a majority of the guests are visiting Iceland for the first time and for the purpose of attending the festival, demonstrating tourism generated by the event and that the attendees engage in other activities and visit other tourism attractions during their stay. The evaluation hence demonstrates how objec-tives have been met and further outcomes achieved than initially planned.

The evaluation results are reported on the IMX website, to primary stakeholders as well as to local councillors and members of parliament and introduced in national media. The evaluation has been utilised in the discussion on interaction between creative art and tourism as well as the importance of revenues that are generated from the tourism for the Icelandic economy through cultural events.

An English version of the evaluation report can be found on http://www.uton.is/frodlei-kur/iceland-airwaves-2011-study

Event evaluation methodologies

12

A range of approaches can be used in event evaluation with many of the more common approaches discussed below. This is not intended as an exhaustive discussion and it should be kept in mind that many event creators will develop their own tailored approach to fit their needs. Each approach has strengths and limitations and given the diversity of the events sector it is important to consider which, and maybe which elements of each, should be used depending upon the context of the event, outcomes and impacts to be evaluated.

Good evaluation ideas and recommended practice can also be found within other fields such as personnel management, product development, education, and marketing, to name a few. In addition, evaluation theory enriched with work by scholars such as Stufflebeam (2001), Scriven (2004), Alkin (2003), Patton (1997) and Mertens et al (2012) is an independent field of study worth exploring for those particularly interested in this important area.

■ Feasibility studies

A feasibility study occurs at a very early stage and acts like a strategic planning document, usually including risk assessment as a part of it (Getz, 2012; Bladen et al., 2012). Hence it is considered an effective evaluation tool to assess the viability of the event and to inform the event design. It provides a considered analysis of the practicality of areas such as those covered in the first two parts of the book, i.e. event objectives and priorities, stakeholders, positive and negative outcomes, and it forecasts the event costs and benefits. O'Toole (2011) provides useful information on undertaking event based feasibility studies and he suggests using checklists, headings and a list of questions to address the important aspects of an event's feasibility study within a deadline.

■ Economic impact assessments

This is a traditional method of calculating economic benefits made from events. Using the multiplier effect it accounts for direct, indirect and induced spending, by using input-output analysis it shows the contribution made to the broader economy by the multipliers as a result of the event occurring (Getz 2012; Bladen et al., 2012). The method would mostly benefit funders, organisers and partners who have a stake in the economic outcomes.

There are limitations to the design of economic studies, such as data being manipulated and not capturing data specific to event attendance, e.g. establishing the actual number of visitors who have travelled specifically for the event as opposed to the total number which includes those who would ordinarily have been there (Getz, 2012). A reason cited for this difficulty is outlined by Davies et al. (2013, p.32) who discuss how there needs to be a clearer articulation of economic impact as meaning 'the total amount of additional expenditure generated within a defined host economy which is directly attributable to the staging of a particular event'. This interpretation of economic impact is demonstrated in the Iceland Airwaves case study, which employs a direct expenditure approach, and it deals with some of the methodological considerations mentioned by Davies et al. (2013). It is a ticketed event therefore the economic impact is more easily calculated as the measurement of attendance is more robust than at free public events and also very few outside traders visit Iceland in the period when the festival is held therefore the local traders benefit from the event with minimal leakage.

■ Cost/benefit analysis method

This is a simple tool but one that requires careful monitoring. It aims to compare the costs incurred in the planning and execution of the event against what has been achieved in real terms. It is not just used to measure the success, but rather as a forecast and monitoring tool to compare forecasts with outcomes, for instance it is a useful management tool to assess for example the value that the PR agency brings to the event. Bladen et al. (2012) discusses how it can be enhanced by including consideration and comparison of tangible/intangible costs and benefits that may not be accounted for in real economic terms. Burgan and Mules (2001) advocate this method claiming that it takes into account costs and benefits for the host community. However the challenge here is that results are completely reliant on the interviewees and where forecasted benefits are intangible such as community pride, the actual costs are tangible, making it difficult for comparisons and analysis.

■ Triple bottom line and values-based evaluation

This is a growing method that offers a holistic approach to calculate the three key areas of socio-cultural, economic and environmental outcomes. Hede (2007) and Tull (2012) advice using a triple bottom line event stake holder map that can identify common interests of stakeholders and thus develop strategies to meet more objectives. Fredline et al. (2005) suggest considering the following areas under each of the headings as illustrated in Figure 12.1 below.

Economic performance indicators	Social impact indicators	Environmental impact indicators
Net income as a ratio over the expenditure The financial contribution of visitors Net benefit to the host community, etc.	Percentage of locals who attended Total volunteers for the event Percentage of local businesses contracted with for supply of goods and services Value of access or access denied to visitors for new facilities Crime reported during the event Traffic counts Crowd management issues Coverage by media, etc.	Energy consumed travelling to and at the venue Carbon footprints Water consumed on-site Waste water and solid wastes recycled, etc.

Figure 12.1: Triple bottom line analysis, adapted from Fredline et al., 2005

This allows the assessment of positive and negative impacts across social, economic and environmental outcomes. Getz (2012) and Bladen et al. (2012)

suggest that this method is more inclusive as it provides the opportunity to consider more stakeholder objectives and to evaluate and demonstrate additional outcomes whereas other approaches concentrate on only one of the areas.

■ ROI methodology

The ROI methodology is useful for both evaluating and planning an event, it provides a particular focus upon business events, but proponents argue it is more widely applicable. It builds upon six levels as illustrated in Figure 12.2.

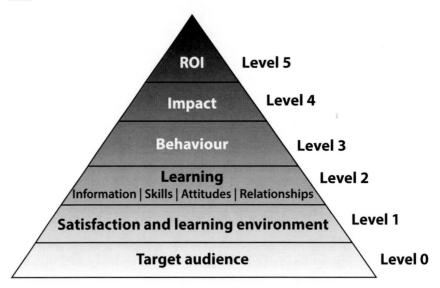

Figure 12.2: The ROI methodology: Source, Phillips et al. (2008)

The lower levels evaluate traditional tangible outcomes whereas higher levels aim at evaluating more intangible outcomes and these levels are often more challenging to include. All levels up until the highest level must be evaluated and objectives set for each of them, and financial measurement is only carried out if the highest level is included (Phillips et al., 2007). An event with outcomes that are not easily transferrable to financial figures would therefore not go beyond Level 4 (Impact) or even Level 3 (Behaviour). The feasibility of the last two levels must be carefully considered and they need substantial planning and time to evaluate. The initiators for the methodology advise that only about 5% of events measure at the last level, for instance very large and expensive events (Phillips et al., 2008). Further information on the methodology can be found on the Event ROI institute website, www.eventroi.org.

■ Environmental impact assessments

Environmental impact assessment is an effective tool designed to calculate carbon footprints, and identify carbon and green practices of events by collecting information relating to event characteristics such as suppliers, venue, food and catering, accommodation, travel, recycling waste method, printing and marketing, and so forth. Checklists and questionnaires are often used to collect such data for evaluating environmental outcomes (Bowdin et al., 2011).

The calculation of carbon footprints at events has become a growing measurement and evaluation tool. A carbon calculator is demonstrated by the Environmental Protection Agency Victoria, Australia called the Carbon and Ecological Footprint Events Calculator (EPA, 2007). The website www.TerraPass.com provides an online carbon footprint calculator with options for the events industry (TerraPass, 2014). In the UK, the management system ISO 20121 has been designed to assist the event creator to manage sustainability throughout the event lifecycle and it helps to improve the sustainability of the event. The system is designed so that it fits with different event sizes, types and budget, and further information on it can be found on www.iso20121.org.

■ Real-time evaluation

A growing area of event evaluation interest is audience behaviour during an event. Brown and Hutton (2013) provide a very useful overview of the development in technologies to enable this. These may not currently be available for all event types but it is worthwhile following given the rapid changes and accessibility to technology. They discuss a study carried out by researchers at Flinders University and Mid-Sweden University which aimed to develop the integrated data survey system (IDSS) for the purposes of evaluating the event experience environment and attendees' physiological response to this environment. Data is collected, for example, attendees' movements tracked by GPS, bio-medical data such as heartbeat and rate of sweating, and observations, interviews, surveys, photos and meteorological evaluation of the event site. This evaluation method allows for a co-creation of the event between event creators and the attendees as they are feeding information on their mood, behaviour and mobility to the creators of the event during it and allowing them to alter the event programme and environment immediately and thereby improving the event experience. The MeetingSphere case study provides an alternative illustration of real time evaluation as well as demonstrating how the approach fulfils the three pillars of evaluation, which informs the design of the current event, capturing and communicating outcomes and impacts, and acquiring learning to enhance future events.

12

Case study: MeetingSphere, a real-time evaluation strategy

A governmental organisation in the USA held a meeting for 400 senior employees in late 2013 with the aim of launching a new strategy. The external event facilitator along with a team of internal event specialists designed an event which would capture the attendees' issues, concerns and questions about the strategy as well as enable an interactive dialogue between attendees. The event was held over two days structured into four 90 minutes sessions, with all of them beginning with a 10-15 minutes introduction on the topic followed by short Q&A. The rest of each session was designed for group discussions, deeper discussion into the practicalities of delivering the strategy and an analysis of the opportunities and barriers to each element of the strategy. Each group of 9-10 attendees were provided three laptops with participant access to the meeting productivity software MeetingSphere. Their discussions were captured, in detail, to ensure all perspectives and views from individuals and the group were considered. All input was anonymous which encouraged people to openly reveal their thoughts without intrepedation. Participants realised that their views and contributions were valid and valuable and reflected what many in the room were thinking. This anonymity is one of the fundamental features when using MeetingSphere; many participants are unwilling or uncomfortable asking questions or commenting publically in front of many people at an event. This way, putting their thoughts through the keyboard, the event creators along with the organisation's leadership team could analyse the data and prepare a response, identify consistent themes and questions raised. The software allows for capturing and processing the inputs (discussion, rating, action tracking) at a very detailed level during the meeting, all fully documented and available instantly. MeetingSphere was also used towards the end of the meeting to evaluate the overall meeting. One quantitative question was asked, 'How do you rate the overall value of the meeting to you?' The mean score from over 400 delegates was 8.2 on a 10 point scale. In addition three qualitative questions were asked, 'What 1-3 things will you do after you leave this conference?', 'What went well?' and 'What needs to be improved?'. The responses to these questions were categorised and reported within a day of the meeting and used to inform the follow up activities and pre-planning of the next event. As demonstrated in this case, using MeetingSphere allowed for the capture of all the ideas, questions and concerns in the room. This was processed by the group to form outcomes, measure consensus and agree next steps and actions. The MeetingSphere tools were also used to evaluate the meeting, measure its value to the participants and check the levels of buy-in to the outcomes agreed. The information on what worked well/needs improving within the meeting, is always used to progress and improve future events. MeetingSphere delivered on the key request from previous events to allow for more discussion time. In the feedback, conventional survey issues, such as facilities, food and other logistical elements were not heavily mentioned.

What to do with the evaluation?

After the evaluation has been designed, and data collected and interpreted, two crucial stages remain. They involve reflecting upon the information and learning from it, and also communicating this skilfully to the necessary stakeholders to satisfy their requirements and safeguard and enhance your relationship with them. In doing this, consideration needs to be given as to whether tailored reporting has to be developed to provide stakeholders with the relevant information they need and not a mass of information. An analysis of this evaluation should be a very early stage in the design process of the next event, in the same way as the presentation of the evaluation to stakeholders should be the first stage in your conversation with them about their future involvement.

Industry voice: Vladimir Vodalov, Director, EXIT Festival, Serbia

Then according to evaluation we decide what will stay the same, what will be created for the first time, what will be abandoned and what will be changed. That process takes a lot of effort and it is very important that it is done by people most suitable and with most experience on the given field or segment, but still there is brainstorming, experiments and a bit of magic.

Concluding remarks

This chapter has made the case for strategic event creators to see evaluation as fulfilling three vital functions, informing the design of the current event, capturing and communicating outcomes and impacts, and acquiring learning to enhance future events. In doing so it emphasises the strategic nature of evaluation and the importance of a considered and multi-layered approach. Evaluation is in many respects the ingredient that underpins event design as it enables event creators to make informed decisions. It must be integral if event creators are to benefit from the opportunity of becoming reflective practitioners.

12

Study questions

1　Why is event evaluation important? What are the challenges for evaluation? What type of information may be required for the consideration of evaluation and for what?

2　What are the factors to be considered for an evaluation method? Discuss some evaluation approaches/methods/tools and the use for each.

3　Interpret how evaluation can be used for ongoing learning. What can be analysed from the MeetingSphere case study discussed in the chapter?

References

Alkin, M.C. (2003). Evaluation theory and practice: Insights and new directions, *New Directions for Evaluation*, **97**, 81-89.

Bladen, C., Kennell, J., Abson, E. and Wilde, N. (2012). *Events Management: an Introduction*, Routledge, London.

Bowdin, G., Allen, J., O'Toole, W. and Harris, R. (2011). *Events Management*, Butterworth-Heinemann, Oxford.

Brown, S. and Hutton, A. (2013). Developments in the real-time evaluation of audience behaviour at planned events, *International Journal of Event and Festival Management*, **4** (1), 43-55.

Burgan, B. and Mules, T. (2001). Reconciling cost–benefit and economic impact assessment for event tourism, *Tourism Economics*, **7** (4) 321-330.

Davies, L., Coleman, R. and Ramchandani, G. (2013). Evaluating event economic impact: rigour versus reality?, *International Journal of Event and Festival Management*, **4** (1) 31-42.

Dwyer, L., Mellor, R., Mistilis, N. and Mules, T. (2000). A framework for assessing "tangible" and "intangible" impacts of events and conventions, *Event Management*, **6** (3) 175-189.

EPA (2007). *Event Ecological Footprint Calculator Checklist*, Environmental Protection Agency Victoria. www.epa.vic.gov.au/our-work/publications/publication/2007/october/1181, accessed 08/08/2014

Event ROI Institute (2014). *Event ROI Institute; Designing effective events.* www.eventroi.org, accessed 08/08/2014

Foley, C., Edwards, D. and Schlenker, K. (2014). Business events and friendship: Leveraging the sociable legacies, *Event Management*, **18** (1) 53-64.

Fredline, L., Raybould, M., Jago, L. and Deery, M. (2005). Triple bottom line event evaluation: A proposed framework for holistic event evaluation, *Third*

International Event Conference, *The Impacts of Events: Triple Bottom Line Evaluation and Event Legacies.* UTS, Sydney.

Getz, D. (2012). Event studies: Discourses and future directions, *Event Management,* **16** (2) 171-187.

Hede, A. (2007). Managing special events in the new era of the Triple Bottom Line, *Event Management,* **11** (1) 13-22.

ISO 20121 Team (2014). *ISO 20121; Event Sustainability Management System.* www. iso20121.org, accessed 08/08/2014

Mertens, D.M. and Wilson, A.T. (2012). *Program Evaluation Theory and Practice: a Comprehensive Guide,* Guilford Press, New York, NY.

Meeting Support Institute (2014). *Fresh; designing effective meetings.* www. thefreshconference.com, accessed 08/08/2014

MPI (2011) *Business Value of Meetings: Defining the Purpose of Your Event and Gauging Its Success,* Meetings Professional International (MPI). www.mpiweb.org, accessed 08/08/2014

MPI (2014). *Meetings Outlook,* Meetings Professional International (MPI). www.mpiweb.org, accessed 08/08/2014

O'Toole, W. (2011). *Events Feasibility and Development: From Strategy to Operations,* Butterworth-Heinemann, Amsterdam.

Patton, M.Q. (1997). *Utilization-Focused Evaluation: The New Century Text,* Sage.

Phillips, J.J., Myhill, M. and McDonough, J.B. (2007). *Proving the Value of Meetings and Events: How and Why to Measure ROI,* ROI Institute.

Phillips, J.J., Breining, M.T. and Phillips, P.P. (2008). *Return on Investment in Meetings and Events: Tools and Techniques to Measure the Success of All Types of Meetings and Events,* Butterworth-Heinemann, Amsterdam; London.

Scriven, M. (1991). *Evaluation Thesaurus,* Sage.

Scriven, M. (2004). Reflections, in M.C. Alkin (ed) *Evaluation Roots: Tracing Theorists' Views and Influences,* SAGE, Thousand Oaks, California, pp. 183-195.

Stufflebeam, D.L. (2001). Evaluation models, *New Directions for Evaluation,* **2001** (89) 7-98.

Stufflebeam, D.L. and Shinkfield, A.J. (2007). *Evaluation Theory, Models, and Applications,* Wiley.

TerraPass (2104). *Terrapass; clear the air.* Available: http://www.terrapass.com/ [2014, 08/08].

Tull, J. (2012). Event evaluation in *Events Management: An International Approach,* eds. N. Ferdinand and P. Kitchin, SAGE, pp. 173-195.

UK Sport (2014). eventIMPACTS website. www.eventimpacts.com, accessed 08/08/2014

12

Wood, E.H. (2009) An impact evaluation framework: Local government community festivals, *Event Management*, **12** (3-4), 171-185.

Worthen, B.R. and Sanders, J.R. (1987) *Educational Evaluation: Alternative Approaches and Practical Guidelines*, Longman.

13 Capturing the Learning

Daryl May and Lindsey May

Learning objectives

- To examine and apply how evaluation can be completed.

- To apply evaluation design guidance.

Introduction

The very nature of events as unique, transient and largely intangible occurrences mean they sometimes do not readily lend themselves to close interrogation to extract learning. However, by applying established and contemporary social science research methods to strategic events evaluation and management, it is possible to achieve successful results that would enable an events organisation to learn and plan for future events. This chapter will explore various methods through which event creators can successfully extract learning from events. It will suggest an alternative approach to the traditional post event evaluation: one in which strategic event evaluation can be embedded throughout the event lifecycle as an iterative process.

Ultimately the central tenet of this chapter is that event creators should consider the evaluation of their progress as a key part of the design process. It should not be left as an afterthought and something to be completed only post event. With some creative thinking, the evaluation should become an actual part of the event, essential to demonstrate that the stakeholders' objectives have been achieved. This chapter, consistent with the previous chapter, argues that the event creator must consider the evaluation as one of the key components during the design process. However, it should be noted that the following content focuses specifically on how the evaluation can be conducted. This is contrasted with Chapter 12 where the emphasis is on the metrics and measurements event creators can use.

Evaluating strategic objectives

Strategic event evaluation should be with the intention of reflecting and learning, either as an institution or organisation, or as part of the event experience, to enhance future outcomes for all stakeholders and for the event creator specifically, as each event represents a point in time in their career. In the context of event evaluation, it is useful to consider evaluation under one or more of three broad objectives. These objectives are the reasons why the evaluation should take place, be strategically planned and embedded within the whole event creation process:

1 Evaluation can be used to inform decisions relating to the effectual on-going design of the event in progress

2 Conducting evaluation enables creators to capture and showcase the event and the important outcomes

3 After reflecting on the evaluation, it can lead to strategic learning, planning and enhancing future event creation (including demonstrating the success or otherwise of the event)

These objectives are discussed in more detail in Chapter 12. However, in exploring the reasons to complete an event evaluation there is one further feature to consider. If events are being increasingly seen as a means to an end, and not an end in themselves, then what needs to be evaluated? As argued in Chapter 1, if organisations are using events as a catalyst to achieve wider strategic outcomes, the event creator needs to carefully consider what should be evaluated. Should the event itself be evaluated or are the wider strategic objectives the aspects to be measured? If so, it poses the challenges of measuring longer term, complex and multifaceted objectives.

Strategic learning

In relation to capturing the learning, it is useful to review the five guiding principles – as set out in Chapter 1 of this book. These also serve as general principles for conducting strategic event evaluation:

☐ *Outcome obsessed:* any evaluation should be aligned to the objectives set. The event creator needs to ask "have the outcomes been met?" If not, why not, and what can be learnt from the event? As event objectives are likely to be varied and take account of different stakeholders, it is a necessity for the evaluation to be pluralistic. The outcomes and objectives of events must be relevant, suitable and achievable. There is little value in setting unrealistic outcomes for an event. Doing the essential preliminary pre-event research allows for confidence that the outcomes are achievable.

☐ *Stakeholder centric outlook:* Not only should the research be objective based, but it should also be pluralistic in nature. By this we mean it should engage with multiple stakeholders to build a fuller picture of the event and not rely on one group of stakeholders - traditionally the participants, attendees or delegates. Instead the evaluation should consider the wider stakeholders, for example the local communities where events are held/hosted. The UK health service provides a useful example of pluralistic evaluation, and the events discipline can draw parallels. Any evaluation should document the different ideas and notions of success from the different groups, but also take account of the different motives and interests – "success is a pluralistic notion. It is not a unitary measure" (Smith and Cantley, 1985, pg.172). Chapter 2 of this book provides a summary of stakeholder engagement with Chapters 3 to 6 considering some of the main event stakeholders.

☐ *Purposeful design:* Chapter 1 puts forward an argument that the component parts of event design need to integrate and align to allow for a cohesive event experience. As described in the introduction to this chapter, the evaluation can be planned in such a way that it adds to the event experience. So in one sense evaluation needs to be planned into the overall event architecture. Furthermore, if we consider the evaluation as one component part, and as a form of research, it also needs careful planning on its own merit.

☐ *Strategic persona:* Evaluation can be done for one or more of the three main reasons, listed above and in Chapter 12. With the focus on event outcomes and the resulting learning, it then follows that evaluation is strategic in nature.

☐ *Reflective practitioner:* By considering all of the above, it forces the event creator to embrace a reflective outlook. Asking questions on what has been achieved (outcomes), from a variety of interested parties (stakeholders), taking a systematic and rigorous approach (purposeful design), with the view to learning (strategic persona) are the key ingredients to becoming a reflective events practitioner.

13

What needs to be captured?

In order to recognise what needs to be captured, first it needs to be established why the evaluation is taking place. The reason for the evaluation will impact upon how the data is gathered. We have already contended that the evaluation can take place for a range of reasons. Completing evaluation during the on-going events phase may take a different form to the evaluation conducted during or post event.

For example, consider completing an evaluation of the participant experience during a music concert. What is the best way to gather data from those attending the event? The temporal nature of most events has consequences for what people may be prepared to do during the actual event. Will individuals want to sacrifice time to complete a questionnaire or discuss in detail how they are feeling? This may force the evaluation towards a post-event design, in which case it can be argued that evaluation is not at all 'during' the occasion but instead is somehow retrospective.

Completing post-event evaluation the event creator needs to be aware of other limitations. The objectives of bringing any large scale mega sporting event to a particular city, region or country (think Olympic Games, Commonwealth Games, Tour de France) may be justified through the often quoted legacy (see Chapter 11 for further discussion). Long term evaluation can be complicated, difficult to manage and expensive. If the event creator wants to complete a longitudinal evaluation with organisations and individuals, how can they ensure continued engagement and limit respondent attrition whilst managing the cost of the evaluation? Again these are key issues that may impact on what the event creator can realistically achieve during the evaluation.

Designing event evaluation often results in a compromise, can be contradictory in nature or produce ambiguous data. Furthermore, it is important to be aware that respondents may have their own agendas and reasons for completing event evaluations. It can also be complex, time consuming and impossible to come to an absolute conclusion. Evaluating objectives from multiple stakeholders – sponsors, participants, venues, local communities – adds further dimensions. It may be that the event creator has to prioritise the key objectives for evaluation and leave others which are less significant.

Many authors consider evaluation as part of the event design process. Table 13.1 summarises some of the prominent views on how data can be collected during an event evaluation.

■ Using existing sources

Information from reports, financial records, market research and journal articles can be used to evaluate events or wider markets. Within general research studies and particularly academic research, secondary data is often collected at the initiation of a project to inform the study design and help contextualise the setting. However, the nature of the events discipline has seen secondary data being used in a much more direct and applied manner. Secondary data has many benefits when completing an event evaluation. These include reducing the cost and time, being able to utilise high quality and large data sets and opportunities to compare data over time (Byrman and Bell, 2003).

Table 13.1: Data collection methods during event evaluation

Author(s)	Data collection methods proposed for event evaluation
Bladen et. al. (2012)	Event documentation (secondary data) Social media Surveys (attendees and staff) Interviews (attendees and staff)
Bowdin et. al. (2011)	Event documentation (secondary data) Secondary data (research bureaux, web searches, journal databases, research reports) Media coverage Surveys Event observation (non-participant, by management/staff/stakeholders) Debrief meetings Focus groups
Getz (2012)	Secondary data (large data sets on leisure and travel) Netnography Surveys (questionnaires) Interviews Observation (structured) Observation (unstructured) Participant-observation Experiential sampling
Shone and Parry (2010)	Event documentation (secondary data) Secondary data (financial reports and accounts) Surveys Interviews Management notes
Tum et. al. (2006)	Event documentation (secondary data) Surveys Interviews

Case study: Business Visits and Events Partnership

The work by the Business Visits and Events Partnership (BVEP) is a good example of the use of secondary data to complete an evaluation on the events industry. Whilst not an example of an evaluation on an individual event, it does highlight a number of key considerations. The initial report titled Britain for Events was produced and launched in 2010 as part of the BVEP campaign under the same name (BVEP, 2010). The report has subsequently been updated by its author Tony Rogers and republished in 2014 under the new title of Events are Great Britain (BVEP, 2014). The report is an overview on the size, value, characteristics, trends, issues and opportunities in Britain's events industry. To help achieve this objective, it summarises the events industry into separate segments: conferences and meetings; exhibitions and trade fairs; incentive travel and performance improvement; corporate hospitality and corporate events; outdoor events; music events and festivals; and sporting events. It places a direct spend value on each segment and provides a total estimated figure for the worth of the industry in Britain (£39.1 billion).

13

Like many associations and partnerships, the BVEP does not have the resources to invest directly in commissioning research to gather new data through primary methods. Instead the report is compiled by making use of the secondary data already available. For example the figure for sporting events (£2.3 billion) is based upon the 2008 data on inbound visitors to Britain to play and watch sporting events. The report includes an appendix showing the data sources, either from research conducted on a regular basis, or from reports and publications produced on a one-off basis. Whilst this example does not show the use of secondary data on an individual event evaluation, it does illustrate how secondary data can be utilised to capture market wide information and showcase a complete industry and its contribution to the UK economy.

The use of secondary data is not without its shortcomings. Using the example above there are questions over the way in which the industry has been segmented. Is Glastonbury Festival an outdoor event, music event or both? Has it been double-counted through research being conducted independently? The sports events estimate uses data from inbound tourist visits, yet doesn't include domestic tourist figures. Similarly the timeliness and therefore relevance of the data can be examined. For example, the research on incentive travel has not been conducted since 1996 – does this still accurately represent this segment of the industry?

Despite the questions raised regarding the BVEP work, it gives a good base in which the same secondary data sets can be interrogated to compare year on year (or revisited periodically). The report provides the events industry with a useful overview and marketing tool, something it has not had in the past.

Documents that are created for purposes other than evaluation can prove to be valuable when evaluating the outcome of an event and these are often easily accessible. Table 13.2 provides an example of sources of secondary data that could be routinely collected at events.

With any secondary data it is important to understand or appreciate where it originated from or how it was collected. If appropriate, caveats should be added to show where data is insufficient or where potential gaps and shortfalls are apparent. Quite often when the gaps are identified in secondary data, it results in new projects or avenues to explore for future research. Ultimately the event creator may have access to appropriate and relevant secondary data that meets the needs of the evaluation and can be utilised without the expense or time spent gathering new information. Event evaluation may involve compromises, one being the reliance on existing sources rather than collecting new data. In doing so this may reduce the resource investment required to complete the evaluation.

Table 13.2: Examples of data recorded at events.

Document	Examples of information they provide/future learning
Evaluation reports from previous years	Value demonstrated, satisfaction improvements year on year
Event budget and balance sheet	Information on the profit/loss, financial evaluation
Ticket sales reports	Visitor numbers, financial evaluation
Crowd estimates, car park figures	Visitor numbers, risk assessment
Registration forms	Demographic details, marketing information
Sales reports of merchandise, food, etc	Revenue, financial evaluation
Safety reporting	Record of the number of incidents that occurred, risk management
First-aid treatments	Record of the number of incidents that occurred, risk management
Reports from other sources such as visitor bureaux, other event creators, etc.	Wider impact of event, showcase of event

■ Gathering new information

The event creator may first need to consider if it is essential to collect new data as it can be costly and time-consuming, and secondary data may already be available. The two types of data are not mutually incompatible. Secondary data can be used to inform primary data collection, or alternatively an event evaluation may involve secondary data plus primary data collected using a variety of mixed methods. If new data is required then the event creator should consider the most appropriate way in which it can be captured.

Event creators wanting to generate primary (new) data as part of an evaluation will be required to gather information from stakeholders. Whatever method is used to gather data it has to align to the objective of the evaluation. Many of the main methods used to gather data during an event evaluation are borrowed from the social sciences. This chapter can only provide an overview of the main approaches with some acknowledgement of the key design features in the context of event evaluation. For a fuller discussion on traditional methods cited in this chapter it is recommended that specific research texts are consulted.

13

◼ Questionnaires

The questionnaire as a method to evaluate an event or as part of a wider evaluation strategy is arguably the most commonly used technique in leisure and tourism research (Veal, 2011). Questions may typically ask about the quality and/or usefulness of the acts, activities, speakers or sessions, the suitability of the venue, catering, social programme, etc. Whilst this approach to post-event satisfaction does have its place, we argue that evaluation should take a more holistic on-going form and not be consigned to the conclusion of the event. Despite the tendency to use questionnaires in this way, they are still an invaluable tool for evaluation. The case study example below shows one way in which a questionnaire can be administered and discusses the challenges that come with this traditional method.

Case study: UK Events Management Trend Survey

The UK Events Management Trend Survey (UKEMTS) has been produced annually since 1993. Currently it is commissioned by Eventia with the objectives to measure characteristics of the business events and conference market from a venue perspective and to provide an estimate of the volume of the market (Eventia, 2013). To achieve this, a self-completed questionnaire is distributed to a sample of venues that all provide space to hire for business events. The venue sample consists of purpose built convention centres (with a capacity over 500 delegates), conference/training centres (with a capacity of less than 500 delegates), hotels, universities, and unusual or multiple purpose sites. The overall sample size included in the 2013 report was 224 venues. The survey has been running in one format or another each year since 1993 thereby allowing the observation of trends over a period of time.

The preface to the report outlines the methodology taken during the work; within this it emphasises a number of potential errors. The sample size and resulting representativeness can lead to questions over the validity of the results. Eventia's own venue database has approximately 3,500 listed, with many more not included. Is the sample size of 224 respondents large enough and does it cover the range of venues appropriately to be representative of the industry?

◼ Interviews

Interviewing is one of the most common and powerful methods used within social research to gain an understanding of human beings (Fontana and Frey, 1994). An interview is a type of conversation or interaction designed to gather data on a particular topic. Whilst the semi-structured qualitative interview is a common approach for many researchers completing evaluations, it does have practical drawbacks when applied in-situ at events.

The temporal nature of a lot of events limits the availability of participants to spend time taking part in an interview. This type of interview should be pre-planned, conducted in a quiet environment to allow for the data to be recorded and should be of adequate length in order for the topic to be explored in detail. People attending many events will find it difficult to justify time spent being interviewed. Instead the interview may be better suited to engaging with stakeholders at other points of the event lifecycle - either pre or post event - when the evaluation can be accomplished without distractions. Alternatively unstructured interviews can be considered at events where it would be deemed inappropriate to try and conduct a more formal approach, for example at an underground rave, on the terraces at a football match or at a cultural event. The unstructured interview can be viewed like a focused conversation, in that the interviewer may not have any set questions or fixed aim for the interview. Instead they allow the interview to flow freely and without a script.

■ Focus groups

Focus groups are widely used as a method to collect data. They have traditionally been associated with market research, but are now used in a variety of settings and industries. The central tenet behind a focus group is to gather data relating to feelings and opinions from a target group of people. The group is selected and encouraged to discuss issues relating to a common theme. This approach can be easily adopted by event creators as part of their evaluation strategy. For instance, pre-event a group of potential festival goers could be asked to discuss possible schedules and acts to be booked at a future music festival. Alternatively a hotel may wish to review its own conference facilities and service offer by contacting a number of key business event clients and inviting them to attend a focus group to review proposed changes.

The format of questions and areas for discussion will be based around a particular theme or area that is to be discussed. The arrangement and layout of the questions may look similar to an interview guide. The advantage of the focus group is that the group situation or dynamic can stimulate discussion that might otherwise not occur on an individual basis.

13

■ Observation

Observation, as an approach to evaluation, has a long tradition in social research. It is useful way to interpret findings and places data from other methods into context. Through observation, a researcher, via a number of methods, can uncover the unspoken rules and informal structures of an organisation (Simons, 2009).

How can observation be practically applied during the evaluation of events? A highly formal and structured approach of observation could be as simple as counting the number of specified occurrences at an event, e.g. ingress/egress numbers, recording the use of a certain service or counting some type of incident through observation. Informal, unstructured observation can be done differently and might be employed to understand something in more detail, in a naturalistic setting. Evaluation of hard to reach groups within society at events may be suitable using this approach, for example drug dealing at a rave or interactions between people attending a pagan festival at a heritage site. With observational approaches the evaluation can pose ethical questions, such as gathering information from participants covertly and without consent.

■ Ethnography

The term 'ethnography' can cover a wide range of qualitative approaches and methods. However it is primarily concerned with the act of 'participant observation'. This involves becoming a participant of the event being studied and includes reflecting on conversations and interactions with others (Veal, 2011). Hammersley and Atkinson (2007) outline the main features of ethnographic work that include the research taking place in natural setting with participant observation as the main way to collect data. They also state that it should focus on a small number of cases but with a high level of detail and involve the interpretation of meanings considered in the context of the environment.

Adopting an ethnographic approach can be viewed as one of the most useful tools to enable an event creator to understand the richness, detail and depth of the human experience. Holloway et al. (2010, pg.79) argue that ethnography is starting to be used "to develop a deeper understanding of the nature and meanings of event experiences for visitors, participants or organisers". What better way to document a participant's experience than by undertaking the activity oneself and speaking to others in the natural setting of the event? An increasing number of studies are arguing and adopting this approach (Mackellar, 2013; Jaimangal-Jones, 2014; Stadler et al., 2013; Holloway et al., 2010; Green, 2001; Borchard, 1998). If a key objective of the evaluation is to learn and 'augment' the event through a variety of extras and additional propositions for future marketing activities, it then follows that gaining insights by way of ethnography allows for a greater understanding of participants' values (Green, 2001).

There are obvious practical design barriers to completing event related ethnography, for example gaining access to a sub-group of participants being studied, how to integrate or pose as a participant (or complete non-covert research), how to sample informants to converse with, how to record the data whilst completing the evaluation (perhaps harder when conducting covert observation) and the general issue of ethics and consent when observing others (Veal, 2011).

New technology has enabled ethnographers to make use of devices to capture data. Small lightweight digital cameras are now available that can be worn discretely and set to take images automatically over a set period (from 120 images per hour to 360 images per hour). This type of device provides a visual record of an event and associated interactions which can later be downloaded into a library of images and notes added to capture the experience. Other ways in which ethnographic data can be captured include making use of specialist dictaphones or recording features that appear on most new phones or hand held mobile devices. Those wishing to capture thoughts, feelings and document their experience at an event may be prompted to do so at pre-set points by an alarm or calendar alert.

Case study: Kentuck Festival of Arts, Alabama, USA

The Kentuck Festival of Arts is held annually and is an event that showcases national and international folk artists and craftspeople (basketmakers, blacksmiths, woodworkers, potters, fibre and fabric artists, quilters, jewellers and glassblowers). In addition to the interactive workshops and live demonstrations, the festival also incorporates live music and story-telling (Kentuck Art Centre Website, 2014). One study on the festival which focused on demographics and trip characteristics, motivations to attend and an assessment of product uniqueness utilised a questionnaire to collect the data (Wooten and Norman, 2008). Participants were approached to complete the face to face questionnaire using a systematic sampling procedure. A total of 144 respondents completed the survey - an estimated 30,000 number of people attended in 2004 (Wooten and Norman, 2008). In order to complement or augment the study further ethnographic work might have been conducted alongside the questionnaire. Either the researchers themselves, or a number of pre-recruited attendees, could have been supplied with a camera to capture images. This would have collected data to show social interactions in the context of the event, illustrate the festival experience and demonstrate the uniqueness of the festival and potentially be used as marketing material for future events.

13

Real time participant experience

With the recent trend to engage and interact with participants at events, embedding evaluation into the experience can enhance the attendees' and participants' experiences in a variety of ways. Using hand held voting units or asking participants to log onto a website and provide feedback using smart phones and mobile devices may appear on one level to be a tool to facilitate interaction, but it also enables the event creator to gather essential evaluative data.

Gathering data about real time participant experience is also a valuable insight into how participants or audiences at events feel whilst in the moment of the actual event experience. If reactions, emotions, situations and atmospheres can be gauged and recorded, and reacted to in a timely manner, it is realistically possible to simultaneously alter subtle facets of a live event accordingly in tune with the expectations of the participants. To put this in context, this is similar, for example to how a professional DJ or performance artist can read a dance floor or festival crowd and alter music/tech/lights accordingly to influence mood, atmosphere and reactions. Obviously any data collected and recorded during the live event should also contribute to post-event evaluation, learning and reflection; it does not have to be limited for use purely during a live event situation. In their conceptual paper, Brown and Hutton (2013) explore recent technological and methodological developments in the evaluation of audience behaviour at planned events and discuss the implications for researchers in this field, particularly the advantages of evaluating in real-time. Their paper argues that real time data collection (evaluation) of audiences provides insights into the effective design and management of planned events, particularly from the event risk management perspective.

A variety of methods, tools and technology can be used to gather real time participant experience of events. From the ethnographic or observational approach to the more technologically advanced and current methods such as event specific apps, interactive live voting systems, increasing use of wristband technology, and of course the use of social media such as live Twitter sites/walls/feeds and Facebook.

Case study: NFL International Series at Wembley, UK

The National Football League (NFL) is the governing body for the sport of American Football. Since 2007, as part of the league's expansion plans, it has hosted regular season games in the UK at Wembley Stadium (there has been talk of one of the existing 32 teams relocating to London to play all their regular season games at Wembley (CBS Sports, 2012)). As part of the pre-game activities a 'tailgate' party is hosted in the car park and surrounding area of the stadium. This is a social event to extend the duration of the sporting event and enables ticket holders to eat and drink at the many catering outlets and buy merchandise from official NFL stalls. The tailgate party is part of football as a spectacle. It has been long associated with American Football and deeply entrenched as part of the cultural experience (Veri and Liberti, 2013). Fans queue to enter the official merchandise stall, during this period they are approached by NFL staff who present them with the opportunity to sign up for exclusive offers and deals. This diverts attention during the period waiting to purchase products. At the same time NFL are able to gather market research information and also conduct an evaluation from individuals during the event.

Social media

One advantage of using social media to gather real time participant experience is its unrestricted access for event organisers, participants, attendees and other stakeholders. At the 20th International Conference on the World Wide Web in New York, Castillo et al. (2011) presented their extensive research on assessing the credibility (power) of twitter tweets. They had analysed microblog postings related to trending topics, and classified them as credible or not credible. Their research found that newsworthy topics (tweets) tend to include URLs and to have deep propagation trees, also that credible newsworthy tweets are propagated through authors (tweeters) that have previously written a large number of messages, originate at a single or a few users in the network, and have many re-posts.

Many events, large and small now rely at the very least on sponsorship from various stakeholders, with medium to larger scale events having more (globally spread) stakeholders such as broadcasting bodies, media companies, advertising businesses, local authorities, governments, councils and volunteers. All of these various stakeholders can have access to social media which, when used appropriately, can be utilised very effectively to create an umbrella forum (e.g. a Facebook/Twitter site) to gather precious real time participant experience of an event. Other important advantages to event businesses using social media sites are the low cost of using the software; and businesses can harness the evaluative capacity of social media to maintain links with stakeholders and investors, and improve the business sustainability (Sigala 2013).

Evaluation design guidance

13

There are many texts that deal with research designs in social settings. The basic principles from most general research designs can be applied with some modification to event evaluation. However, the design guidance in Figure 13.1 provides an overarching framework for event creators to exploit and represents the main issues raised in this chapter. The evaluation guidance should be built into event design and lifecycle as standard rather than left as an add-on or afterthought. The framework is presented in a sequence, although in reality many of the issues will need to be considered in parallel and at the same time.

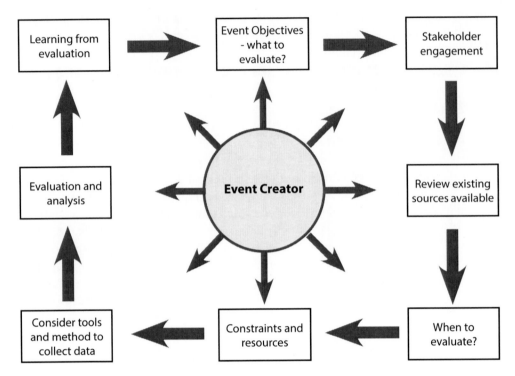

Figure 13.1: Evaluation design guidance

The event creator should consider, in context of the event objectives, what needs to be evaluated and the reasons for doing so. The motivations for the evaluation could be to inform on-going event design decisions, creating evidence to showcase the event, reflecting to enhance future events, or demonstrating the success or otherwise of an event. Since stakeholder engagement is a central tenet in strategic learning, the event creator should plan the evaluation in order to engage with different interest groups. This doesn't necessarily mean all the stakeholders. The scope of the evaluation must be prioritised against the available resources and most evaluation will be completed within a set of constraints. Event creators will have access to limited resources which may mean some compromise on the design of the evaluation. For example an evaluation may need to be completed within a certain time period in order to produce marketing material to showcase future events. Furthermore, most evaluation will be accomplished within a set budget.

The timing of the evaluation will be largely dependent on the reasons for doing so and objectives to be met. For example using evaluation to inform the on-going design is likely to be done pre and during an event. The data collection in order to evaluate an event and showcase will take place during the event, but the report or output is completed and produced post event.

The temporal nature of events has implications for the design of an evaluation. Evaluation completed in-situ, especially when the context and natural environment is critical, can only be achieved within a limited time period during the event itself. This will impact on the choice tools and methods to collect the data. Making use of data already in existence to complete the evaluation can reduce the cost and time involved. Alternatively, sources already available may help to inform the event creator on the design of the evaluation or to act as a point of reference or benchmark against which their own event can be compared.

Of the foremost questions an event creator should ask when considering the most appropriate approach to collect data is "why is the evaluation taking place and what does it hope to achieve?" If the event creator is wishing to understand the complex human experience then methods to gather rich, in-depth and detailed data may be appropriate. Alternatively, if the objective is to measure the event success using economic or financial metrics, then wider, larger scale approaches which produce data capable of being statistically manipulated and generalised may be suitable. As a result, the analysis will be dependent on the type of data gathered. An evaluation to measure tangible, objective outcomes is likely to be analysed in a quantifiable way, leading to statistically robust and perhaps complex reports. Experience-based outcomes that focus on the human experience at events will result in narratives and discourse that capture the phenomena in detail. This type of analysis may include multiple sources such as images and photographs alongside the text to complete the rich picture.

Concluding remarks

Event evaluation, and the subsequent learning, is often seen as something of an add-on and considered post-event. This chapter argues for event creators to consider evaluation as a core part of the design process. Chapter 1 proposes that event creators should be outcome obsessed, and if that is the case, they should also be obsessed with gathering the evidence to prove the outcomes. With some creative thinking event evaluation can be seen as part of the whole event experience and embedded in all stages of the event life cycle.

13

Study questions

1   If evaluation is viewed as an on-going iterative process that is embedded within the creation of events, then what are the potential advantages of this in contrast with evaluation post event? Are there any drawbacks?

2   Review the following journal article Wooten, M.H. and Norman, W.C., (2007), "Differences in Arts Festival Visitors Based on Level of Past Experience", Event Management, 11 (3) 109- 120. In particular, critique the way in which the data was collected.

3   Think about the last time you carried out an event evaluation. How many of the following points have you considered and how can they influence your evaluation design from now on?

☐   Sampling strategy

☐   Ethical considerations

☐   Data analysis

☐   Sharing the learning with stakeholders

References

Bladen, C., Kennell, J., Abson, E. and Wide, N. (2012). *Events Management: An Introduction*, Routledge, London

Borchard, K. (1998). Between a hard rock and postmodernism: Opening the Hard Rock Hotel and Casino, *Journal of Contemporary Ethnography*, **27**, (2), 242-269

Bowdin, G., Allen, J., O'Toole, W., Harris, R. and McDonnell, I. (2011). *Events Management 3rd Edition*, Elsevier, Oxford

Brown, S. and Hutton, A. (2013). Developments in the real-time evaluation of audience behaviour at planned events. *International Journal of Event and Festival Management*, **4** (1), 43-55.

Bryman, A. and Bell, E. (2003). *Business Research Methods*, Oxford University Press, Oxford

BVEP (2010). *Britain for Events*, BVEP, London

BVEP (2014). *Events are Great Britain*, BVEP, London

Castillo, C., Mendoza, M. and Poblete, B. (2011). Information Credibility on Twitter. Proceedings of the 20th international conference on World Wide Web, p 675-684. New York, NY, USA.

CBS Sports (2012). NFL's move to London could come soon; Jags a target. www.cbssports.com/nfl/writer/jason-la-canfora/20724077/nfls-move-to-london-could-come-soon-jags-a-target, accessed 08/08/2014

Eventia (2013). *UK Events Management Trend Survey 2013*, Eventia, Birmingham

Fontana, A., and Frey, J.H. (1994). Interviewing: The Art of Science, in N.K. Denzin and Y.S. Lincoln (eds.), *The Handbook of Qualitative Research*, Sage, London, 361-76

Getz, D. (2012). *Event Studies: Theory, Research and Policy for Planned Events, 2nd Edition*, Routledge, London

Green, C.B. (2001). Leveraging Subculture and identity to promote sports events, *Sport Management Review*, **4**, 1-19

Hammerlsey, M. and Atkinson, P. (2007). *Ethnography*, Taylor and Francis, Oxon

Holloway, I., Brown, L. and Shipway, R. (2010). Meaning not measurement: Using ethnography to bring a deeper understanding to the participant experience of festivals and events, *International Journal of Event and Festival Management*, **1** (1) 74-85

Jaimangal-Jones, D. (2014). Utilising ethnography and participant observation in festival and event research, *International Journal of Event and Festival Management*, **5** (1) 39 - 55

Kentuck Art Centre Website (2014). Festival page. www.kentuck.org/festival.html, accessed 02/08/2014

Mackellar, J. (2013). Participant observation at events: theory, practice and potential, *International Journal of Event and Festival Management*, **4** (1) 56 - 65

Shone, A., and Parry, B. (2010). *Successful Event Management: A Practical Handbook 3rd Edition*, Cengage Learning, Hampshire

Sigala, Marianna (2013). Customer involvement in sustainable supply chain management: a research framework and implications in tourism. *Cornell Hospitality Quarterly*, **55** (1) 76-88.

Simons, H. (2009). *Case study Research in Practice*, Sage, London

Smith, G. and Cantley, C. (1985). *Assessing Health Care: A Study in Organizational Evaluation*, Open University Press, Milton Keynes

Stadler,R., Reid, S. and Fullagar, S. (2013). An ethnographic exploration of knowledge practices within the Queensland Music Festival, *International Journal of Event and Festival Management*, **4** (2) 90-106

Tum, J., Norton, P. and Nevan Wright, J. (2006). *Management of Event Operations*, Elsevier, Oxford

Veal, A.J. (2011). *Research Methods for Leisure and Tourism: A Practical Guide 4th Edition*, Pearson, London.

Veri, M.J. and Liberti, R. (2013). Tailgate warriors: exploring constructions of masculinity food, and football, *Journal of Sport and Social Issues*, **37** (3) 227-244

Wooten, M.H., and Norman, W.C. (2008). Differences in arts festival visitors based on level of past experience, *Event Management*, **11**, 109-120

13

Part V
Strategic Persona

14 Industry Insights

Phil Crowther

Learning objectives

- Interpret the connections between the practitioners' words and the themes of the book.

- Identify the links between their different stories.

- Reflect upon how their accounts differ from your views of the role of event creators.

Introduction

Throughout this book we have tried to make the voice of industry prominent. This chapter is the pinnacle of this with anecdotes from six senior event professionals sharing their personal reflections about the business of event creation. The world of events is rich with exceptionally talented people designing and delivering incredible events. Refreshingly these people also recognise the importance of guiding and inspiring the event creators of the future (you) and have kindly taken time to contribute to this book.

In such an experiential area as events there is always a danger that a divide opens up between the classroom and what is sometimes referred to as the 'real world'. It is very important that students of events engage with both, to ensure their learning is grounded and applied. The theory, concepts and arguments introduced in books cannot justifiably exist without connection to the practicalities of the event industry. It is hoped that the views of professionals expressed below support readers to interpret their event management education in the context of the real world.

The commentaries are not displayed in any particular order and are largely copied and pasted directly from what the authors provided. They have not been edited so as to preserve emphasis and meaning. At times they read as a stream of consciousness as the authors simultaneously reflect upon their experiences as they write. Similar to students who struggle to find opportunity to put their learning into practice, practitioners often struggle to find time to reflect upon their practice. It is therefore hoped that this has been, and will be, an equally useful exercise for both writers and readers.

The contributors were asked to share their insights, gained from years of event creation experience, and to openly express their views with the event creators of the future. It is notable when reading through the accounts below that the writers come from varied and specific event contexts; corporate, agency, festival, and destination marketing. A challenge for readers is to interpret their views and assess how they can be transferred to other event contexts. For the most part this is entirely possible and useful.

Industry insights

Mark Shearon, Managing Partner, Proscenium, New York
www.proscenium.com

With regards to event strategy and event design we ALWAYS start at the end. What do our clients want to happen at the conclusion of their program? With clients like Harley-Davidson, Walmart and Boeing the stakes are high, millions and sometimes billions of dollars are in play.

Therefore the business outcome of any program is paramount. That is the value we bring as live event producers to our clients' events. So those goals and objectives need to be agreed with the client up front. What do they want their target audience to commit to do? How do we get them to commit to buy a product or service, or if an internal audience, how do we get them to commit to a vision or a plan? Gaining commitment from an audience is our primary reason for existing. And it is much more powerful than experiential or engagement. One can be engaged but actually not do anything. Only to commit is to truly act. And action should be the outcome of any event that we as strategists take if we are going to help the companies that we work with to obtain business outcomes from their live programs.

How do we extract those business outcomes? Well, great questioning technique is very important. Asking the right questions and the right proportion of closed and open questions is key, but the most important skill you will need as an event strategist and designer is to be able to LISTEN. You have two ears and one mouth; please use them in that proportion. Listen closely to your clients and really get to the core of what they are asking of you.

Once we have a draft of desired outcomes we need alignment, so we socialize those internally within the client company. All stakeholders (and influencers) must sign off on the objectives of the program before we move forward with the strategic direction and design concepts.

Once we know the desired end result, only then can the design process start. We assemble strategists, creatives, writers, designers, art directors and producers. Event design is not a solitary sport; it is a collaborative process between teams of subject matter experts and our clients.

So know what you want people to say and do after your event. Know what stakeholders expect as a result of the program. Create 'filters' that you can pass through any of the ideas that you come up with. In this way you can ensure that you do not waver from your strategic plan. Objectives come first then strategy then design and execution comes last.

Many people have asked me, with strategy and execution, which is the most important? Let me leave you with a little fable: Strategy and Execution walk into a bar and immediately spot a Client. They both do their best to impress, but Client lets them know, "Tonight it's all about Strategy." Dejected, Execution starts to walk away, but Client says, "Wait, your day will come." And that was the start of a beautiful Partnership. Oh, and for a "twist"– Strategy and Execution turn out to be twins so Client could never tell them apart – and never really needed to.

Ann Palmer, Director, Event and Roadshow Marketing, Barclays Bank
www.barclays.com

Excellence in execution will always be fundamental to producing successful events, however true added value for stakeholders comes when event teams engage at a more strategic level. In simple terms, strategic input means translating the business objectives into memorable and engaging live experiences for hosts and guests. In addition to understanding a wide breadth and depth of event solutions, events teams have to invest the time to learn about their respective industry and stakeholders in order to match the business objective with the event solution, and serve credibly in this strategic advisory capacity.

Acting as a strategic advisor begins with first understanding the business products and services as well as the nature of interaction with clients and prospects. With a broader understanding of the client relationship, event teams can make targeted recommendations about the best type of event solution to bring to life a particular message in a meaningful way that will attract the client's attention, enough to attend and ultimately retain the message.

14

The 'strategy' might come in the overall event solution or sometimes in a single element, i.e. the speaker. The opportunity for impact lies in determining what is 'meaningful and engaging' for each audience; and rarely do we find it is the same. Events have to be increasingly clever about what 'creativity' looks like, bringing fresh ideas at competitive costs. Remember also that events are not static activities. The events teams have to work with the business from concept to completion, continually monitoring progress, delegate interest and adapting as needed as the event approaches.

Beyond single event touch points, event activity should be integrated with wider communication and marketing campaign plans to achieve a greater, longer-lasting impact where it makes sense. With knowledge of the client life-cycle, and working collaboratively with the business, event teams can again offer strategic guidance as to how and when to promote various event initiatives.

It is important to remember that strategy is important for all events regardless of scale and format. The same principles apply.

Maurice Fleming, Managing Director, Shelton Fleming Associates Ltd
www.sheltonfleming.co.uk

A working day in the events industry is as changeable and varied as the array of events you will produce. Just as each event is an individual in shape, size and style, so is maintaining the relationships with varying clients and partners, each coming with their own set of values and challenges.

The core tasks of producing a high quality event revolve around strategy, implementation and delivery on a brief. However, the essential skills to maintain a successful business in events rely upon your ability to also continually please your clients. In most cases these two challenges run in opposition to each other. Often the client can be an obstacle to their own desired results, for example, requesting last minute changes, rethinking design preferences, cutting finances, questioning strategy, changing timings and limiting staff. You will never face quite the same set of obstacles with a client.

Different events and live experiences have very different methods for measuring their success. The events industry is as transitional and diverse as the experiences you create. As well as creating these continually different environments you must also adapt and recreate a form of analysis in order to feedback to clients, making it more complicated than other single discipline marketing outlets each with their own standardised ROI indicators.

When running an event the pitch is what sets you apart from others but the result is what you are remembered for. After winning a brief, in the middle of the project, there is just mayhem of changes, action, reaction and adaptations to make an outcome possible. The formula for successful event management is to expect the unexpected, always maintain standards, communicate, and continually focus upon and aim to exceed client and also audience expectations

Each client has a different focus on indicators for success (key performance indicators). These can be identified by analysing where their concerns were raised during the pitch and implementation phase of the project. So typically, in the event industry, the evaluation phase does not easily follow a fixed set of steps to deliver an evaluation. Instead it is an organic learning process, built throughout the duration of the project where by observing the client and their areas of concern you can learn where they will want to see justification and evidence of success. The delivery of an event evaluation must address the areas of concern raised and valued by the client and clearly justify the reasons behind decisions made outside of the initial brief. The success of such decisions must also be quantified or qualified. Make sure you include some instructions to record such data during the event duration so that you are able to provide this invaluable evidence.

It is also imperative to focus on building the future relationship with a client at this point by highlighting your extra efforts and your ability to exceed delivery on a brief. Return on investment is always key in an evaluation so be prepared to justify your spend rationale. One way to start with the evaluation and feedback is to mimic how you approached the brief and pull-out key points that were repeatedly raised by the client from your event working document. By addressing these in an upfront manner you are showing your awareness of their concerns and immediately building trust. It is all too easy to give into a desire to brush issues under the carpet but doing this will never go unnoticed.

A tendency of clients is to request long, drawn-out reviews of events after they have taken place. If at all possible avoid such painful nit-picking situations by delivering a concise, bespoke evaluation document that gets straight to the facts they want to see and takes away the opportunity to delve into unnecessary or irrelevant discussions that can become detrimental to your future working relationship.

Just remember this survival mantra: "With every project, client relationships should be considered the main event."

14

Claire O'Neill, Senior Manager, Association of Independent Festivals (AIF) and Co-founder, A Greener Festival
www.aiforg.com www.agreenerfestival.com

The past 10 years has seen a rapid increase in the number of festivals taking place in the UK and many other territories globally. Whatever the reasons for the growth of festivals, the industry has developed and professionalized, with more services and contractors being supported by the festival events and vice versa. Greater competition amongst festivals brings a sophistication and expectation amongst audiences who are, to a degree, spoiled for choice.

In addition, there are new audiences attending festivals who would not have done so 10 plus years ago. More families and 'glampers' might expect a certain level of comfort and facilities at the events they attend. Events must meet these expectations to compete, and when they succeed to meet expectations more new audiences are attracted. In addition to requiring convenience and comfort, people are more and more used to being participants as opposed to spectators. Looking at events such as the Secret Garden Party, there is a fine line between audience and entertainers, with areas such as the Colosillyum instigating mud wrestling, bungee battles, and the infamous Suicide Sports. Through social media we star in our own show, and have our virtual stage for expression. 20 years ago TV was a main source of entertainment and was entirely a spectator sport. Even TV shows since the late 90's have been based on so called 'reality' subjects, and now we have the 'red button' too.

Sponsorship has also become more sophisticated and has evolved alongside event creators and audiences. It is not a branding exercise but a shaper and creator of content and experiences. What is important is to identify value to improve the event and audience experience, in turn having far greater positive impact for the brand in question associated with the activation. Most sponsors' main objective is to ultimately achieve a connection with the event participants. Sponsors also wish to be a part of the wider opportunity for communication and connecting with audiences outside of the event itself. Sailor Jerry's bring the Ink City to Bestival celebrating the tattoo shops of Hotel Street in Honolulu's Chinatown along with the loud music and bars that entertained sailors crossing the Pacific. A fun way for audiences to engage with the brand, that fits with Bestival's own style, and generates value for all involved.

It is right to highlight that the event does not begin and end when it physically starts and finishes. There is often a year round interaction with audiences or followers, which relates to the earlier point about niche 'bubbles' or scenes that we view and create through our interaction with media channels and peer groups. It is necessary for event creators to view this whole process as a combined part of the event. Tomorrowland by ID&T is an incredible example of the scale that an event can reach beyond its physical borders. Tomorrowland aftermovie 2013 received 3 million views in one day! Now over 75 million have viewed the video.

It is not just audience engagement, but also data analysis that is important pre and post event activity. Due to the ability to monitor clicks and online interactions we are able to gauge the effectiveness and reach a campaign, activation or interaction has actually had. With opportunity for analysis comes the ability to set clear targets, expectations and goals – a quantifiable ROI. In order to effectively use data analytics it is important to consider having competent analysts working with the data gathered. On an efficiency level, real time data can be very useful. WOMAD were able to adjust their food supply for crew meals by monitoring the number of crew coming for each meal with RFID. This in turn reduced the level of food waste.

AIF organize seminars for those involved in event creation from structural safety and crowd management, to marketing and sponsorship, to financial management and sustainability and so on. This highlights the breadth of understanding necessary to deliver a successful festival. One key point is that it is not possible for an individual to be expert in all of these areas. Part of creating a successful festival with longevity is building the right team with competent persons in decision-making roles, and bringing a variety of skills and strengths to the table.

As well as the internal skill sets and abilities, the wider impacts of events are also an intrinsic factor that must be part of the events overall strategy. In 2005 I completed a dissertation about festivals and the environment, and struggled to find any academic reference to this topic. This research later formed *A Greener Festival*, which assesses and advises festivals around the world on the subject of environmental sustainability. By contrast, today it is difficult to find a festival that does not have some policy to minimize its environmental impact.

It has always been important for events to maintain a positive relationship with the local community, not least in order to avoid objections to their licenses. There are regional events that have a very strong connection with the local community and draw part of their unique identity from that. An incredible example of this in France is Le Cabaret Vert Festival. They don't even sell orange juice on the bars as they don't grow oranges in the region! Luckily they do produce champagne in the region so they are in a good position.

14

Richard Waddington, Chairman of Event Marketing Association' (EMA)
http://www.ema-uk.com

Event marketing covers many specialisms, personally I come at this subject from the position of many years of creating B2B events on behalf of clients around the world.

20-30 years ago events were generally reactive, all about hospitality and having a good time – the boss wants to throw a party, hold a conference (tell people), sponsor his pet sport etc. it was ill thought out and the business held the power, things have changed, those days are well and truly over.

Events today are (or should be) a strategic led marketing/communication initiative. There is still much to learn, evolve and achieve, however in my opinion Event Marketing is quickly becoming the 'New Advertising'. The power has now shifted to the audience, customer centric, employee engagement, etc. we must focus on their needs, requirements, feelings and align our event strategy, communication to these to be able to communicate with them, influence them.

Strategy, creativity and operations are three interlocking circles of success. Success lies at the centre of getting all three of these elements correct.

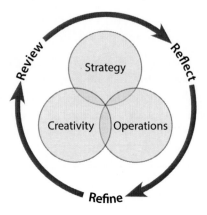

Figure 14.1: Three interlocking circles of success

No strategy = no thinking. The focus needs to be upon objectives, desired outcomes, the audience, the client brand. Segment, challenge, develop a crystal clear focused brief with measurable objectives – you have to be able to measure, otherwise how do you know you've been successful… again this does not need to be complicated, however defined, measurable objectives crystallise the brief.

Once you have a clear brief then you can be creative. The challenge for creativity is to know the boundaries, be conscious of the objectives, the audience, and the brand otherwise all will be lost. The Audience is everything – you have to understand them, get under the skin, into the minds of your specific target audience. Know what makes them tick, what they want to achieve by attending this event.

Example: A (hypothetical) leading city investment house holds a Christmas party at Café de Paris in Leicester Square – high octane party, lots of champagne, food, cabaret show and loud music. However it was too dark, too noisy no one could hold a conversation – what was the point? Whilst a few junior brokers may have had a great time, the people who really count, senior hosts and attendees would find it a waste of time and totally off brand.

Strategy is not rocket science, the questions that should be asked, delved into and documented are:

☐   Who is the audience?

☐   What are our objectives?

☐   What will success look like?

☐   What are our options?

Answer the above and you have the tools to develop your strategy.

Creativity is what makes the event memorable. Creativity can be many things, it's not just the big WOW. It can be content, entertainment, food, venue, destination and many more – in all it's the integration and interconnectivity of many of these elements. You've got it right when an attendee either thinks WOW that was great, or more formally in a B2B environment, something along these lines – that was a good use of my time, I learnt something, had good dialogue with my hosts, met some interesting people (which could be useful contacts in the future) in an extremely pleasant environment.

The role of technology – you must look at technology as an enabler, an enhancement not the answer. The greatest enhancement technology allows is the ability to engage and involve audience, prior, during and after, to engage the full audience, not only the people that were able to attend the event – what do I mean here? Generally the initial invite list may go out to 400 people to get 100 attendees (the maths depends very much on the audience and reason for the event) however, generally there is a larger percentage of people who can't attend the event than can – technology allows you to engage, inform, involve these people in some form or another.

14

Interaction with the audience should be exactly that, interaction – two way communications not one way. On-line forums, discussions, chats pre and post, voting, live tweet/question walls, there are many possibilities.

Whatever your solution it has to be consistent and reflective of the host brand. Guests who know the brand should be able to tell it is their event, even without the brand name being present. Great events have the brand DNA running through them. It's easy to visualise (close your eyes) events for consumer brands such as Apple, RedBull, Standard Vodka. But it's harder for B2B events, but they to have their own DNA.

Reflections

Although each writer is absorbed in their particular event context, the consistency of message is striking and connects very well with the idea of Strategic Event Creation. The repeated focus upon outcomes is prominent, as is the opportunity presented by relationships, partnerships and generally seeing events as collaborative multi-stakeholder endeavours. A recurring theme is the necessity to inject creativity into event creation and the dangers if you do not do this. It is certainly pivotal, and an even defining question for the event creation community, as to how creativity remains central to their event design.

In Chapter 1 the following point was made, "…event creators must resist the inclination to routinely fixate on the 'here and now' and instead pause to ensure they possess a considered appreciation of the 'why and how". This resonates throughout the industry voice above and of the many things discussed in this book seems to encapsulate the spirit of Strategic Event Creation.

One respondent, who also contributed a case example in Chapter 1, succinctly captures the mood of other writers, so this chapter fittingly concludes with the reflections of Carol Bell.

Carol Bell, Head of Culture and Major Events, NewcastleGateshead Initiative
www.newcastlegateshead.com

I've been involved in creating, producing and developing cultural festivals and events at NewcastleGateshead Initiative for over nine years. The objectives, budget, scale and scope of each event has varied dramatically, each bringing different challenges and rewards – and incredibly varied learnings along the way.

If I had to distil what I've learnt from this and many other events, and therefore the approach that I would advocate - no matter what the sector - I'd sum it up as follows:

1   Nothing is impossible: an initial idea for an event can sometimes appear unachievable or perhaps too ambitious or outlandish to put into practice – but there is always a solution and a way through if the vision is strong enough. It is entirely possible to marry practical and logistical considerations with extraordinary event aspirations; it just takes the right preparation, expertise and a good deal of perseverance along the way.

2   Effective partnership working is essential: no matter how focused the brief or how singular the objective, it is always necessary to consider, consult and communicate effectively with all stakeholders in order to deliver a successful event.

Study questions

1   Compare and contrast the accounts of two different professionals, identifying three key conclusions.

2   Claire O'Neill and Maurice Fleming come from very different event contexts. What key points in Maurice's piece would be useful to Claire in delivering music festivals?

3   Take each of the five facets of Strategic Event Creation (outcome obsessed, stakeholder centric, purposeful design, reflective practitioner, strategic persona) and identify how each is supported by the views of the industry professionals.

14

15 Concluding Remarks and Future Gazing

Howard Lyons, Phil Crowther, Liz Sharples, Chiara Orefice, and Daryl May

This chapter offers some closing reflections by the book's editors and then provides a valuable future perspective through an interview with Howard Lyons, who as a futurist shares his thoughts on the future and events.

Editors' reflections

Our intent has been to communicate the step change in the events industry, and particularly the changes this demands in the approach and behaviours of individual and teams of event creators. As we reflect on the many contributions to this book we recognise that for some readers the shifts that we are announcing, and advocating, will feel considerable and perhaps alien. For others, such as the industry voices conveyed throughout the book, there is no change at all as this is quite simply the business of event creation as they already know it.

For the most part this book has taken a strategic perspective. Yet many of the readers will, so far in their events careers and studies, have a much more operational basis to their experience. Their reading and consideration of the many ideas is no less important. For event creation to provoke the best outcomes 'operational' must be galvanised as the delivery mechanisms for the many strategic considerations and aspects considered in this book. As stated by Mark Shearon in Chapter 14;

> Strategy and Execution turn out to be twins so clients could never tell them apart -- and never really needed to.

Therefore the creator(s) of any given event must repeatedly instil this, and the operational individuals and teams must learn to intuitively recognise it. Perhaps this is a remaining barrier to the professionalisation of the events area.

A lurking danger for students of events and event practitioners alike is that operational becomes detached from the strategic. It is taught in different modules, undertaken by different people, and talked about in different meetings. Therefore some of us are strategic, others operational. The dynamic and inter-related character of events makes that an unpalatable situation. It undermines the spirit of Strategic Event Creation and presents a significant challenge to the individuals and teams at the heart of the process.

Event creation is inevitably the totality of the efforts of many and disparate individuals and teams that contribute to the event project. The ability of the event creators to identify and instil clarity of purpose, and also spark synergies between these many protagonists, is often the acid test of Strategic Event Creation. Too often a strategically sound vision does not exist from the event creators, and when it does it is distorted by a failure to effectively influence the disparate operations that strongly determine the event's execution.

This book is therefore offered as an antidote to the above scenario, and our undertaking is endorsed in the previous chapter by leading industry professionals who re-emphasise this perennial challenge of uniting strategic and operational. In many other respects, Chapter 14 provides an encouragingly fitting conclusion with the informed views of the contributors convincingly endorsing the DNA of Strategic Event Creation.

The below concluding discussion returns to the five interwoven principles which embody Strategic Event Creation and considers how they are particularly revealed in the discussion throughout this book.

■ Outcome obsessed

The need for event creators to take time to interpret the ambitions and concerns of stakeholders and use this knowingly as the bedrock for event creation reverberated through many of the chapters. The frameworks and ideas introduced in Part 2 are very influential in revealing the variety of interests that inform and shape an event. Chapter 5, for example, examined the opportunity to consciously bring together stakeholders with a commonality of interest, and how these synergies can be of benefit in successfully aligning the overall event purpose.

Whatever the composition of the stakeholder mix, their combined interests are perceptively reflected in the purposeful design expressed in Part 3 of the book, through key areas such as eventscape design, marketing and so forth. The circle is incomplete unless the evaluation examined in Chapters 12 and 13 are undertaken to both capture and communicate these outcomes and also learn from them for future event creation.

15

■ Stakeholder centric

From the beginning of the book, particularly in Chapter 2, the stakeholder centric ethos was conveyed as a fundamental aspect of Strategic Event Creation. The suggestion, in Chapter 2, to 'flip the norm' and place *locality* at the centre of the thinking process is a direct attempt to evolve the thinking away from the outdated language that is exclusive rather than inclusive. It provides a foundation for longer term development as expressed through the portfolio ideas debated in Chapter 11 and the need for event creators to think beyond the here and now.

Chapter 6, in discussion of the host community, introduced the very appealing notion of event creators as 'community animators', positioned at the intersection between the host community and the event funders and other stakeholders. This extends the remit of the event creator with a focus beyond the immediate and a requirement to engage wholeheartedly with a wider range of stakeholders and in so doing interpret their concerns and hopes, and facilitate activities to mitigate event related risk and to trigger opportunities. The alternative is that they are not stakeholder centric, pay lip service to the community, and wider stakeholders, and in so doing destabilise the current event and also future relationships and opportunities. And, of course, also behave in an anti-sustainable manner.

■ Purposeful design

The output of both of the above principles is that they combine to provide a holistic rationale for the event(s) and an explicit internal logic that steers the purposeful event design. The ideas introduced throughout Part 3 of the book can only prosper if this considered purpose exists. Chapters 4 and 7, for example, focus heavily upon the experience of attendees, and the considered and skilled role of event creators in interpreting and influencing this. Through the development of the eventscape discussion in Chapter 8, food in Chapter 9, and marketing in Chapter 10, we see how each event has its own strategic event context (as depicted in the diagram in Chapter 1). It is evident how a close understanding of this strategic event context is a pre-requisite to event design decisions.

The plethora of variables available to event creators is both an opportunity and a risk. The following interview with Howard Lyons (Futurist and Visiting Fellow at Sheffield Hallam University) refers to 'me too' events, where he alludes to the ever present risk, given the multitude of events that exist, of event creators (un)intentionally achieving replication rather than differentiation. The challenge for event creators is to wield more purposefully, and skilfully, the many variables of event creation. In doing so we should note the important early content in Chapter 8 which calls for a renewed focus upon competencies of creativity, risk taking and innovation in the skill-set of event creators.

■ Reflective practitioner

An undercurrent in the book is that there is a requirement for a considerable realignment in the emphasis from 'doing' towards 'consulting, thinking and then doing'. Consider the marketing related discussion in Chapter 10, or the legacy oriented content in Chapter 11, which both convincingly set progressive agendas for event creators in how they consider and undertake their activities in these areas. The necessity to pause and engage in considered dialogue and thought before acting is palpable.

Chapter 12 makes a strong case for strategic evaluation throughout the event creation journey. It also emphasises the integrated nature of this evaluation to have meaningful implication during the creation of the existing event, immediately post event, but also a much longer term resonance to positively affect the event creators and their future events through providing rich learning. A reflective approach underpins Strategic Event Creation, for without it much is lost.

■ Strategic persona

The totality of this book presents a significant challenge to event creators. It demolishes the traditional stereotypes of event creators as low-grade organisers with a more short term and restricted remit. The discussion in all chapters commentates upon a maturing of the event creation role from junior to senior and from operational to strategic. Event creators, as indicated in Chapters 3 to 6, are architects of strategic outcomes, deliverers of returns for funders, designers of human experiences, and animators of communities. Re-read the conclusions to each chapter and envision the persona and competencies required for the event creator of today and the future, they look very different from the stereotype.

This book has far reaching implications for both the individuals who are, and aspire to be, event creators, for event stakeholders (in the broadest sense), and also for educators who are challenged to rethink their academic delivery to ensure it is appropriate. The interview below is a fitting conclusion.

15

Interview with Howard Lyons, Futurist and Visiting Fellow, Sheffield Hallam University

Howard, you have been involved with futurology (the study of our futures) for more than a quarter of a century. As an academic what are your thoughts about the timeframe in which this book sits?

It is useful to look at this book by placing this new (events) framework within a continuum from the historical to the future. Most students reading this book will have nearly fifty years of work ahead of them and events tutors typically also face many years of work. If we consider the development of service sector management over the last fifty years and then consider fifty years into the future we can understand that our time perspective may be as long as one hundred years. Anything that can be done to unpack what a future in events management may look like should be helpful. I can suggest the following thoughts:

Experts can make tolerably good forecasts of <u>what</u> can and will happen over the next ten-seventy years, but they are still poor at forecasting <u>when</u> things will occur. There is reasonable evidence of this in the UK Technology Foresight Report that used a Delphi study (Loveridge,1996).

As this is a textbook we must avoid the impression that all of the ideas presented here flow together seamlessly. Although they all relate to the markets and industry practices, these do not represent universally joined-up thinking. All that we can assert is that matters correlate; they may typically follow one another or occur concurrently but that doesn't actually prove cause and effect.

Our study of events creation is of a process that typically follows some form of life cycle. For example the discussion of establishing objectives and managing stakeholders to organise events is the result and reflection of the preceding lack of direction and goals (in the events sector) in the past. ROI and ROO have quite rightly become useful standard measures of events success, at the moment. However we need to remember that its primacy is a phase that will pass (as all things do!) and other forms of measurement may be used in the future.

Howard, in Chapter 1 we discussed the shifting landscape in which events are being created. How can an understanding of futures and strategy help us when operating in this changing real world?

First let us look at the difference between *strategy* and *futures*. Futures are concerned with developing long-term pictures of what the future might look like. Some scenarios look fifty or more years into the future and the important variables are when something may happen, and what is the probability of the future? Trying to estimate the probability of both the futures and when they happen is a major part of the process. Once such pictures are created then people may begin to plan to ensure that an organisation benefits from the future. Strategy horizons vary between industries. The forestry industry needs strategy based on how long it takes to grow trees, which is a long time. Despite appearances the computer industry has at least a five-year time horizon for strategy, and large manufacturers will have at least two generations of product ready for market. So planning the launch event for the next but one product is feasible. Often some launches are of a modified version of an existing product with a subsequent launch covering a very new and updated technology. Mobile phones, tablet computers and games consoles all have this profile. Whether the event creators that are involved in an interim product launch are aware of the need for a bigger launch for the next really innovative product depends on the secrecy standards applied by the technology company.

Colin Beard in Chapter 7 explored the world in which events attendees function, and his examples are taken from many parts of the world that have disparate cultures. A large part of his discussion looks at corporate events associated with outdoors recreation, and the dominant paradigm seems to be a global Western corporate world-view. However there are other competing world-views and one aspect that organisers of events may wish to consider is how this paradigm may develop or change?

Similarly looking at the wedding market in the UK, a significant proportion of Asian weddings reflect the Islamic cultures of, say, Pakistan and Bangladesh, or the Indian culture, a large percentage of whom are of the Hindu faith. Weddings are typically large, elaborate, and can last several days. Companies associated with mainstream weddings in the UK may anticipate that more clients will become westernised at some stage. Equally firms with skills in UK Asian weddings may seek to capitalise on these and expand into other geographic markets. Some UK hotels seem to depend on Asian weddings and might consider growing abroad. However the Western wedding may also take root in these communities, providing further opportunities for mainstream wedding organisers. Clearly each of the alternatives has massive implications for companies involved in the industry. Forecasting for the next five years may be problematic, whereas forecasting for, say thirty to fifty years, might be more certain, notwithstanding the uncertainty around when in the next thirty to fifty years a pattern may emerge? Conventional analysis suggests that secular weddings may become more important in immigrant communities. However concerns in faith communities may actually lead to a move against the secular, towards an increase in faith based weddings. So even the UK wedding market has a large area of uncertainty associated with the multiculturalism of the UK.

15

Citizens born of second-generation immigrant parents may have a different view of weddings when their own children reach marriageable age (or celebrate other partnerships). This may have implications for the construction of new wedding venues.

Even the location of what are currently perceived to be immigrant communities is a movable feast. London's Brick Lane was the scene of fascist attacks on the Jewish community in the 1930s. Since then many other communities have moved into Brick Lane as the Jewish community moved on, became anglicised and relatively assimilated. How far their gradual integration changes their behaviour as events consumers is a matter of conjecture. Different communities integrate in different ways, some of which are based on culture, religion and observance, as well as economic success. However assimilation is a two way process, and immigrant consumer preferences often change the host community. This is highly visible in music, and fine art. However it is also important in most other aspects of our culture that range from language to food. For example, legal highs may become more regulated and embedded. This may change the nature of social events. On the one hand if we see the legalisation of, say, marijuana this will bring in new custom. However young people who are typically drawn to counter culture will then need different forms of entertainment that are unlawful or apparently illegal, in order to express their need for rebellion. It could be argued that rebelling is a need for some young adults, yet how we organise events to meet this need is challenging.

When we look at *futures* we usually identify a range of possible *futures*. Some may be mutually exclusive, and others may be part of a progressive development as a future develops. For example attending live sporting events may continue or even grow in popularity, or alternatively new technology may diminish attendance as three-dimensional virtual reality may provide a more acceptable experience, meaning that sports stadia shrink to be little more than the pitch. The future is not an inevitable progression and organisations seek to behave in ways that create futures that are advantageous to them, as well as remodelling their organisation to benefit from the future.

Howard - What should we be aware of with regards to the strategic direction of the Events sector in the wider economy?

All demand is derived from other people, industries or countries. For a steel producer there is a clear link in downstream demand from industries such as motorcars and arms manufacturers. Up-stream steel makes demands on primary mineral extraction industries, particularly coal and iron ore, as well as on electricity supply. Demand for events is equally linked up and down stream, but events are primarily intangible and their markets are based on strong but nebulous drivers of demand. We can see the tangible inputs into events, which may include consumables ranging from food and drink to publications and other paper goods, but some costs associated with events may be harder to estimate.

When the motor industry is busy there is clearly an increased demand for steel and plastics, and all of the other materials that make a car. However services such as events do not have so clear a linkage between the business cycle and demand. *Within* the events sector however there is linkage, so holding events increases demand for, for example, accommodation, catering, travel, and all manner of other related products and services.

Another difference between specialist events companies and other industry sectors is that many typically have a relatively small fixed investment base. If a hotel chain or conference venue has event specific staff, then those firms have a relatively large investment base when compared with agencies. So a hotel costing several £ million may use its facilities for business events on weekdays and for celebrations such as weddings at weekends. Each event will represent a small percentage return on investment (ROI) for any particular event. By way of contrast a small events organiser may have a couple of laptop computers and use a rented office and leased cars and vans. Small firms have difficulties in raising capital to grow the business and as we know the events industry is dominated by small firms 'without a balance sheet', i.e. lacking substantial fixed assets. However good their cash flow, and profitability, a small events company may find it almost impossible to borrow money from banks. If the small business is run from a property that is owned they will have less of a problem. Plotting the future trajectory of the business is therefore hard when compared with, say, banks, motor manufacturers or mobile phone companies.

A small firm with a small capital investment base is, however, very flexible and has much less need to plan for the long term when compared with very large enterprises. Furthermore the rapid decline of many large manufacturers, airlines, banks etc. indicates that their long-term view has in many cases been deeply flawed through having insufficient accurate forecast data. As the events sector develops there has been a very large growth in the human capital base of the industry, with a rapid increase in expensively educated, graduate, events management personnel. In many ways this is more valuable than fixed assets, although it isn't conventionally bankable. Large enterprises have a large resource that can be invested in trying to make long-term forecasts, whereas small enterprises depend on their large clients for information. Does the events manager in a large bank know what picture of the world the bank has in, say, ten years' time? How much information does the events professional have access to?

15

Howard – so in your opinion – what next for the Events sector?

In seeking to design and create new events, an essential starting point for any company is to determine if it is really a leader or follower in the market. It is exciting to think of oneself as an innovator and fashion leader, but there is limited space for such enterprises and they must have both amazing instincts for new ideas as well as excellent timing. Creative approaches in business seem to be rarely timed right, and timing is key.

Mostly events are *'me too's*, and differentiation is of a relatively minor nature. Weddings and funerals are both in part regulated by the state, and religious weddings and funerals are subject to additional social regulation. Furthermore they typically include a wide range of age groups and people from varied backgrounds, so there is homogeneity about these events. Business and professional conferences and exhibitions, which have fewer constraints, may be more flexible as may music, arts and sporting events, as attendees are typically more homogeneous.

Corporate events can be innovative, but concerns for companies' stakeholders means that care must be taken when innovating, particularly when a decision is made about which aspect of the event can be subject to a highly innovative approach. Location has been a typical variable that has been managed. Lawyers have long held their major events in the Asia pacific region having exhausted European and North American honey pot locations. The variety of locations have been widely exploited, probably leaving space flights and 'under the sea' as the new frontiers. However one can only eat one meal at a time, drink one drink and sleep in one bed. So opportunities for the creative design of events experiences have limitations placed on them by human biology. Culture, taste, or any other psychological or sociological factors operate beyond these fixed constraints of biology.

Business events are often about making more profits. Giving stakeholders a good time in Hawaii may be passé, and what many senior people may now need is quality time with friends and family rather than the stress of travel and conspicuous consumption. Innovative design for an event is an opportunity. For even Haj is changing as Saudi Arabia redesigns the holy places so that foreign pilgrims are safer and can be better accommodated both at religious sites and hotels.

■ Further reading

Julia Rutherford Silvers *Event Management Body of Knowledge* project (EMBOK) was a good starting point for those involved in events education as educators and students with lists describing the boundaries of the field (http://www.juliasilvers.com/embok.htm). This initiative was a reflection of the development of the field of study that other professions typically undertake. For example in hospitality we saw the publication of *The Corpus of Knowledge* in the 1970s. (Johnson, 1977). Having been a member of the marketing team working on that project it is clear that we provided an excellent basis for the development of the field, although the detail of marketing has changed immeasurably over the past decades with the growth of the web and more recently social media. Understanding how the web will continue to develop requires us to look outside of any user industry such as events; look for example at sources dealing with what is called 'Web 3.0'. One example is http://computer.howstuffworks.com/web-30.htm visited 10/8/14. The importance of Web3.0 cannot be understated although it is challenging. However failure to consider its implications for events creators will be problematic to those who seek to shape the industry. A simple activity that will highlight this is to review four sources on Web 3.0 and identify three possible opportunities and three threats for events enterprises. There are no 'right answers', just an exciting challenge.

If readers want to see what the UK Government sees fit to publish as important up-coming trends, then see *Future Identities, Changing identities in the UK: the next 10 years*. It is freely available at https://www.gov.uk/government/uploads/system/uploads/attachment_data/file/273966/13-523-future-identities-changing-identities-report.pdf and has huge implications for all aspects of life, not least the events sector. Engagement with multiple social media in addition to complex society is a major consideration in the report, and has profound and largely unpredictable implications for the events creators of the future. Events may become partly or wholly virtual reality, or they may grow as a reaction to the virtual. However that is something for you to determine as part of your career plan.

The uncertainty associated with the future makes a long view hard to deal with in the context of small firms or the classroom. However having an opportunity to think about the shape of the industry and of events creation in the next ten, twenty, or thirty years will help you to appreciate the possible implications of business or career choices made now.

References

Loveridge, D. (1996). Technology Foresight: the Delphi survey for Science in Parliament

Johnson, P. (1977), HCIMA, The Corpus of Knowledge: The Final Report of the Research Fellowship to e stablish the corpus of knowledge in Hotel, Catering and Institutional Services.

15

Index